Get a **better**
boat

Also from Phoenesse
www.phoenesse.com

After the Ego: Insights from the Pathwork® Guide on how to wake up

Blinded by Fear: Insights from the Pathwork® Guide on how to face our fears

Living Light: On seeking and finding true faith

Spiritual Laws: Hard & fast logic for forging ahead

Walker: A memoir

Word for Word: An intimate exchange between a couple of kindred souls | By Jill Loree and Scott Wisler

The *Real. Clear.* spiritual teachings series

Holy Moly: The story of duality, darkness and a daring rescue

Finding Gold: The search for our own precious self

Bible Me This: Releasing the riddles of holy scripture

The Pull: Relationships & their spiritual significance

Pearls: A mind-opening collection of 17 fresh spiritual teachings

Gems: A multifaceted collection of 16 clear spiritual teachings

Bones: A building-block collection of 19 fundamental spiritual teachings

Nutshells: Snippets from *Pearls*, *Gems* and *Bones*

The *Self. Care.* how-to-heal series

Spilling the Script: A concise guide to self-knowing

Healing the Hurt: How to help using spiritual guidance

Doing the Work: Healing our body, mind & spirit by getting to know the self | By Jill Loree with Scott Wisler

Keywords: Answers to key questions asked of the Pathwork® Guide By Eva Pierrakos with Jill Loree | www.theguidespeaks.com

Get a **better boat**

Trustworthy teachings
for difficult times
Spiritual essays

Jill Loree

Published by Phoenesse LLC
www.phoenesse.com

ISBN: 979-8-9872876-0-6 hardcover
ISBN: 979-8-9872876-2-0 paperback

Cover image by WikiImages from Pixabay.

phoenixe

Jill Loree & Scott Wisler

Walking this path **together**

Dedication

For Scott. My essays, like my life, are better because of you.

About the cover

The piece of art on the cover is commonly known as *The Great Wave off Kanagawa*. It's also just called *The Great Wave* or *The Wave*. It is a Japanese wood-block print created in 1831 by the artist Hokusai, and may be the most reproduced image in the history of all art.

The Japanese interpret *The Great Wave* by viewing it from right to left. Because traditionally, Japanese text is read from right to left. This means the slender, tapered boats—especially the top one—are facing into the wave. Life is just like this, giving us a better boat anytime we have the courage to face directly into our challenges.

During such difficult times, it helps to remain aware of a calm presence—like Mt. Fuji in this print—standing firm during rough passages. That awareness alone gives us a better boat. After all, this print is part of series is called *Thirty-six views of Mt. Fuji*, not *Thirty-six views of struggle*.

What's more, we get a better boat when we open ourselves up and share our gifts. That's what Japan did when it became willing to open its borders in 1859, ten years after Hokusai died. In doing so, Japan shared Hokusai's gifts with the world. This brought new inspiration to American and European artists like Whistler, Van Gogh and Monet. In other words, this print became an inspiration for the Impressionist era.

In a profound way, this image reflects the way something old can become a new inspiration. How something formerly hidden can suddenly make a difference, all around the world.

The spiritual teachings in this book are now 50 years old. Yet these timeless teachings are proven and deeply trustworthy. They chart a highly spiritual—and, at the same time, very practical—way to journey through the seas of life. If you let them, they can become your better boat.

Contents

Introduction

When the Pathwork Guide gave a talk, he opened with a spiritual blessing for everyone coming to listen to his teachings. It was a spiritual force containing strength, truth and love capable of penetrating deep into our souls.

This personal connection and blessing from the Guide is available to all of us in this moment, coming through these essays. The spiritual power of this blessing works to help open our *inner* knowing. For while the Guide's teachings help us grow our intellectual understanding about how life really works, they also penetrate deep into the soul.

I hope that as you take in this body of work, these teachings will collectively point you towards a deeper understanding of what it looks like to walk a spiritual path. To become more spiritual.

– Jill Lore

We all wear jewels in the heart. Some of them are polished and some of them aren't yet.

WWW.PHOENESSE.COM

phoenesse

Essay 1

Jewels in the heart

The teachings from the Pathwork Guide were transmitted by Eva Pierrakos over a period of 22 years. After she died in 1979, those who loved her created a collection of remembrances called *For Eva*. Judith Saly, one of the people who edited the original Pathwork lectures, shared that she felt Eva's presence very strongly in the days following her death.

So she had a "conversation" with Eva, asking Eva where she was. Eva replied that she was in Paradise. Judith asked what it was like there, and Eva said it was wonderful. No one had any transference!

Transference is what happens when we harbor certain feelings we aren't aware of towards one or both of our parents. We then go about life directing these same unresolved, conflicted and often contradictory feelings on other people. Our demand is that they fix their problems so we won't have to feel this way.

Eva seemed to be saying that everyone there was wearing "jewels in their heart," or something like that. Some of these jewels were already polished and others weren't yet. But nobody was hiding the ones that weren't polished. They wore them openly, holding them with the right kind of pride.

Everyone went around admiring each other's jewels, saying things like, "So this is what you still have yet to polish." But it was all OK. The unpolished stones were just those that someone still had to work on.

In Paradise, everyone saw everyone else for who they really were, with nothing else between them. There was so much love. And this love gave clarity so that everyone could see the ultimate possibility of the spiritual being in front of them.

It seems that's what Eva was asking each of us to do: To see each other as we really are. And to let everyone be who they are.

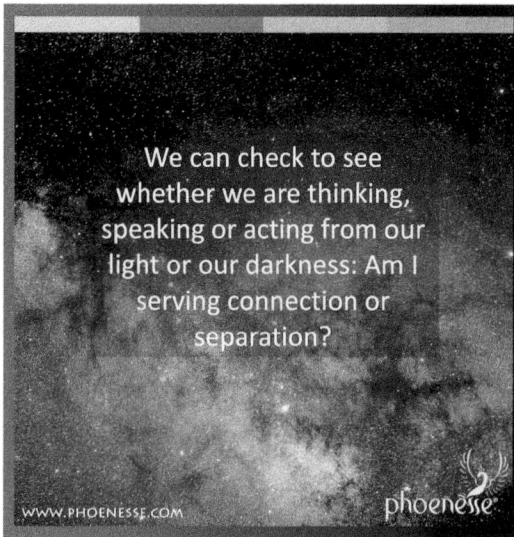

We can check to see whether we are thinking, speaking or acting from our light or our darkness: Am I serving connection or separation?

WWW.PHOENESSE.COM

phoenesse

Essay 2

A simple test for life

At the core of every created being, we are all the same: We are light. This light holds a prism of wonderful qualities, including truth, calmness and harmony, beauty, wisdom and love. At this level of our beings, these qualities are intimately interconnected.

So where there is truth there will be calmness; where there is harmony there will be beauty, where there is wisdom, there will also be love. Jumble the last sentence into any order and the equations will still always balance. At this level of our being, all is already one.

The hallmark of seeing these divine qualities in action? Connection.

In contrast, on the surface of every human being are various layers of darkness. All our faults, wrong conclusions and destructive tendencies live here, discoloring our ability to connect.

The hallmark then of these negative qualities? Separation.

We can always check to see whether we are thinking, speaking or acting from our light or our darkness by asking this simple question: Am I serving connection or separation?

For example, when we build a case against someone, we are aligning with separation. Then we view everything that person says and does through our warped filter. We don't see the totality of this person, which includes both their strengths and their weaknesses. Instead, we focus on their faults and reject the person for them—especially if we have the same fault but don't realize it.

When our goal is to serve connection, we give people the benefit of the doubt. If we feel disharmony with them, we check things out: *Here's what I'm noticing, what are you noticing?* We work towards understanding and we bring compassion, knowing everyone is wounded in some way. We make whatever effort is needed to clear the air.

Whenever we align with anything other than our inner light, we keep creating disharmony in the world. But equally important, we create discord within. For when we serve separation, we are no longer at one with our own selves.

During difficult times, it's important to remember that everything we think, say and do has an effect—on us and those around us. Each moment is an opportunity to slow down and choose the light. To choose connection.

Both our Higher Self and Lower Self are real. But only one is in truth.

WWW.PHOENESSE.COM

phoenesse

Essay 3

The Real Self vs the True Self

In our quest to wake up, our mission is to travel the surprisingly long distance from our ego to our Higher Self. We could also call our Higher Self our Real Self or True Self. To reach our Higher Self, our ego will need to clear away the inner obstacles created by our Lower Self.

Like our Higher Self, our Lower Self is part of our Real Self. But it is most definitely not our True Self. And if we want to wake up—to become enlightened—it's vitally important we understand this distinction: Both the Higher Self and Lower Self are our Real Self, but *only the Higher Self is in truth.*

What does it mean to be real?

If something is real, that means it is highly charged, or alive. And since both our Higher Self and our Lower Self are energized by our life force, both can be considered real. The energies of our Higher Self flow in a positive direction. But along the way, the energies of our Lower Self have gotten twisted, or distorted. So our Lower Self temporarily operates in a negative, or opposite, manner, flowing against life.

Since our Higher Self works in alignment with the flow of the universe, it is known for things like harmony, peace, connection, compassion, forgiveness, willingness, wisdom and courage. This is the light-filled part of us that's in truth. As such, the Higher Self doesn't need to shout. It quietly sits at the center of our being, patiently waiting for us to wake up and listen to it.

Our Lower Self, on the other hand, is the part of us working in opposition to the light. It's our shadow self, or darkness. Some classic moves of the Lower Self are resistance, rebellion, destruction, withholding, separation, cruelty, spite and hate.

What's holding all this negativity into place? Untruth. In other words, in the area of our Lower Self, there is ignorance we are not yet aware of.

The origin of ignorance

All children go through painful experiences at some point. Based on these experiences, we draw conclusions about life. Then we go through life using our self-made beliefs about how life works to navigate the seas of life. Our goal? To keep ourselves safe from further pain.

But since we form these understandings using the limited logic of a child, they are always *misunderstandings*. They seemed true to us at the time. But as children, we have a very narrow view of the world. Which is why the conclusions we drew then are not true in the greater reality.

As we emerge from childhood, our wrong conclusions about life sink into our unconscious. Now our untruths are hidden, even from our own awareness. And there they sit, motivating our Lower Self behavior.

Since Lower Self behaviors are based on buried wrong beliefs, they create real disharmony. Even more problematic, since we are now separated from our own mistaken conclusions, we can't see how our struggles in life connect with us.

This is why the work of self-healing is all about developing more self-awareness. We must find the faulty understandings inside us and establish more truthful understandings about life.

Covering ourselves up

Because our Lower Self is real, we get a rush from activating its twisted energy when we live from this part of ourselves. But when we activate our life force this way—by acting from our Lower Self—our inner dishonesty goes unchecked. Then conflict and disharmony grow.

Living this way makes it extra hard to sift the truth from untruth *outside* ourselves. In fact, since untruth is what's now driving us, we line up behind untruth in the world. For we like the way it excites us. We actually resonate with the low-frequency vibration of untruth.

Of course, we may have figured out by now that people don't respond well to those who behave badly. So out comes our Mask Self. We call this part a mask because the Lower Self hides behind it. One could say the Lower Self hires the mask to do its dirty work. For unlike our Higher Self, which is always oriented toward connection, the Lower Self serves separation. And the mask does a beautiful job of keeping us separate.

Our mask is made up of our defenses. And, in a nutshell, we use our defenses to demand love and keep ourselves safe from being hurt. In reality, all three defensive strategies—aggression, submission and withdrawal—do nothing but push people away and cause us more pain.

As such, if we are operating from our mask, we are not in truth. For it's simply not true that our defenses are effective in bringing us love or keeping us safe. Boiling it down, our defenses are really just manipulative strategies designed to control others. This is why we would say our defenses, or Mask Self, are not real.

Finding the truth of who we are

Our first step in self-development must be to dismantle our defenses. We do this by coming to understand our mask, and then using our positive will to change our behavior. Then, and only then, we can we start to slowly transform our Lower Self back to its original truthful nature. This is how we restore ourselves and get more of our life force flowing in positive, feel-good channels.

In the beginning, it may seem we are getting worse, or going backwards. For once we stop operating from our defenses, we will start seeing the real behavior of our Lower Self. Our ego will now need to learn to pay attention to our reactions and begin to unwind our inner distortions.

We must find our mistaken beliefs and reorient our thinking. We must also release our pent-up feelings of old, unfelt pain so warmer emotions can flow. And believe it or not, we'll need to uncover our negative intention to stay stuck. Then, after we've made some progress in clearing away these inner obstacles, we must learn to let go of our ego and begin to live from our Higher Self.

Over time, we will gradually learn to give our best to life and live in harmony. As we grow and mature, life will reflect more and more goodness back to us. Eventually we will find our way through all parts of our Real Self and into the truth of our being.

Then, having found our True Self, we will find we can live in peace.

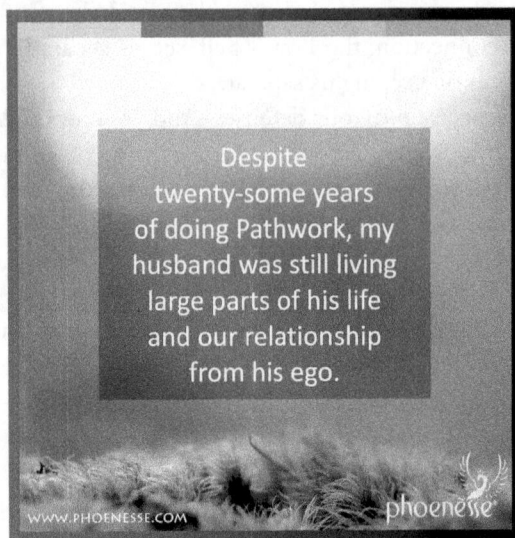

Despite
twenty-some years
of doing Pathwork, my
husband was still living
large parts of his life
and our relationship
from his ego.

WWW.PHOENESSE.COM

phoenesse

Essay 4

Finding the light switch:
My husband, the ego and imposters

The journey of finding our light is not an easy path. It's a winding road that leads through difficult territory. It's also the most worthwhile thing a person can ever do. This is a short story about the journey my husband and I were on in 2020, pulling together and finding our light.

Shortly after publishing *Salty* for my cousin, a new book of rewritten Pathwork Guide material came barreling through. It started with an urge to look more deeply into what the Guide had said about the ego. With this in mind, I rounded up four lectures with "ego" in the title (one had already been included in a previous book, *Gems*). Then I heard an inner call to search for lectures about consciousness.

As I scrolled through the list of hundreds of lectures, various titles jumped out at me. By the time I was done, I had 17 lectures in a queue to work with. For the next several weeks, I woke up very early and worked for 12-14 hours straight, rewriting the Guide's teachings. The energy running through me was intense, and the messages unfolding through my fingers were remarkable.

This treasure trove of teachings reveals the importance of creating a firm connection with our inner divine self, or Higher Self. For the journey of a human being—the journey that all the lectures from the Pathwork Guide are pointing to—is exactly this: It's about waking up from the domain of the ego and establishing a firm connection with our inner source.

We must transition from being lost in the illusion of duality to maturely living in unity. This is neither trivial nor easy to do. It requires us to surface and transform all the parts of ourselves that are blocking our light. This, in fact, is specifically what the bulk of Pathwork teachings guide us in doing. Then we must actively work to let go of our ego and align with God's will.

Slow and steady progress

What I can see, in hindsight, is that despite how much farther I have personally developed over this past decade, I was well underway in connecting with my Higher Self back in 2013 when I dove into this task of making these teachings easier for others to access. In fact, it was only by listening intently to the intuitive guidance I was receiving that I had the impetus and confidence needed to: leave my corporate career, sell my house, move far away and start writing these books on a full-time basis.

My intuition guided me to live off my savings and develop a level of trust I hadn't known was even possible before. It also led me to meet a wonderful man, Scott, and move to a remote part of New York state. Here, we would keep growing and healing together, and create a beautiful new life.

This process—transitioning from an ego-centric life to centering ourselves in something greater—is long and it is arduous. It involves a lot of personal healing work and requires tremendous tenacity. As the Guide says over and over, self-development happens slowly and gradually. Awakening, then, is not a one-time event.

We are all somewhere on such a healing spectrum. And wherever we are in our journey, our ego has an active role to play. It's really just a question of where our ego is getting its direction from. Is it from itself or from a greater place within?

This leads me to share an important piece of work that has been unfolding with Scott and me. I am sharing this story with Scott's full permission and involvement as it may have value in helping others. This is the same reason we both shared our personal healing experiences in *Doing the Work*. Our desire and intention is to be of service in furthering the Guide's teachings so they can help other people heal and grow, the same way they help us.

So there I was, nearing completion of *After the Ego*. As I was steeping in the rich lessons of this book, I came to this clear understanding: That despite his twenty-some years of doing Pathwork and practicing a number of other healing modalities—for real, he has been doing the work, not doing spiritual bypass—he was still living large parts of his life and our relationship from his ego.

The ego can do great things

By way of background, let me share a few things about Scott. He has an intelligence that runs extremely deep. When he understands something, it is solid. In college, he didn't just memorize complicated equations for the test, like some of us. Case in point, thirty years later the man can still use calculus.

Suffice it say, his ego mind has served him well in the fields of aerospace engineering and power generation. What's more, he has a highly developed ability to read people's energy and the interactions of energies in a room. More than once he has sensed I was upset before I was fully aware of it myself.

Such qualities are certainly part of what I love about him. But these things are not his Higher Self. And so, while his inner light shines through in many ways, and while he has greater self-awareness than a lot of people, his ego was still basically running the show in many areas. I shared with him what I was noticing and frankly, this was a bitter pill to swallow.

After a few days to process this, I shared another difficult truth with him. Not only was he largely operating his life from his ego, his ego was dropping the ball in doing a big part of the job it's intended for.

The role of the ego

In *Spilling the Script*, I summarized the role of the ego like this: "It is the part of us that thinks, acts, decides, memorizes, learns, repeats, copies, remembers, sorts out, selects, and moves inward or outward. In short, the ego is really good at taking things in, straightening them up and spitting them back out. What the ego can't do is add deep meaning to life or produce creative solutions, as it has no profound wisdom of its own."

Using the various tools in its kit, the ego plays the important role of self-observer. To do this, it must learn to identify our many inner voices. Then, as we develop and grow, we can make new choices about which part we are identifying with.

In broad strokes, our work is to transition away from identifying with our Lower Self. This is the part that is fearful, destructive, stuck in old trauma patterns, and not aligned with truth. And we must start identifying with our Higher Self. This is the part that holds our wisdom, courage and love, and fully aligns with truth.

It's our ego that shifts our identification, and it does so by first seeing what the current inner situation is. In short, we must dismantle our defenses so we can begin to understand how our Lower Self operates. The ego then leads the effort to clean our inner house of any light-blocking obstacles.

The ego's next job is to surrender and let go into the light—our inner light. In reality, the process isn't quite this linear. After all, the work of clearing away Lower Self obstacles is always an act of our Higher Self. Nonetheless, it's the ego that makes this transformation by the Higher Self possible.

What living from the ego looks like

In an effort to illuminate what I'm talking about when I say "Scott was living from his ego," let me share an example. First, a little history. Years ago, I was trained over the course of five-plus years of study to become a Pathwork Helper. This was *after* roughly five years of being a Pathwork Worker. Because a key requirement was to first rigorously apply the Guide's teachings to myself.

For to be an effective Helper—to help someone else do their healing work—we must be able to tap into our own Higher Self. Then, by listening inside, we follow the guidance flowing from within to navigate the healing process. To do this, we will need to have cleared enough of our own inner obstacles. And we will need to have learned to surrender our own ego to align with our own Higher Self. A person simply cannot be very effective in helping others apply the Pathwork Guide's teachings if we're still operating mainly from our ego.

One way I have practiced tapping my own inner divine guidance is by learning to tell when a project is ripe, and then sensing how to proceed. This is something I did while working in marketing communications, which is a career comprised mainly from a long list of small tasks. And I also did this during a home-makeover project in Atlanta, shortly after graduating from Pathwork Helpership training.

Jumping back to the year 2020, in January, Scott and I embarked on a home improvement project that was fairly extensive. We had finished the first two phases over the winter and spring, saving the remodeling of our entryway for warmer weather. More importantly, whereas I had been filled with guidance over the winter for the various parts we were working on, I hadn't received a single idea for how to proceed on the entryway. And so we waited until that project became more ripe.

Creativity flows from the Higher Self

With other projects finally complete, ideas started to bubble up for the next home-improvement phase: our new entryway. Scott and I began talking about what we wanted, and I started feeling the familiar flow of creativity. But as I was collecting ideas for things to consider, Scott was busy raising concerns and creating hurdles.

It's not that he shouldn't have been contributing suggestions or asking questions. But it seemed his "guidance" wasn't jibing with mine. Instead of fleshing out, adjusting or building on the ideas I was bringing forward—which we were essentially in agreement on—he was mostly throwing out obstacles and roadblocks. This was both confusing and frustrating.

One of the teachings in *After the Ego* is that our Higher Self is never in conflict with the Higher Self of another. But on the level of the ego, there will often be discord. This is the reason we need to have courage to do our own healing work. For when we follow our own inner guidance, we may run smack into the face of someone else's ego. In developing our entryway plans, Scott and I were bumping up against each other a lot.

Letting go looks like "I don't know"

Further, as noted in that definition of the ego from *Spilling the Script*, the ego is not equipped to bring forward creative solutions. This doesn't mean the ego can't solve a problem, but it can only deal with known formulas. It simply doesn't have the depth to allow for original, creative problem solving. It's our greater being that provides a conduit to universal forces where the possibilities are truly infinite.

Does that mean, since I was following guidance and Scott seemingly was not, I'm saying I was right? Here's where this gets tricky. Over the last five years, since quitting my day job and selling my house, I've often referenced an old saying, "In for a penny, in for a pound." Meaning, once I let go and left Atlanta, I had to keep paying out more and more rope from my ego in order to follow my intuition. For my ego was not in the lead.

I continue to marvel at the enormity of my ego's ability to let go and hang out in the space of "I don't know." As in, I don't know where my life is heading, I don't know if I will run out of money, I don't know if these books will ever find an audience, I don't know, I don't know, I don't know.

Yet it's within the spaciousness of my "I don't know" that I listen within. My open mind allows me to hear more clearly. And over time I've developed a quite reliable channel to my inner knowing. I can tell when something feels right.

That said, our intuition will never be a fence we can lean on. We need to always be checking out our inner guidance and fine-tuning it using our ego. But our inner guidance will never lead us to self-righteousness. Because it can only surface through the relaxation of our ego mind. Further, whereas the limited ego thrives on rules and rigidity, our greater self is fluid, agile and adaptable. It doesn't get fixated on only one right answer, since it's tapped into an infinite resource.

So, no, I wasn't demanding to be right. I was trying to understand: *Why aren't our ideas flowing together?*

Creating an open avenue for imposters

When I shared what I was seeing with Scott—namely, that he was operating mostly out of his ego instead of tuning in to his Higher Self—he didn't just open up and hear the truth of this. Instead, as happens so often in life, he deflected what I was saying into the defensive inner wall he had long ago built to protect himself.

To be fair, Scott came by this wall honestly. Briefly, his mother died the spring of the year he turned 12, after a multi-year battle with leukemia. During the years of her illness, no one spoke with him about what was happening—that she was ill and would likely die—even as a depressing pall hung over their house.

At the end of that same year, his father married a woman Scott had barely met, and nine months later a new baby sibling came along. To accommodate this growing family of seven—which included Scott's sister and two step-siblings—his parents built a bigger house. But since it was just across the district line, this meant he also had to change schools.

The integration of all this was brutal, especially with no resources to help him process the shock of the trauma. On the family front, things continued to go downhill for him, from there. It's no wonder he put up thick inner walls to defend against all that pain. And yet, as it goes for everyone, such protective walls later turn into a magnet for inviting more pain.

In this situation, by deflecting what I was saying—the awareness that his ego was preventing him from becoming his best self—he created an opening for spiritual imposters to access his psyche.

What are imposters?

Imposters belong to the legions of dark forces that come to tempt us into aligning with our Lower Self. In the Lord's Prayer, we are asking for help in the face of these temptations. Our goal is to learn to make better choices—choices aligning with the light. Ever since the time of Jesus—following Christ's victory in the war with the dark forces after Jesus Christ died—spiritual laws have been in place that essentially limit their range.

In short, over the last two thousand years, dark forces have only been allowed to tempt us to whatever extent we still have faults. In other words, if we don't do our personal healing work to transform our Lower Self, we will attract dark forces. And the agenda of dark forces is always to keep us from living from our inner light.

But unlike "normal" dark spirits, imposters have a different agenda. They tempt us, but they want to also teach us. They do this by encouraging us to go down obviously wrong paths. They can sound convincing, but they aren't leading us anywhere that's good. Ideally, the rather absurd choices we make in following imposters will help us wake up. We will hopefully realize we are going the wrong way and thereby correct ourselves.

Imposters, then, are essentially teachers who are coming to help us see something important. They operate by whispering bad ideas into our inner ear, and if we are not connected deeply within, we will mistakenly believe these voices are coming from our conscience, or Higher Self.

For when we are living from our ego and are not connected with our inner divine self, we can't tell where these voices are coming from. We can't sense if they are from our truthful essence or not. Remember, the ego doesn't have truth-teller as part of its job description.

To be clear, imposters can't inspire us to do something against our will. But they can find our faults and leverage them, enticing us to use our own will to act against our own best interest. For instance, one way Scott started to be influenced by imposters was by making jokes or comments that really weren't funny. "That's not who I want to be," he later said.

If we trace Scott's story back a bit, we'll find an influential family member who enjoyed practical jokes, which Scott also engaged in when he was younger. One can see the origin in this lifetime of twisted wiring around humor mixed with cruelty, and the unhealed fault line that remains. It was into this crack that the imposters slid.

Nothing stays hidden forever

During this same winter-to-summer timeframe, Scott had been dealing with a frozen shoulder following a torn-tendon injury. I had been encouraging him to explore what was really frozen: *What is being out-pictured here?*

It was becoming clear to me that his habitual identification with his ego had become so frozen he literally couldn't see it. Regardless of his remarkable intelligence and his ability to sense energetic patterns in himself and others, he was blind to this.

I have witnessed Scott's incredible devotion to doing his spiritual healing work. He has been digging deep for decades to clear away the kind of obstacles that prevent a person from transitioning from their ego to their Higher Self.

Now he essentially needed to go inside and find the light switch—to turn on the light. The problem was, his ego was so in command of his life, he didn't even know there was an inner switch. And he had no idea where to find it.

One place he started looking was by examining his expectations. Through daily review, he would simply notice how each day had gone. Where were there bumps? And did they happen to match his expectation of what would happen? We need to stop using the challenging experiences in life as confirmation that our expectations were right.

Instead, we can begin to notice the way our ego has set us up for struggle through its tightly held expectations. *This is how things should go or will go.* Then we create from this belief. Such an approach does not leave any room for fresh ideas, or for things to unfold with divine timing. This is a switch we can learn to pay attention to.

Eventually, through his persistent work on his spiritual path, Scott's plugged-up inner portal to the divine began thawing and opening. Correspondingly, mobility in his shoulder was being restored.

We can learn from ourselves

Keep in mind, this journey from the ego to the deeper self is gradual, and we are often uneven in our development. Unfortunately, such unevenness is very hard on our psyche. Truly, it can tear a person apart. To heal, we must keep surrendering and shifting our identification, practicing this persistently in all areas of our lives. Some open more easily than others.

For example, Scott does the cooking in our house and he consistently does so from an ego that is surrendered and listening to his Higher Self. He feels into the meal as it almost assembles itself, rarely from a recipe. So he knows what that feels like. And there are places professionally where his Higher Self shines through, particularly in working with teams. That too is a familiar flow of the divine.

Although Scott's light was already shining through in many ways, his Higher Self was calling him to take this next big step. This is why imposters started appearing. They are performing a valuable service and are very good at what they do. Imposters find a way to inspire us using just enough truth to get us to bite the hook, but their messages are not fully aligned with truth. Their intention is to help us see this.

If we are connected with our greater being, we will know when we are being visited by an imposter. Without that inner connection, our ego will fall for their tricks and we will be the ones looking foolish. Worse yet, when we are over-identified with our ego, all our questioning about *"What is the truth?"* will only lead to more questions. We will never find peace if our ego has us running in such circles.

Further, if we are trapped in our ego—unable or unwilling to let go into the arms of our own inner divine self—our ego will find false ways to let go. Addictions are a prime example of this. Whatever our ego uses to distract itself—in a misguided attempt to avoid uncomfortable feelings associated with old unhealed wounds—will always bring us more heartache in the long run. Moreover, these ploys can never bring us to the doorstep of our true inner self.

Waking up and finding the light switch

The ego needs to wake up and see how it is trying to cheat life by attempting to find a shortcut to happiness. We must see how hanging on is not the answer. And we must accept that finding our light means letting go.

We must realize that letting go requires us to clear away our inner walls and dark areas, and we must take the apparent risks associated with healing: becoming vulnerable, transparent and flexible. And then we must consciously surrender.

Yes, finding our light is hard work. But in the end, is this really a hardship? For truly, our brilliant inner light by far outshines our ego and is the true source of everything good. Our divine nature is to flow and find our way, following the path that will lead to everyone's highest good.

True enough, this is often the way that requires *more* effort, not less. (By contrast, following our Lower Self can also be called following the path of least resistance.) But since our Higher Self is connected with the source of all that is, when we're in the flow of it, energy flows freely from within us to replenish us. Our efforts then become seemingly effortless.

Our Higher Self is creative, abundant, resilient and fearless. It knows deeply, loves openly and can carry us to freedom. Our ego, on the other hand, is but a limited, temporary aspect whose destiny is to serve our greatness.

When the ego gets it right, we start living from our greatness; we access our full potential. It is the awakening ego that eventually figures this out and starts tackling the challenge of finding our light.

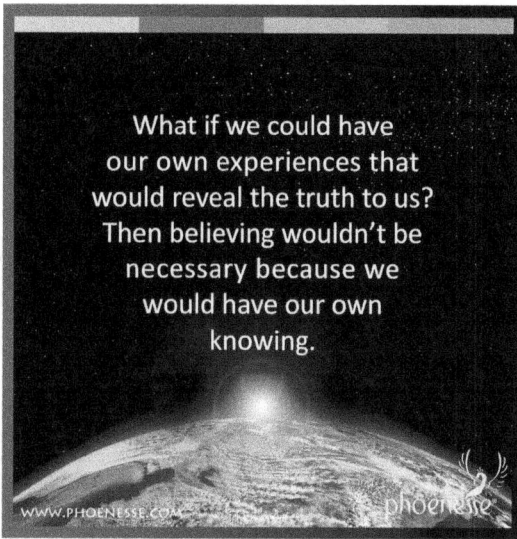

What if we could have our own experiences that would reveal the truth to us? Then believing wouldn't be necessary because we would have our own knowing.

WWW.PHOENESSE.COM

phoenesse

Essay 5

From believing to knowing:
The trip of a lifetime

Reading the long-winded but well-considered treatise *Why We All Need Philosophy* by Mark Manson, author of *The Subtle Art of Not Giving a F*ck*, got me thinking: Are the Pathwork teachings—and in turn, my Phoenesse writings—essentially a philosophy? Perhaps yes. For according to Manson, "Philosophy is the inquiry into our understanding of reality, knowledge, and how we should live." Indeed, that describes the Pathwork teachings to a "T". And *believing* isn't part of the program.

As he skillfully weaves together a brief history of philosophy, Manson touches on the work of David Hume, who in Manson's view "demolished the idea of cause/effect and or the assumption that we can predict anything at all." Since the reality of cause-and-effect is one of the basic tenets of the Pathwork Guide's teachings, this intrigued me.

"Bear with me here," writes Manson, "as this might sound insane. Hume said, logically speaking, that it is impossible to *prove* that anything will occur in the future, no matter how often or how regularly it has occurred in the past. If the sun has risen in the east every day for millions of years, that still doesn't *prove* it will rise again in the east tomorrow. It simply makes it insanely probable that it will rise in the east."

It's hard to imagine a time when people had to rely on *believing* the sun would rise each morning. That the sun rising daily in the past was all they had to go on. It's future rising couldn't be proven, so people had no choice but to believe it would.

Understanding means knowing

Isn't this what Christian religions do? They ask us to believe in something, without any proof. But what if we could have our own experiences that would reveal the truth to us? Then believing wouldn't be necessary because we would have our own knowing.

That is basically what's happened in the case of the sun rising. We no longer *believe* "the sun rises in the east," because that's simply not what's going on. We now have proof—thanks to some very smart people who built a little rocket ship to go see for themselves—that in fact the Earth is turning, and the sun is sitting in a relatively fixed position. We're the ones in motion. And as long as this planet keeps spinning, we're going to see the sun again tomorrow morning.

Not once has the sun actually ever "risen," even though it appears that way to us. And now we know the truth of the matter. In the case of sunshine, then, we have a collective knowing about how this works. We *understand* now, so there's nothing we must *believe*. Cause-and-effect is solid.

In the case of Pathwork, and now Phoenesse, we can have a similar experience. We can look within and uncover the reason for the patterns in our lives. We don't have to wait for the stars to align. We can start doing our work today, and then one day we'll understand ourselves.

The truth about what we believe

Manson goes on to say that one thing the world's great philosophers have uncovered is that we can't believe everything we believe to be true. This is much like the philosophy of the Pathwork Guide—and therefore also of Phoenesse—which says: We believe many things—in our unconscious mind—that are untrue. But since we aren't aware of them, we don't think to question whether they are true.

And yet our life will reflect our hidden untrue beliefs. Any time we say we want a certain thing—a relationship, job, car, experience, whatever—and we don't have it, then somewhere deep down inside us we don't want it. Or we fear getting it. And make no mistake, we all have unconscious beliefs that are the opposite of what we say we believe.

This is how human consciousness—including the unconscious—works. It's a reliable dial that points, without fail, to our hidden inner problem areas. It's this piece about the unconscious that so many are blind to. And it makes us unsure about what to believe.

Unconscious untrue beliefs bring us back

When Descartes landed on his preeminent realization, "I think; therefore I am," he was equating his conscious ability to think to proving his existence. Yet ironically, it's what we *unconsciously* believe that's responsible for our many return visits to circle the sun.

Each lifetime we're given another chance to see the unconscious misconceptions—the mistaken beliefs—we're holding onto. And if we look at our life in the right light, we can start to see what we've lost sight of. By doing our personal work of self-knowing, we can start to slowly excavate our own inner landscape.

And that's when we'll discover something truly revolutionary: *This*—our own wrong beliefs—is the source of all our conflicts. *Here* are the untrue conclusions we've drawn about life—along with the pain associated with those mistaken beliefs—and so *here* is the magnet attracting more of that same pain.

Said another way: Here are my hidden untrue beliefs that make me behave in ways that make them appear to be true. It's only by realizing that we are somehow responsible for what's happening in our lives that we start to say: *Oh, I see.* And once we become clearer about our life, this world starts making more sense.

Shifting our world view

Unfortunately, we won't have a once-in-a-lifetime epiphany and be all better. We'll need to dig into all the nooks and crannies of the whole ancient city that's buried down there in our unconscious. But if we persevere—if we unearth all the faulty bits of immature logic and find every uncomfortable feeling we've been avoiding—we'll come to an entirely new view of this world.

Then we'll move from *believing* we could someday be happy and free, to *knowing* freedom is our undeniable destiny. For we're not meant to be miserable. But with so much discontent hidden in our unconscious, it can't be otherwise.

Cause-and-effect is alive and well, friends, and it doesn't miss a beat. Every disharmony in our lives can be traced back to an origin. And it always begins within us. This is an ironclad truth. In fact, cause-and-effect is as reliable as our knowing we'll see the sun again tomorrow. Because that's how this world works.

And just like the people who journey into space, proving it's so, we can journey within. We can discover for ourselves that if we follow every disharmony far enough, we'll see it in a different light. We can see for ourselves how our own inner darkness—and any associated untrue belief we've locked away in our unconscious—colors our lives.

Truly, our own inner darkness is the cause of our existence as human beings. But also know this: We have the ability to overcome it.

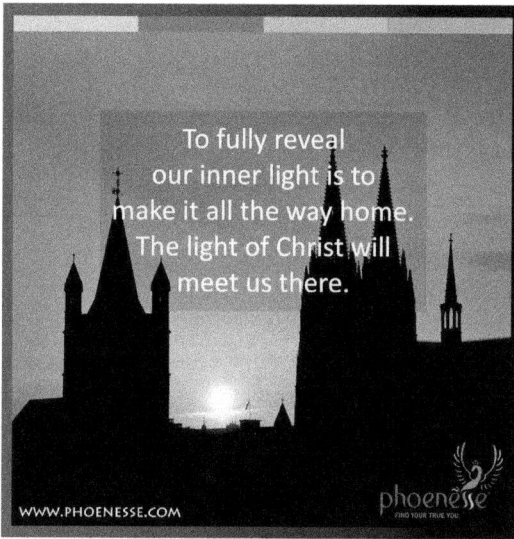

To fully reveal our inner light is to make it all the way home. The light of Christ will meet us there.

WWW.PHOENESSE.COM

phoenesse
FIND YOUR TRUE YOU.

Essay 6

Taking the more mystical way home

Years ago, when my two boys were very little, we visited some friends one Christmas and exchanged gifts. Upon being handed his gift, their four-year old looked at me and asked, "Why did you use dreidel paper?"

"What's a dreidel?" I replied. As far as I knew, I'd wrapped Daniel's gift using Christmas paper with little spinning toys on it. Come to find out, a dreidel is a four-sided top bearing four Hebrew letters. These letters form an acronym for a Hebrew saying which translates to "a great miracle happened there," referring to the miracle upon which Hanukkah is centered. For someone raised Lutheran in Northern Wisconsin where Jewish people were few and far between, this mistake was understandable—and also pretty funny.

Even more funny, fifteen years later I would wind up studying Kabbalah for four years. But interestingly, not once did we talk about things like Seder, Rosh Hashanah or dreidels. Kabbalah is a form of Jewish mysticism that one can study without touching into mainstream Judaism.

Following a mystical path

During my four years of studying Kabbalah, we learned about things like the Hebrew alphabet from which all of creation arose. Or as it says in the Bible,

"In the beginning was the Word, and the Word was with God, and the Word was God." We danced with the energy in the mother letters and father letters. Really incredible stuff! When our class graduated, the leader gave us each a silver necklace with a Hebrew letter on it. My letter is *lamed*, meaning "teacher."

We also spent a lot of time sitting with the ten divine qualities embodied in the Tree of Life. As an example, a person might be struggling with something in life that relates to an imbalance of Gevurah and Chesed.

- *Chesed* is "Kindness": Loving grace of free giving/love of God/inspiring vision
- *Gevurah* is "Severity": Strength/discipline/judgment/withholding/awe of God

In pairing these qualities, we can think of a river and bank. The water needs to flow and move and let go, but it can only do so if there is a bank to hold it. The bank, on the other hand, needs to be firm and still, creating an open space for the river to exist.

If we have too much or too little of either quality, problems will arise in our life. A healing would involve sitting with a person while resonating with the already healed state of these two sefirot, helping the person bring them back into balance with each other.

In a similar way, there is a mystical form of Islam called Sufism. This mystery school emphasizes the inward search for God, focusing on meditation while shunning materialism. A whirling dervish may show their love for the divine through their spinning Sufi dance, and we may know some of their wisdom through the wise words of the famous Sufi poet, Rumi: "Your task is not to seek for love, but merely to seek and find all the barriers within yourself that you have built against it." Or this one: "Out beyond ideas of wrongdoing and rightdoing there is a field. I'll meet you there." I may not know much about the Islamic faith, but I know I love that.

Finding a Christic mystical path

It's a bit harder to find a mystical path that dovetails with Christianity. We might point to the Franciscan Friars, but their ways align very closely with those of the Catholic Church. Beyond degree of devotion, I'm hard pressed to tell them apart.

A better candidate might be the path of Phoenesse, which is built on the profound teachings offered to humanity by the Pathwork Guide. This fits better from the perspective that both Phoenesse and Pathwork are Christic paths that don't resemble Christianity at all.

One can, in fact, whirl their way through decades of deep spiritual healing work by following these teachings and not once bump into anything that looks or sounds like Christianity. In my own twenty-plus years of involvement in the Pathwork community, I'd say the whole topic of Christ was danced around so beautifully, it was barely even mentioned.

Snipping out the teachings about Christ was really quite easy to do. After all, of the 250 Pathwork lectures, only a very small handful are directed toward the topic of who Christ is, who Jesus was, and why we should care. In short, in walking this Christic path, a person has the option to just do what Rumi suggested and just seek out all the barriers in ourselves we've built against love, and that will be enough.

What we'll leave on the cutting room floor, though, is an understanding of how we came to be this way. I don't mean, "How did I come to be separated from other people and my own self?" for that we will uncover during the course of our self-discovery work. I mean, "How did I end up *here*? Why do we have to deal with duality? What caused evil to come into existence?"

These are huge questions, and we can't get to the bottom of them without bringing up the teachings about the Fall and the Plan of Salvation. And in order to understand those two important concepts, we have to talk about Christ. But this version of the story varies enough from what I was taught in Christian Sunday school that *everything* now falls into place. The origin and plight of all humanity now make far more sense to me.

Christic, not Christian

1700 years ago, when Christian church leaders played fast and loose with the truth about reincarnation, they were defining what would and would not be in the Bible. And they really did us all a disservice. To be fair, distortions have wound their way into all the world's major religions, and yet the Pathwork Guide says they all still contain enough truth to serve our personal development.

That said, at this point, people have been leaving organized religions in large numbers and churches have been closing their doors left, right and center. Why? Because people are no longer buying what they're selling. The stories don't add up. Our minds want real answers and not empty threats of going to Hell for all of eternity.

It's logical to assume that if Christianity is off base, there must be something wrong with Christ. After all, Christ is at the heart of the Christian faith. Yet by looking more deeply, we can start to understand that Christ isn't the one who's gone sideways, Christianity is. The problem, as is so often the case, lies with us humans and our feet of clay.

It's important to recognize that there are valuable, true and important teachings in Christianity. But what's missing is the deeper reason for Christ's incarnation as Jesus. Christ came to open a door so we—*all* of us—could return to spheres of light, rather than continuing to be trapped in the dark spheres of Hell from which we are all rising.

In order for us to gravitate toward the light, we must make choices that remove our inner obstacles. For these are what block us from creating loving connections. These are the walls that are tearing us apart and which need to come down. The way home can never involve putting up *more* walls and creating *more* division.

Yet this form of destructiveness is what so many of today's evangelicals support. Our current sad surroundings in the US are the fairly predictable tragedy that lies at the end of a 1700-year dance with untruth.

Does this make Christianity all wrong? Of course not. Sacred truths can certainly be found in church. But the wheat must be sifted from the chaff and too often, that's not being done. Similarly, Pathwork leaders weren't all wrong when they sidestepped the Guide's teachings about Christ. A lot of authentic, transformative work has been done over the last 50 years.

But anytime we cover up and deny a truth, we smother a flame. When that truth is a light the size of Christ, darkness develops.

Revealing more and more light

Earth may be our temporary home, but heaven is our true home. And Jesus was famous for trying to tell us that—really and truly—heaven is *within*. So it is by doing our personal healing work that we are finding our true selves. We are clearing away what's blocking our inner light. This is what opens a pathway for more of our own light to shine out into the world. But it takes more than a single lifetime to complete this journey.

To fully reveal our inner light, then, is to make it all the way home. The light of Christ will meet us there.

The Pathwork Guide on self-development

"A group like yours contributes more than vast masses of people who preach doctrines, who force away the emotions, who feel they must be good, while their true state of being is removed from such goodness.

"A group of only five people, who face reality as it happens to be now, contributes more to the entire world—not only to your Earth sphere, but to all spheres—than the best intended teachings and ideals that reach merely the surface intellect."

– Pathwork® Guide Lecture #105: Humanity's Relationship to God in Various Stages of Development

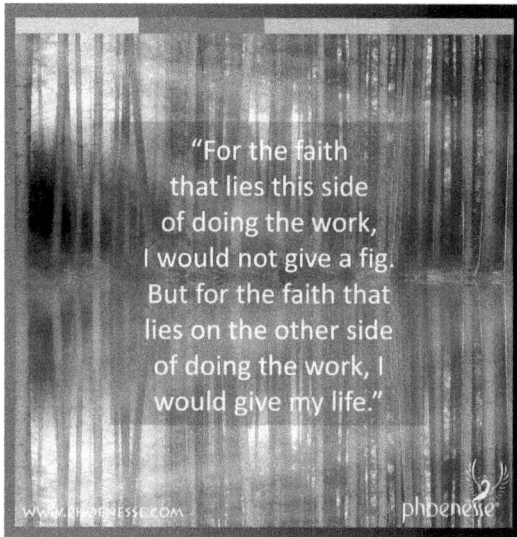

"For the faith that lies this side of doing the work, I would not give a fig. But for the faith that lies on the other side of doing the work, I would give my life."

WWW.PHOENESSE.COM   phoenesse

Essay 7

Two Martin Luthers, two kinds of faith

I was raised in the Lutheran faith in a small city in northern Wisconsin. This region was populated by settlers from such diverse areas as Norway, Sweden and Germany. So we had more than our fair share of blonde people. By the time I arrived on the scene in the early 1960s, we were basically all just a bunch of white people with interesting foods to eat during the Holidays.

When I was twenty-five, I moved to Atlanta where I would settle down for the next twenty-five years. Not long after arriving in Atlanta, my parents came for a visit, and we attended a church service at Ebenezer Baptist church. My mother had long been the organist at our Lutheran church in Rice Lake, and my dad taught vocal music at the University of Wisconsin two-year college in Barron County. So they were both particularly keen to experience the music, and we were not disappointed.

As I recall, we were the only white people attending the service that day, and the congregation couldn't have been kinder in welcoming us. Dr. Martin Luther King Jr's daughter was giving the sermon, and afterwards, we waited a short while for recordings of the service to become available on a CD. My dad would go on to use it in one of his music classes at the college.

This came to mind recently when my mom sent me a clipping about Dr.

Martin Luther King Jr from her daily devotional book. It clarified something that had always confused me: Why did Dr. Martin Luther King Jr and Martin Luther, the founder of the Lutheran religion, have such similar names?

Here is the explanation, according to the clipping: "Dr. Michael King Sr, a prominent preacher in Atlanta, toured the Holy Land and Berlin in 1934, sponsored by his church, Ebenezer Baptist. In Germany, Hitler was in power, and Dr. King's church stood against him.

Dr. King was deeply moved by his visit to the land of Martin Luther and by the reformer's proclamation of salvation by grace alone through faith alone in Scripture alone. When he came home, King changed his name from Michael to Martin Luther.

His oldest son, Michael, was five. His father changed his son's name also, to Martin Luther King Jr."

First we believe

I am struck by the reference to the Lutheran tenet that our faith alone will save us. Most likely, both Dr. King and Dr. Luther understood the deep, unshakable truth about this. But I am guessing that for some people today, the real understanding has gotten lost.

This reminds me of a quote from Supreme Court justice Oliver Wendell Holmes: "For the simplicity that lies this side of complexity, I would not give a fig, but for the simplicity that lies on the other side of complexity, I would give my life."

In this case, simplicity is faith, and complexity lies in doing the work of healing. In other words, "For the faith that lies this side of doing the work, I would not give a fig, but for the faith that lies on the *other* side of doing the work, I would give my life." For that far faith is true faith. And discovering it is what life is all about.

To go on a healing journey is to remove the obstacles that are blocking our inner light. Keeping in mind what Christ taught, which is that heaven is within. Before we can embark on such a journey, we can only believe with our ego mind. And belief as a mental concept has no spiritual value. It's hardly worth a fig. For the ego is a shallow resource. It does not have the ability to comprehend the whole truth.

The ego, in fact, is forever trapped in duality, not unlike the fragments of ourselves caught in child consciousness. The ego, then, can only hold one-half of a whole truth. But in the center of our souls, where we are in unity, we hold all aspects of the truth. Meaning our Higher Self is comfortable holding opposites.

For many people, including many who are deeply religious, having faith and doing the work of inner healing are opposites they can't reconcile. Left to choose, the ego opts for "faith"—an easy-to-come-by mental idea—and rejects the notion we must do any work to heal ourselves. But ego "faith" is a flimsy boat that's not worth a fig in the great waves of life.

Then we will know

The daily devotional goes on to say: "Today we remember the founder of our church, Dr. Martin Luther (d. February 18, 1546), his faith in the Gospel, and his declaration of the free gift of salvation given to us unworthy sinners, by grace, from God."

As the Pathwork Guide teaches, Christ did indeed come to Earth in the form of a man named Jesus. His mission was to open the door for *all of us* to get back to heaven. That was essentially a free gift. But salvation we must work for.

For as the Guide clearly said, "If you do not meet that in you which freezes and paralyzes the living spirit, it is impossible to be moved and lived by the living spirit."

We simply cannot transcend duality while living from our ego. To transcend duality, we must discover the living spirit at our core, and then our ego must surrender and learn to live from there. Only then can we have a deep inner knowing of the truth, including the truth about how worthy we each are.

That's how we save ourselves. We save ourselves by finding our deeper true selves, for that is where we find heaven.

Half-truths get us nowhere

If we look around, we see that Christianity is in a state of decline. Lutherans are no longer filling the pews. To understand this, we can turn to the Pathwork Guide's teaching about the three principles of evil, one of which is confusion. And few things confuse us more than half-truths. More than that, when something is not fully in truth—when we embrace only half of a truth and reject the opposite half—it can't keep growing. For all untruth equates to negativity, and all negativity eventually grinds things to a halt.

In the case of Christians, many embrace the need to have faith, welcoming the light of Christ in their hearts. But then they fall short in clearing away whatever is blocking that light. There is recognition that we have sinned—none of us are perfect—and that we feel unworthy. These things are true. But that is not the truth of who are. In truth, we are each worthy, because at our core, we are all light.

Our work is to use our free will to find and free up that light. We had the right idea when we sang in Sunday school: *This little light of mine, I'm gonna let it shine.* But the follow-through wasn't there during the rest of the week.

People started to see the hypocrisy that resulted. Worse, many people—myself included—were affected by various kinds of abuse that festered in the unhealed darkness.

As such, many people are turning away from church and gravitating to spiritual paths that face what's not aligned with the light. This is the growing "Spiritual but Not Religious" group. For a time, riding this wave—maybe even helping to create it—Pathwork communities were thriving in many regions across this country. Significant healing work was done as people worked to transform their Lower Self.

And then the wave started to recede.

For many who were drawn to Pathwork had strong negative feelings about church. To avoid offending anyone—to keep people from leaving Pathwork—the topic of Christ was rarely mentioned. Seldom in my own decades of Pathwork experience was it acknowledged that the whole point of doing all this inner cleaning work is to live in a clean house—a house that Christ built.

Letting the light of Christ shine

The Guide teaches that transforming our Lower Self is always an act of our Higher Self. It is our inner light that inspires us to become better. It is our own faith that there could be more to life that compels us to search for deeper meaning. In the end, it will be our willingness to take self-responsibility for what disconnects us from our own core that will bring us home to God.

Christ is going to come again, but not as a person. The next time Christ comes it will be through each one of us when we do the necessary work of clearing away our negativity and calling forth our inner light. When we do that, we will learn how to live together in harmony and in true faith.

Humanity is just now emerging from adolescence. It's time to grow up.

WWW.PHOENESSE.COM

phoenesse
FIND YOUR TRUE YOU.

Essay 8

It's time to grow up: Maturing through stages

As we enter a new era—the start of a new epoch, really—we are going through a time of crisis. But the clashes going on now are just a normal part of growing up. Ready or not, it's now time for humanity to step fully into adulthood. Let's look at where we are heading next.

During transitions, turmoil is inevitable

When all that is negative is stuck and deadened, the destructive forces appear to be quiet. But then, during a growth process—which is a fundamental aspect of living—there will be a temporary time of turmoil. This is what is happening now.

Over the last century or so, there have been many, many more souls arriving here. Many of these souls are highly evolved, more so than in former times. At the same time, many are also arriving who are lower in their spiritual development. In the world today, we can these two groups clashing. This conflict, while unavoidable, has also been absolutely necessary for moving us all forward.

It works the same in the individual as it does in the collective. For example, if a person has been doing their personal self-development work, they will expect their life to gradually get better. Problems and pain should diminish. And while this will indeed be true in some areas, it won't be true where deep-rooted problem remain. There, the conflict still exists and it must come all the way out into the open in order to be eliminated. Simultaneously, positive creative forces are being mobilized in the soul, and the two will clash.

This will necessarily create an inner tension and frustration. Unless this is brought into a person's conscious awareness, they won't understand why they feel all this unease. The person may doubt their progress and become discouraged. But in truth, these opposing forces must both be mobilized—brought into conscious awareness—and then clash before unification can happen.

This same thing is happening with humankind as a whole right now. A tremendous development is going on. Strong, new forces are coming into this earth plane—positive forces that haven't existed here before. And they are being obstructed and feared by the negative forces—present to a greater degree in those who are less developed—that are also becoming doubly strong.

The more we can recognize the truth of what is now happening, the more we can relax and create a healing climate to support this transition. For when we know the truth, we create a special feeling, and that feeling generates a special atmosphere that is very healing.

Clarity and understanding are key

As we usher in this new era, we will recognize spiritual values more and more, and we will live by them instead of deny them. The cold, mechanistic, materialistic approach many have developed toward life will soften and transform. There will be upheavals, but we will be able to overcome them.

We will learn to move past the darkness in our souls that blurs our connection with our inner divine self. We will begin to see that what concerns one concerns all. For currently, in our three-dimensional state, we make a distinction between me and you and God, between this and that, up and down, here and there. But all these are illusions. Whatever is inside us is also everywhere else.

So any tiny step we take toward unfolding our inner wisdom, courage and beauty—where we connect with our own divine nature—is incredibly significant for everything and everyone that ever was, is, or will be. What we each do every day counts.

The deep insights that come by way of self-confrontation can truly set us free. We can liberate ourselves from compulsions and choose a new course. But such change is only possible when it is our free choice. And for us to make the best choices, we must have clear understanding.

There are spiritual laws that God has created and which guide each of us. We need to get to know them. Humanity too, as a whole, is an entity that is governed by certain laws. And just as there are aspects of ourselves we don't yet understand and can't control, humankind contains hard-to-understand aspects that work to destroy union and disrupt peace.

At first, as we each grow, there will still be times of confusion and depression. But gradually, as we master our own inner darkness, the negative periods will become shorter and less frequent. Peace, freedom and joy will deepen. We will realize that the negative times contain lessons. And if we master those lessons, we will be able to pass the tests.

The gift of growing up

Long ago, Earth was in its infancy. It had to go through millions of years of evolution before the first primitive humans could appear. Like a human baby, primitive humanity had no sense of itself back then. Everything came down to an immediate reaction to sensations of pleasure or pain. There was little logic or knowledge of cause and effect. Everything was physical, just like for an infant.

It's still this way in the parts of our psyche that are immature. While various parts of us have grown up and know better, somewhere there remains a selfish, self-centered, limited infant that is in conflict with the rest of our personality. The only way for these parts to grow up is for us to stop suppressing them. We must see our immaturity so we can transform it.

For to whatever extent we hold onto infantile attitudes—wherever we are neurotic, conflicted and immature—we remain dependent. These are what rob us of our freedom. Being self-centered, then, and being dependent are linked. What an inner conflict we create for ourselves by insisting on staying self-centered while we struggle against being dependent on others!

So maturing means developing a sense of self, which paradoxically leads us to become more concerned about others. This is what leads to creating fairness for all. Then we become capable of foregoing an advantage for ourselves if it creates an unfair pain or disadvantage for someone else. As such, we move into an awareness that surpasses bouncing between pleasure and pain. This is how we begin to transcend duality.

Such mature people are free and independent, but not omnipotent. They have a social sense and a feeling of responsibility that leads to creating a harmonious whole. Whereas primitive humanity fluctuated between ruling and being ruled, today we have the choice to discover healthy interdependence, if we are willing to grow up.

Growing and going through stages

The transition from being utterly self-centered to having concern for others marks a crucial period in development, both for a person and a society. But every growth transition is fraught with crisis. Let's consider a human baby. The birth process itself is a crisis, for both the mother and the infant. Then the infant is weaned, which is also a crisis. Starting school is another crisis. Leaving the parent's protection, too, is a sort of crisis. Teething and puberty are other forms of crisis that lead to individuation.

If we fight against these growing periods, they will be painful and filled with conflict. But to the degree we embrace them, life brings us new experiences and challenges.

By now, humanity has left behind infancy as well as childhood, having transitioned into adolescence roughly two thousand years ago. When the spirit of Christ incarnated in the person of Jesus, there was the kind of upheaval and turmoil we associate with puberty. At that age, young people have lots of idealism and strength, while at the same time having cruel, violent and rebellious impulses. All this was going on during the time of Jesus Christ.

Development periods are uneven

It may seem odd that so much time lapsed on Earth between humanity's infancy and childhood, and between childhood and adolescence, while only two thousand years have gone by since we went through puberty. And now here we are, standing on the brink of maturing. But the phases of growth for the overall Earth entity can't be measured in the same fixed way as for a human being.

Consider too that an individual may be more or less a mature adult yet retain destructive and immature elements within. No doubt, the average adult has a number of mature, responsible aspects that operate freely, while also harboring problem areas where a selfish child reigns. So while growing up and maturing is bound to bring a great deal of betterment—to both the world and to a person—it doesn't automatically make the destructive aspects go away.

In our world, there are groups, countries, religions and sects that have different outlooks and attitudes. We lack peace due to their split aims and conflicting ideas. In the same way, we each have contradictory inner convictions we only learn about through the work of self-exploration. After we discover our inner splits, it's no longer so hard to see why we feel disturbed—why we are at war with ourselves.

All of humanity is divided within itself. As long as we hold onto self-centered pursuits and harbor wrong conclusions, we will continue to operate unfairly and blindly. We will continue to be destructive and wasteful.

It's darkest before the dawn

It's time now for humanity to leave the stage of adolescence. But that doesn't mean our societies are any more harmonized than the average adult. Yet just as with a person who lives maturely—in spite of immature trends remaining in their psyche—we could reach a more mature state of living. For the more we grow, the less confused we will collectively be about what's constructive and what's destructive.

In the past, when we were in the child and adolescent stages, we couldn't always tell truth from lies. We couldn't spot crass injustices and we would allow cruelty to parade as being done for a righteous cause. (*Remember public hangings?*) After all, a child's mind can't be discerning and it refuses to make the effort needed to sort out difficult situations. But as each person outgrows their destructive, childish trends, they develop the ability to reason and understand. So too, then, will humanity grow and grow up.

As a result, we are now perched on the threshold of greater maturity. And we can feel the state of crisis we're in looming over us, like a great wave. We are in the darkness before the dawn.

We must dig deep to find real solutions

Life is not a process that is separate from us. Humanity is the sum total of all its people. The two are identical. Just as each person must go through tests in their own lives, we must start to work together to navigate this great test that is life. By understanding this, we will understand this world we live in much better. And we will deepen our own self-understanding.

Everything that is split becomes sick. In order to heal, we must come to see our own inner darkness and how we are projecting it onto the world. Then, the more we come to understand our own selves, the more we will understand the workings of the world. The deeper we go within ourselves, the more will we have fruitful connections with others. The less we know ourselves, the more will we withdraw from the world.

When humanity was younger, we didn't have the ability to look more deeply into ourselves. We couldn't look inward to find the inner causes behind the effects happening in our lives. So far, humanity as a whole hasn't done much better in this regard. For looking at outer factors alone seldom fixes anything. It leads to short-lived solutions and bigger problems down the road.

But when we make the effort to truly look beyond outer appearances—to really face into issues, even when it's unpleasant—we soon see the situation's not hopeless at all. We find wonderful, realistic, creative ways forward that people have the ability to manifest. When the collective spirit of this world starts operating this way, all existing problems will find genuine solutions.

The more we each overcome our resistance to finding and facing the truth inside ourselves, the more will we each contribute to all of humanity reaching the phase when we resolve our problems through reason and fairness, rather than trying to triumph through the use of brute force.

After the whole span of humanity's existence, we are just now emerging from adolescence. The maturing process will certainly take a long time to reach the full individuation of the spirit. For all individual parts must mature in order for the totality of humankind to live in harmony. And don't forget, this integration must always respect the free will of every person.

Yet the faster we mature overall, the faster will the progress go for those who limp behind. Over time, as this evolutionary process continues, each person's emanations will become finer and finer. As our matter becomes more subtle, we will eventually be drawn to a different world that is a match for our finer matter.

Then we will no longer be drawn back to this dualistic sphere, which is currently a match for our split inner selves. Then we will have passed the test of living on Earth, and we will graduate to living life without the difficulties of duality. Then we will all live together in peace. And doesn't that sound like paradise?

Blessing from the Pathwork Guide

"My dearest friends…receive very special blessings for your continuous development and self-realization…go your way in peace. Keep the inner light burning so that further growth, further individuation, can proceed within each one of you, thus enabling you to reach out and contact others in their true inner state. You will become more independent, more free, more responsible, less isolated. Our love, our blessings go to all of you. Be in peace. Be in God!"

– Pathwork® Guide Lecture #120: The Individual and Humanity

Adapted from *The Guide Speaks*, Q&As with the Pathwork Guide on Earth Conditions, and Pathwork Guide Lecture #120: The Individual and Humanity.

Many people go through life in a state of isolation, stranded on an ego-centered island.

WWW.PHOENESSE.COM

Essay 9

After isolation:
Approaching the Great Transition

There are basically two currents that flow through the universe. One of them is love, which leads to union. It does so by reaching out to others. Love communicates and rises above the limitations of the little ego. For the ego lives on an island of isolation. And while the ego is only a part of a much grander whole, it thinks it is the center of the universe.

Beyond our limited ego, then, and beneath the distortions of our Lower Self sits our true self, or Higher Self. It is from here that love unfolds. Although our true self rests calmly at the center of our being, it never considers itself to be the ultimate end. And yet, it is only by finding and connecting with this true essence at our core that we can reach the height of our potential.

Our goal then is to transcend our ego and start experiencing life from the vantage point of our true innermost self. Then we will no longer be limited by the barriers we create for ourselves through our false, limiting beliefs. After all, it is these wrong conclusions about life that block the flow of love. So it is our own misconceptions that separate us and hold us back. But once we break free from our own self-created barriers, we will be able to create union with others.

Two forces in the universe

The other basic force in the universe is the one by which most people still live. It's the principle that puts the ego at the center. In this state, we "enjoy" life alone. And by enjoy, we really mean suffer. Regardless how many loved ones surround us and share our life with us, when our ego is the center of our existence, we will essentially feel separate.

As we stand firmly planted in the shoes of our ego, we think we're the only ones who experience *this*—whether we're talking about *this* particular pain or *that* particular joy—in quite this or that way. And this self-centered separateness feels unshakable.

Our work then is to transition from this state of ego-centric isolation to the state of union with all that is. This is the most essential step we can take on our evolutionary journey.

For each of us, this transition has to come, whether in this lifetime or in another one. When it occurs will vary from person to person. But when walking a spiritual path such as this one, it must come sooner or later. The hope is that each of us will swing from living an ego-centered life to living from our true center *while we are still here*, in this particular incarnation.

Developing greater self-honesty

If we want more love in our life, we need to head in the direction of becoming more honest with ourselves. Or as the Guide so elegantly put it, "Self-honesty is the first step toward love."

Here are the first four steps that anyone can take. They will help us develop a greater connection with our own inner light by clearing away all the dishonesties that are blocking it.

STEP ONE: Uncover our faults

For starters, we must begin to notice our own faults. This is our first step in getting to know ourselves. Yet for most of us, seeing our shortcomings—even as they appear on the most easy-to-spot level—isn't easy. For we're largely untrained in the skill of self-observation.

Remember, all our faults stem from one of three main roots: self-will, pride or fear. No matter what fault we uncover in ourselves, if we dig deep enough, we'll see how it comes from one of these three things.

STEP TWO: Find our misunderstandings

Digging a little deeper, we'll move onto the second step and start to uncover our wrong conclusions about life. We'll gradually come to realize we harbor misunderstandings that are connected with all our conflicts in life.

STEP THREE: Unwind the misunderstandings

Now we're ready for the third big step on our spiritual path. We'll need to see how our faults are embedded in our misunderstandings. Said another way, we need to see that our misunderstandings seem to justify our faulty thinking and behaving. For while we may have made some progress by now in overcoming our faults, we'll now likely see they have deeper roots than we realized.

STEP FOUR: Go deeper

Next it's time to circle back and discover where we are still proud and fearful, selfish and withdrawn. To find these weaknesses, we'll need to look deeply within. We must search every inner conflict for these traits. For even if, on the outside, we're outgoing and able to cover these things up, it's still important to see where they remain hidden within.

Going through the great transition

Now let's look at why we should go through these necessary but difficult steps. What will making such a change really mean for us? After all, those four steps sound like a lot of work. Is it really worth it? In fact, the ultimate aim of any spiritual path is to make this Great Transition from one state to the other. We want to transition from centering ourselves in our ego to living from our own inner light.

Note, to say that people today are mostly self-centered may sound critical. But this word is being used here in a philosophical way. It's the basic state of being that most people are in. Also keep in mind that transitioning from one state to another is not at all like flipping a switch. Along the way, we may have isolated moments of feeling fully awake, only to have it vanish. So we will have to take many steps on our path before this transition becomes permanent.

But there is a key to having this transition permanently stick. The key is to find and resolve all our hidden conflicts. In other words, we must go through those four steps until all our inner riddles have been solved.

There are two different states?

Many people don't even realize there are two distinctly different states. In fact, most don't realize they're still living in the old state—the undesirable ego-centered state. And this lack of awareness makes going through this transition all that much harder.

How about some encouragement: Here are the promises of what lies ahead for those who do the hard work of spiritual healing. First, we'll feel freedom. For our walls of isolating self-centeredness are very confining. Second, we'll feel that life has a deep purpose. And not just our life, but all life!

Third, we'll understand the reason behind all our experiences, even the hard ones. For we'll see our life from a new point of view. Fourth, we'll have a feeling of unity with everyone. And we'll sense the importance of their purpose too, not just our own.

Beyond this, we'll feel a joy and security we haven't known before. This new security won't carry any delusion about the end of all suffering. At the same time, we won't cringe from such suffering. We will have a deep knowing that in the end, our suffering can't harm us.

Adopting a whole new perspective

For many, there will be a feeling that whatever we're experiencing in this moment has been felt by millions of others. Millions in the past have felt this way, and millions more will in the future. All our feelings, we'll come to realize, have always existed. Be they happy or horrible, welcome or awful, we're not the only ones who have experienced them.

The fact that we seem to produce our feelings doesn't, in fact, mean we actually do produce them. What we really produce for ourselves is the condition of tuning into a particular force of an already existing emotion. It might sound like we're splitting hairs here, but really this is a vitally important distinction to make.

As long as we harbor the illusion that we are producing a particular emotion that goes along with a certain life experience, then we think we're unique, and alone, and separate. But we can start to see that we're just tuning into what is already there. Then we automatically become part of a bigger whole. In which case, we're not such a separated being after all.

Now, just hearing these words is not going to immediately create this new state of being in us. But by tuning into this perspective, we just might be able to accelerate our transition to this other way of being in the world. Because seeing what we have in common with everyone else can go a long way in widening our horizons.

Rather than feel sorry for ourselves for being less than perfect, and rather than beating ourselves up for finding our faults, we can make more constructive use of our negative inner findings. And believe it or not, this will open up our creative abilities.

Tuning into union vs. isolation

The great longing of all humanity is to participate in the life that follows *after* going through this transition into union. Meanwhile, in our ignorance, we fight this transition. Nevertheless, the longing always remains, because the state of union is the natural state of all God's creatures. And in that state, there's no loneliness anymore.

In our present state, however, many of us still feel essentially alone. In this state of isolation, the best we can hope for is a feeling that others are also feeling utterly alone. But that's not at all what the new state really feels like.

In the new state, we know deeply that all thoughts, all feelings, and all experiences already exist. And we are flowing along in those currents due to the conditions we ourselves have produced. Like radio waves, these forces are all around us, and within us. It's up to us which ones we will tune into.

It's our frame of mind, our emotional state, our level of development, our passing moods, and how we relate to our outer life circumstances that affect which stream we will experience. While tuning into one, we might also tune into another conflicting one. If we start to see things this way, we are bound to become, little by little, the being we actually are—a divine, deeply connected ray of light—instead of a separate, self-centered person.

The grand illusion: I don't matter

Instead, we operate under the illusion that we are just one out of billions, and therefore we don't count. We feel we're just a cog in a wheel, and so we cling to our uniqueness. This, we think, gives us dignity. This, we believe, is the avenue to happiness. For if we're just one among many, well then, our happiness must not be important.

What's more, we misinterpret our right to being an individual. By buying into the illusion that we are a separate being, we lay claim to being essentially alone. At best, we believe that everyone suffers from this same uniqueness. As such, we are all fighting a tragic and unnecessary battle.

We think we have to fight against giving up our right to be an individual in order to be happy and feel important. But all we're really doing is struggling to maintain our separateness. If we could clear this up, the fight would be much easier.

Because the truth is this: sharing *something that already exists* with others makes us happier people. We are each no more and no less than a part of a whole. And we all have the right to be happy. This fact gives us more, not less, dignity.

Moving toward me *and* the other

If we feel we are a separate individual, we assume that in order to have more for ourselves, we must take something away from others. That's the error and the conflict. And in the old state, that's how it actually works out. But to the extent we leave this state and transition to the state of union, the fullness and richness of life will grow.

In the new state, it's no longer true that it's me *or* the other. Now it's me *and* the other. Once we glimpse this truth, even if for only a moment, we'll no longer be torn by the conflict that either we have a happiness that is selfish, or we give up our "selfishness," meaning our happiness isn't important.

In the end, this misunderstanding makes us feel deeply guilty about our desire to be happy. But that conflict can vanish the minute we train our attention on a new outlook. From this new perspective, we'll also see how steeped in separateness we were.

That old state of separateness was, and still is, the world we live in. But once we recognize this, our desire to leave that old world behind will blossom.

Gradually changing from the inside out

We're all so afraid of changing. But in truth we don't have anything to fear. Paradoxical as it may sound, we can go through this Great Transition and remain largely the same, even as we change.

For as we transition from being in isolation to being in union, our values are bound to change. We won't just adopt new opinions, but a natural, organic inner growth will occur. Our outer opinions may not even change all that much. Yet we will experience them completely differently.

As we go through the Great Transition, what remains the same are the aspects of ourselves that are valid and valuable. Whatever is essentially us, at our core, will only be enriched. And what is not part of our core essence will slip away.

Best of all, as this transition occurs, creative forces will flow from the center of our being that we didn't even know were there.

Allowing creative forces to flow

Many people go through life in a state of isolation, stranded on an ego-centered island. In this state, when love or creative talents try to flow forth, they get turned back. For due to our erroneous notions, such movements are withdrawn, held back and made inactive. But this goes against the grain of our true nature! So we rebel against the frustration we feel. Because instead of streaming out and reaching others, our essence is going backwards.

We cause many conflicts for ourselves with this basic rebellion. Sorry to say, these conflicts can't be totally resolved just by finding our faults and unwinding our internal misunderstandings. True enough, our wounds created in childhood must be worked with and dissolved if we want to step into a new state of being.

But resolving our childhood conflicts is not the end goal. For if we stop there, we will fail in our mission of achieving deep self-fulfillment. The greater aim needs to be this: To transition from the self-centered state of isolation to living in a state of union with everyone and everything.

As part of this transition, we must come to see that we ourselves are an integral part of creation. And as such, it is our right to keep striving toward greater and greater fulfillment. There's no limit to how far we can go.

The thing that blocks the great creative forces from streaming through us *is us*. Instead of developing all our capabilities and having health and strength, our outlook on life has gotten distorted. Not only do we have a wrong perspective on the real meaning of life, but our ignorance, confusion and lack of awareness all work to halt the vital flow of life-giving forces.

Only by adjusting our outlook—by developing more self-honesty, fixing our faults and straightening out our wrong thinking—will we be ready to make the Great Transition. Then, living in this new state, creative forces will naturally flow through us. They will reach out and touch others who are able to tune into them. At the same time, we will be continually renewed by the replenishing forces that will flow into us.

These words may sound abstract. But try to let them melt into you. Let them become a revelation for you. Then a new doorway will open through which you are longing to step. When this happens, you will be able to sense how long you have wanted to cross this portal. You will recognize how long you have been going through this battle that now brings you to this threshold.

Yet this is such a senseless struggle! The fact that what we're reaping is unhappiness should alone prove that the direction we've been going is wrong. *Now is the time to change direction.* And our first steps must take us toward greater self-knowledge and self-acceptance. Everything arises from this.

Truly, we will never solve our problems unless we can envision going through this Great Transition.

May these words crack open a window in your soul.

Blessing from the Pathwork Guide

"With the special blessing of Christ who was love, and is love, and who will always be love, I leave you with strength and our love, and with our wishes that you may continue to struggle on this one path, this path of finding yourselves and developing yourselves to become the person you are meant to be.

"For there is nothing more worthwhile and purposeful that you could possibly do, as long as you are truly honest with yourself. Self-honesty is the first step toward love. So be blessed, my dearest ones, be in peace, be in God!"

– Pathwork® Guide Lecture #75: The Great Transition in Human Development from Isolation to Union

Adapted from Pathwork Lecture #75: The Great Transition in Human Development from Isolation to Union.

If our lives aren't currently running well, our ego is not yet ready to wake up.

WWW.PHOENESSE.COM

phoenesse

Essay 10

Paying attention:
The life-changing process of waking up

The human psyche is made up of many moving parts. Waking up means we start paying attention to them, sorting them out, and gradually shifting which part is in the lead. To do this, we must get to know how the ego, the Higher Self and the Lower Self operate and interact. There is also a Mask Self, which we touched on in Essay 3.

The part that needs waking up most, in the long run, is the Higher Self. In most people, it lies dormant in the center of our being, rarely seen and seldom consulted. It's not so much that our Higher Self is asleep, but we're simply no longer aware of it. It's patiently waiting for our ego to consciously access it and operate our lives from this deeper place within. We have arrived at a separated sense of ourselves precisely because our ego has lost contact with this highly connected, inner domain.

The ego, by contrast, is the part of ourselves we're very familiar with. In fact, we always have full access to our ego. This is the part that needs to do the heavy lifting of surfacing our Higher Self. Hence, having a well-developed ego is fundamental to the process of waking up.

Meet the Selves: Qualities of the
Higher Self, Lower Self, Mask Self, Ego
From *Spilling the Script: Meeting the Selves*

Unhealed Ego

Immature • Lives in duality: Can't hold opposites
"See me, I'm better than you, love me for it."
Competes to be better than others • "Me versus the Other"
Uses drugs, distractions to avoid, escape, try to transcend itself
Demands to be master

Shame | Outer Layer of Mask

Don't expose • Must hide
"I'll be so embarrassed, I'll die"
"I'm the only one" • "I'll be rejected"
A lid that lifts off with appropriate exposure

Mask Self | Defense Strategies | Not Real*

Does the dirty work of Lower Self • Furthers separation
Uses defenses to mask pain of not getting needs met:
    Aggression • Submission • Withdrawal (none work)
Three defense strategies: Power Mask (Attack),
    Love Mask (Submit), Serenity Mask (Withdraw)
Judges others to avoid feeling affected by them
Signs of mask: Urgency • Secrecy • Denial • Projection
Uses forcing current or collapses • Resigns to hopelessness
Blames • Is a victim • Gives away power • No boundaries
Uses rationalizations • "Shoulds" • Excuses
False pain: "Don't do this to me, life!"
False guilt for getting pleasure from destruction,
    for competing and maligning
False conclusions: "It's not safe to love" • "If I'm perfect,
    I'll be loved."
Impossibly high standards • Perfectionism

*"Not Real" means this is a strategy, a manipulation of life,
that is not energized by our life force.

Meet the Selves: Qualities of the Higher Self, Lower Self, Mask Self, Ego
Continued

Little-L Lower Self | Young Split-Off Fragments | Real Self in Distortion | Untrue Self

"I Can't" • Tense • Scared • Anxious
Has immature Emotional Reactions
Inner soul split is transferred onto parents
Holds unconscious wrong beliefs, unfelt pain
Wants 100% perfect, exclusive love • Can't win
Always wants its way • Feels frustrated, rejected
Wrong conclusion: I'm not enough, don't matter, am not worthy
Attaches pleasure principle to pain • Must recreate painful
    atmosphere/experiences to come alive • No way out
Caught in duality • "Me versus the other" • Life or death
Feels: Pain, Helpless, Rage • Blocks pain by freezing feelings
Pain creates resentment • Child fears punishment for hate
Adult recreates childhood hurts • Reacts immaturely
Vicious Circle: Rejection > Pain > Hate > Shame >
    Guilt > Self-Punishment> Self-Rejection…repeat
Transfers painful experiences onto others
Lives in a trance

Big-L Lower Self | Real Self in Distortion | Untrue Self

"I Won't" • Cruel to self and others • Highly charged
Harsh • Raw • Misuses will: "I'll hurt me, and I'll hurt you"
Faults: Self-Will, Pride, Fear • Fears humiliation • Must rule
Strategies to rule: Bully, Betray, Seduce/Reject, Hold back
Stuck in blindness • Blocked • Numb • Keeps secrets
Not willing to pay the price or make the effort
Demands to get love • Gives to get • "My way!"
Follows Path of Least Resistance • Attaches pleasure to pain
Builds cases against others • Maligns • Judges
Bad moods • Pessimistic • Inner critic • Tyrant • Victimizer
Hidden No-Current says No to life • Rigid • Inflexible • Stubborn
Withholds • Won't give or give in • Rebellious • Resistant • Defiant
Negative Intention is to stay separate • Uses untruth to justify itself
Uses materialism to avoid the work of self-knowing
Uses half-truths to deceive • Creates confusion
Is destructive • Is not in truth

Meet the Selves: Qualities of the
Higher Self, Lower Self, Mask Self, Ego
Continued

Healed Ego

Makes peace with duality
Mature • Prays to know the truth
Sees and unwinds mistaken beliefs
Connects Higher Self with split-off parts
Aligns with God's will • Focuses • Commits
Surrenders • Lets go • Desires to be a servant
Willing to pay the price and make the effort
"Me and the Other" • Eventually dissolves

Higher Self | Real Self | True Self

God is in me • I am Light• Divine spark • Inner Essence
Never comes, never goes • Just is • Trustworthy • Flows
Abundant • Creative • Orderly • Yes-Current that creates
Nature • Life • Life force • Courage • Wisdom • Love
Unity • "Me and the Other" • Balances active & receptive
Accepts imperfection • Feels remorse for hurting others
Experiences real guilt • Feels pain of blindness, sadness, grief
Holds opposites • Holds whole truth • Transparent • Authentic
Comfortable with paradox • Compassion *and* self-responsibility
Self-Autonomy *and* selflessness • Humility *and* strength
Emptiness *and* fulfillment • Giving *and* receiving
Guidance • Intuition • Inspiration • Discerning
Pleasure • Joy • Beauty • Humor • Harmony • Fluid • Flexible
Willing to give, to be of service • Is present in the Now
Enjoys the peace that surpasses all understanding

The power of paying attention

Humanity has been focusing on developing our egos over the last few hundred years. We've learned to use our ego minds in important and powerful ways. We've also learned to make the effort necessary to live a functional life. Now that many of us have become accomplished at applying our egos in the right way, we're in good shape for the challenge of waking up.

Nothing is stopping us from starting today on the life-changing process of waking up. Our ego just needs to start paying attention. We must pay attention to trustworthy spiritual teachings such as these from the Pathwork Guide. For they can help us understand the landscape of the psyche.

Then we must start paying attention to ourselves.

But take note, if our lives aren't currently in reasonably good working order, our ego is not yet ready to wake up. For waking up is not an easy task, and an underdeveloped ego is more apt to slip into spiritual bypass than make any serious progress. Spiritual bypass is what happens when the ego attempts to look "spiritual," but is really just avoiding doing the hard work of self-development.

Getting there, from here

What keeps the ego from aligning more fully with the Higher Self? The Lower Self. In a nutshell, the Lower Self is made up of layers of negativity and destructiveness that block our light, and which cause every disharmony in life. So, we can't let go from our ego and live from our inner light, or Higher Self, before we have transformed our Lower Self.

Truth be told, the average person is going to have to cover a lot of Lower Self ground before shifting from the ego to the Higher Self. We must clean out all our dark inner closets, so to speak, as part of the waking-up process. This is the only way to transition from an ego-led life to one that's grounded in the greater truth of our being.

When we live from our ego, we do battle with life. Living from our Higher Self, by contrast, means we clear away the untruth of our Lower Self, so we can live in harmony. For harmony is what naturally occurs when we see the truth in its entirety.

When this happens—when we gradually learn to live more and more from our Higher Self—we drop our cases, let others off the hook, reconcile opposites, and find more peace. All self-development, then, is really about unwinding our inner negativity, or Lower Self, and rediscovering our Higher Self. So to find ourselves is to find our Higher Self, which is the truth of who we are.

Guidelines for self-healing, page 10, offers tips for telling which part is in the lead—the Higher Self or the Lower Self—along with clues about what the ego should be watching for.

Living from our ego

The ego is a limited aspect of ourselves. It performs certain important functions, but it lacks depth. For example, the ego may learn something and spit it back out, but it can't come up with new creative ideas on its own. Perhaps the biggest deficit of the ego is that, like the Lower Self, it's perpetually stuck in duality.

Here's how it works: The ego divides everything into right or wrong, good or bad, black or white. For the ego can't hold both sides of really anything. It can't hold opposites. So the ego must always take one side or the other. Typically, the ego scrambles for the good while running from the bad. (Although sometimes, out of sheer hopelessness, the ego will turn and embrace the bad, kidding itself that this is a good idea.)

Guidelines for self-healing

Higher Self	Lower Self	Ego
Mature	Immature	Pays attention and notices when we're in an emotional reaction. Then takes action to sort ourselves out.
Quiet, calm, centered, patient	Loud, angry, fearful	Pays attention and notices when we're being hateful or anxious. Then takes action to sort ourselves out.
Relaxes while in motion	Controlling or hopeless	Pays attention and notices our alternating forcing current or resignation. Then takes action to sort ourselves out.
Healthy No	Rebels, resists, defies, denies	Pays attention and notices our destructiveness. Then takes action to sort ourselves out.
Healthy Yes	Submits, gives to get	Pays attention and notices when we're not standing on our own two feet. Then takes action to sort ourselves out.
Present in the moment	Withdraws, runs, escapes, hides	Pays attention and notices our avoidance, distractions and addictions. Then takes action to sort ourselves out.
Builds consensus	Builds cases	Pays attention and notices when we're serving separation, not connection. Then takes action to sort ourselves out.
Holds opposites	Opinionated self-righteousness	Pays attention and notices when we insist on being right. Then takes action to sort ourselves out.
Aligns with God's will	Aligns with self-will	Pays attention and notices our lack of trust and ability to let go. Then takes action to sort ourselves out.
Fluid, resilient, free flowing	Rigid, harsh, judgmental	Pays attention and notices when we are stuck on a position or hard feeling. Then takes action to sort ourselves out.
Lives in harmony	Thrives on conflict	Pays attention and notices disharmonies in our lives. Then takes action to sort ourselves out.
Fights the good fight	Follows the path of least resistance	Pays attention and notices when we are being lazy. Then makes an effort to heal.

As such, if we are living primarily from our ego, we will be lost in duality. Meaning, we will be missing half the picture; we will not be able to see the whole truth. This leads to conflict with others, especially if *they* can only see the *other half* of reality. The Higher Self, on the other hand, resides in the unitive state where opposites are necessary to complete the entire picture.

The wrong way to "win"

With our dualistic, ego-oriented approach, we take on life with a "me versus the other" attitude. But the bigger truth about life is that it's always "me *and* the other." This is why we say that conflict is an inherent part of the illusion of duality. It's only by giving up our fighting stance towards life that we can overcome the pain of separation and the untruth it stands upon.

Further, the ego tends to go for a hard-lined, fixed position. It likes rigid rules, lots of control and ironclad opinions. It especially likes to be right. This, the ego thinks, is the way to win. But crouching in such a fighting stance—which is the ego's version of strength—creates stress and anxiety, and tension in the body.

This makes it hard for a body to stay healthy. What's more, it's not even true that we can come out ahead—that we can "win"—when we approach life this way.

The promises

In short, waking up is what happens when we clear away our inner disturbances, resolve our problems in life, learn to stand on our own two feet, and align with the divine. Conflict is what happens when we remain isolated from our own Higher Self, living primarily from our ego and avoiding our dark inner corners. All the while, we're demanding the world shower us with light.

But waking up is not the job of the world. It's what each of us is being called to do. Once we do our all-important inner housework, we'll find ourselves shining more light into the world. And the world will then reflect light back to us.

When that happens, we will discover that life can be lived with grace and ease. After we clear away our resistance and the untruth that underpins it, our lives will naturally become more manageable. We will cooperate with life and help bring an end to chaos.

It's our inner light—the part we must work so hard to free—that goes on forever.

WWW.PHOENESSE.COM

phoenesse

Essay 11

Living on the good side of life

I grew up saying the standard Lutheran prayer before meals: "Come Lord Jesus, be our guest, and let this food to us be blessed. Amen." At my friend's house, where they were Methodist, they said: "God is great, God is good, and we thank him for this food. Amen." In my head, I always questioned if "food" really rhymed with "good."

But that second prayer also raises an even better question: Is God *all* good? This seems fair to ask, given the way we live surrounded by duality. Where good and bad are always a package deal. If you ask for salt, life will also hand you pepper.

Per the Guide's teaching in Chapter 5 of *After the Ego*: "We have been geared for century after century to see the world through the lens of good or bad. It's understandable that we've gotten lost in our confusion...Only in truthful perception do we accept both opposites, allowing them to mutually aid one another...Religion itself has furthered this division, making God good and the devil bad. This is, at best, a half-truth."

Consider the fact that the devil, Lucifer, was among the first created beings. No matter what water has gone over the dam since the Fall, under all those dark robes remains a magnificent light. More brilliant, in fact, than almost any other. To miss this truth is to be blind to half of reality. And the minute we believe seeing half a truth is the same as seeing the whole truth, we are involved in error.

The teaching in *After the Ego* goes on, "And all error can lead only to more error and misinterpretation of life. Eventually, we get incredibly lost in this maze." Perhaps this can serve as a good reminder that no matter how "bad" someone may seem, if we try, we might also glimpse their inner goodness.

Going back to God and that dinner prayer, is it true that God is *only* good? Said differently, does God also have a bad side?

There's a good side and a bad side

Eons ago, long before the beginning of time, something bad happened. And in a nutshell, human beings—who were spiritual beings at the time—got in trouble. Our punishment was a bit like being sent to our room. In this case, we were sent into darkness. Which raises at least two questions: What did we do that was so wrong? And who handed out this dreadful punishment?

Where we went wrong

The long and short of what we did wrong is quite simple: We got sideways with God. We did this by not supporting the leader God had given us. And we did this knowing full well that doing so defied the will of God. And that really was the rub. Call it insubordination. Disobedience. Sedition. Poor judgment. In the end, God was not happy. And this is what led to the Fall. But let's not get ahead of ourselves.

Before any of us came along, God had created the very first being. And as the first, this being was slated to be the one in charge. To this end, this being was created with more light than anyone else. Actually, this being was created with so much more of God's light that this highest-ranking spirit has both feminine and masculine characteristics, all rolled into one.

This was the only way that such a being could be capable of creating all the other divine beings who later came into existence. For any creation requires the presence of both the "let it happen" and "make it happen" energies embodied in the receptive and active principles, which we may also think of as feminine and masculine aspects.

After a time, it was Lucifer—the second in command, if you will—who eventually steered us all into the ditch. Eaten up by envy over the magnificence of Christ, Lucifer began an eons-long campaign to become king himself. He was clever, charismatic, persistent and patient, and over time gathered an enormous following.

What Lucifer failed to account for was this: God was backing Christ. And

God never wavered. From the very beginning, God had clearly and nicely requested that everyone look to Christ as their king. For this was God's plan. This was God's will. And as it turns out, aligning our will with God's will is always going to be in our own best interest. Every time, staying on God's good side brings us to our heart's deepest desires.

Yet as it was then, so it is today: We always have the choice about whether we align our will with God's will. Or not.

Who handles discipline?

Disciplining children well—even when done with the very best intentions—is not easy. Add in our shortcomings as humans, and most parents fall short in how well we discipline our children. Yet raising a child without any guard rails at all isn't just poor parenting, it's dangerous. Kids needs boundaries, guidance, reminders and corrections.

It must be said we shouldn't limit God to having human parental qualities. God exists within, above, beyond and outside the human form. Or as the Pathwork Guide succinctly put it, "God is life and life force." So while not a "person" kind of parent, it could certainly be said that God is the guardian of us all. As in: God has created an infinite number of spiritual laws that guide us.

They operate, in short, by making it painful in the long run to make choices that go against God's will. This is called cause and effect. There's no old man in the sky handing out rewards and punishments. Spiritual laws, in fact, work much like gravity. They function automatically, the same for everyone.

Going back to the time when Lucifer drummed up his rivalry against Christ, Lucifer overlooked one important thing. His defiance was not really aimed at Christ. Lucifer was going against God. Which brings us to the point in the story when we witness the wrath of God.

In essence, by aligning with Lucifer, we all got on God's bad side. And we are still paying a heavy price for it. Now, as we painstakingly work our way back home to God, we must work our way up from separation. To do this, we must stop aligning with darkness.

In other words, our work now is to consciously make choices that align with the light. We can only do this by sifting out truth from untruth and unraveling our self-created negativity. And here on Earth—where both light and dark are present in everything—this is no small task.

God never left us

It is true that God's punishment was severe, casting us out of heaven and into the dark depths of Hell. (It's obvious God doesn't want us to make *that* mistake again!) But it's also true we had plenty of chances to make a better choice before God triggered that event.

To be clear, we've brought this discipline onto ourselves through the choices we made. To be even more clear, whatever difficulties we experience now, we are somehow still contributing to their creation. All our various prisons are of our own making. It is God's plan and desire that we each break down our walls of separation, so we can live in freedom and unity.

For although God did indeed banish us, God never abandoned us. Living here in this land of duality, this may be hard for us to reconcile. But in truth, God continues to provide us guidance and inspiration for getting back home. It arrives in the form of the spiritual guidance and protection that surrounds us and encourages us to go the right way. The more we tune into this, the closer it can come.

Restoring our good side

Our inner light begins and ends with God. Therefore, it has no beginning and no end. This light is our essence, and it can never be destroyed, only dimmed. We can twist, distort and deny it, yet the light remains. So we can always fully restore it. When we do the work of spiritual healing, this is what we are doing. We are restoring our inner light to its original bright and truthful form.

Once we get this ball rolling, things get easier. But starting out, the way may be hard. This is due to our accumulated inner clutter. As we progress, we will align more and more with truth. And this will organically bring us into alignment with God and God's will for us. When this happens, we will open more and more to living and being in truth. Then we will clearly see how the roots of all our problems—which roll up to create the world's problems—lie within.

We'll start to realize that all disharmony comes—in one way or another—from an untruth. And untruth always leads to pain. We cover pain with hate and anger. This leads to avoidance and denial, control and manipulation. All of which create more disharmony, which further hides the truth of the matter. The longer this vicious circle goes on, the more difficult the work of unwinding it will be.

Light is truth

Eventually, when we're shining and sharing the same authentic light as God, God will see we are ready to return, for good. But there's no faking true light. For God always knows the truth. Because God *is* truth.

When we become filled with light, we will know truth and we will feel at peace. And when *that* happens, we will feel like we're already home. It's our choice whether to head in that direction.

Don't forget, we are all made in the image of God. Meaning, like God, we have free use of our will. The question is, are we willing to use it in service of doing our work of healing, of unwinding our hidden untruths and their associated disharmonies?

Are we ready to start living on the good side of life?

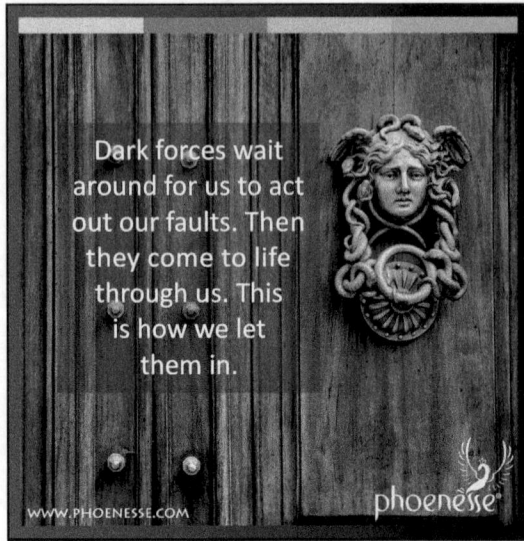

Dark forces wait around for us to act out our faults. Then they come to life through us. This is how we let them in.

WWW.PHOENESSE.COM

phoenesse

Essay 12

How inner obstacles let in dark forces

We moved the summer I turned seven, going from the tiny town of Barron, Wisconsin to the small city of Rice Lake. I had just finished second grade and didn't yet know I would attend third grade in a whole new world. After living close to no one my age, we would now be surrounded by over a dozen neighborhood kids.

Instead of playing with my brothers in the field behind our house, there would now be kick ball games most summer nights. Whereas in Barron, we rode the school bus, we would now just walk the two blocks to school, since Jefferson Elementary, Hilltop Middle School and Rice Lake High School were all just around the corner.

A lot of changes were unfolding that summer, and many were for the good. But here's the thing that hit me the hardest: I was the last to know about the move. When I did find out—whether hours, days or weeks after my two brothers were told, I don't know—I was crushed. This sense of not being included—of feeling left out—and of not being spoken to would echo throughout much of my life.

54

Setting the stage for struggle

It turns out, being seven is an important age in the life of a child. Because although we don't yet understand how the world works, we are old enough to start projecting into the future. As a result, we begin to draw wrong conclusions about life: "So *this* is how life is," we think. "And this is how it's always going to be."

In my case, I secretly concluded, "I am always left out." After all, I always felt like everyone else had gotten the directions, but I was left in the dark. Armed with such unspoken statements, we now feel a bit more prepared to face life. "Now," we think, "I see how this world works."

It will take most people an entire lifetime to realize that such conclusions formed early in life are based on misunderstandings. If they get it at all. Indeed, many will go to their graves believing their hidden wrong conclusions were right.

In fact, by the time we become adults, we're no longer aware we even formed such conclusions based on our childhood experiences. Nonetheless, they have by now become so woven into the fabric of our being that our attitudes and behaviors reflect these beliefs. And then the world responds in a way that makes our wrong conclusions seem true.

Our faults create connection points

Since we can no longer see our mistaken beliefs, it's easy to assume they must be harmless, right? No, they're not. For they form hidden obstacles in our system—tight knots made up of wrong conclusions and the painful feelings associated with them—that today are the root cause of all our daily disharmonies. Because they are at the root of our faults.

And what's wrong with having a few faults, you ask? After all, everybody has them! Or perhaps we think that since our faults aren't as bad as someone else's, they don't matter so much. But we are still responsible for each one, even the minor ones. And the higher our level of development, the greater is our duty and responsibility to keep cleaning up our side of the street. For the greater our light, the bigger the shadow we cast with our remaining inner obstacles.

Too often we make allowances for ourselves, saying, "I'm not the only one doing this," or "Surely others are doing worse." Or we say, "the devil made me do it," as though it's just a coincidence that dark forces were influencing us. No, we're the ones who open that door by ignoring our own hidden inner obstacles.

How we connect with spiritual spheres

According to the Pathwork Guide, the universe is filled with these spheres that are invisible to us. They exist on the planets in our solar system, and also in different stellar systems. On Earth alone, we harbor all kinds of overlapping spiritual spheres of different vibrational frequencies, spanning from the lowest levels to the highest.

This means that as a human being, we can be in a room on Earth, and at the same time be connected to a particular distant spiritual sphere. Meanwhile, another person in the same room might be connected to a different spiritual sphere that's at an entirely different level.

The spiritual sphere we're in contact with will be the one that corresponds with our overall spiritual development. And since none of us are completely harmonious in our development—if that were the case, we wouldn't have to live here—the spiritual spheres we connect with will vary over time.

For as our moods shift, we emit certain currents from our soul. These come from both our conscious mind and the parts of ourselves we're unaware of. And depending on the makeup of these currents, they can link us with quite different spheres.

We're always making connections

We know from other Pathwork teachings that every human being is comprised of both a Higher Self, which is our original divine spark, and a Lower Self, namely our faults and destructiveness, rebelliousness and resistance. In the areas where we have restored our Higher Self to its fully functioning capacity, our inner light shines through.

When this is the case, we must have already done the necessary work of shedding the Lower Self layers that surround us. Then our Higher Self will reach out and automatically connect with the most radiant spiritual spheres. This can—and must—happen while we're living here on Earth.

But wherever our Lower Self is stronger, it doesn't let the Higher Self shine through. When this is the case, we connect with the spheres and forces of darkness that correspond to our own attitudes and our own level of development. For, to be sure, the Lower Self of one person may be lower than another's.

Spiritual specialists influence us

Each spiritual sphere is richly populated by spirits that are a match for that sphere. Earth, for example, is a sphere that's a match for beings who are some parts light and some parts dark. Due to our varying levels of development, wherever there are people, we are surrounded by beings who are linked to widely varying spiritual spheres. And in these various spheres there are all kinds of specialists. This applies to well-ordered, light-filled spheres as equally as it applies to the chaotic dark spheres.

Each of us then attracts the specialists that are a match for the particular qualities we possess, whether they are good qualities or bad. For inevitably, like attracts like. Birds of a feather, as they say, flock together.

As we grow up, we are surrounded by guardian spirits who belong to the divine order of light. And if we are inclined to strive higher and try to align with divine truth, they can come close to us. If not, they must stand back and keep an eye on us from a distance. They can then only step in to protect us based on the past merits we have accumulated.

At the same time, a number of other spirits also surround us who are not part of the divine order. Some of these may belong to the world of darkness. If we are not a particularly sinful soul, then very evil spirits will not come near us. After all, they wouldn't be able to succeed in their specialty with such a person, so why bother?

Minor faults have major impact

That said, even the specialists of everyday human faults—those so-called minor faults—belong to the dark spheres. So if we are, let's say, selfish, we will have a selfishness specialist attached to us. Or if we're inclined to make furious outbursts, we'll have a specialist nearby just waiting for us to let it take over and effectively live through us.

When such a specialist succeeds, it feels a great deal of satisfaction. For not only did it fulfill its task, it got to indulge its own particular weakness. If we do not have a particular fault, such as envy, then we won't have an envy specialist attached to us. Meanwhile, a person standing next to us—who may even be further along than us in their overall development—may have an envy specialist close by because they still have this fault.

Keep in mind, it is our own faults that are pulling particular specialists close to us in the first place. All the specialists do is wait around for us to act out our faults. Then they come to life through us. This is how we collude with them and contribute to the darkness.

Being aware of our faults is the first step

How can we rid ourselves of these dark spirits? By working to overcome our faults. The first step is to recognize what our faults are. For too often we are unaware of them simply because we don't want to have the burden of knowing such unflattering information. Few folks indeed want to know what their own faults are. Most will admit that they probably have some faults, but only do so in a superficial way. Becoming fully aware of our *particular* faults, however, is an entirely different matter.

If we wish to protect ourselves from dark spiritual specialists, we must learn to face ourselves in utter honesty. After all, if we are nursing a certain fault, possibly even turning it into a pet we praise and joke about, we are also carrying the corresponding spirit specialist with us. And that spirit is just waiting for a chance to encourage us to give in to our fault.

Granted, it often doesn't take much effort on their part, as aligning with our faults is the easiest and most comfortable way to go. The Lower Self, remember, follows the path of least resistance.

We must find the root

Any time we are in disharmony, such as when we feel a storm brewing with someone, we can have the presence of mind to remember to pray. When we do this, we are reaching out for God—who is already within us—and asking for spiritual guidance. After all, our Higher Self is a divine ray of God's light.

Prayer, of course, only works when we have the presence of mind to remember to do it. In reality, we don't always have such presence of mind. Sometimes we're tired and we once again become prey for dark influences. The only true and lasting protection, then, is to tear out the bad growth at its roots. That's the approach we're taking when we search to find the root of our faults.

Our attitudes chart our course

Let's imagine for a moment that all of humanity—every single person on Earth—decides to follow the path of least resistance. We all opt to give in to our Lower Self, nursing our faults instead of fighting them. What would happen, from a spiritual point of view?

All our overlapping spheres would change in appearance, because we would make the disharmonious spheres bigger and stronger. These would then dwarf the harmonious spheres of love and light, of truth and happiness, pushing them into the background. In short, humanity would constantly feed the world of darkness, and in turn, it would have an ever-increasing influence over us.

Now let's imagine that all of humanity—each and every person—starts to walk a path of self-purification. Although such a path would be different for every individual, if we were to each try our best, we would cast off and dissolve the spheres of hatred and prejudice, war and greed, evil and envy, darkness and disharmony.

The good news is that divine creations of light cannot be dissolved. They can only be pushed into the background. But as long as negative attitudes remain in control here, God's spirit world of light can't positively affect the material world. They can't help us. Disharmony, on the other hand, with all its unpleasant facets, can eventually be destroyed and must ultimately be dissolved.

Seven signs we need to search within

When our young self was hurt, we took steps to defend ourselves. This is understandable. These steps included formulating conclusions about how life works—with the intention of keeping ourselves safe going forward—and stopping the flow of feelings. Then we adopted a strategy for getting the love we wanted, using either aggression, submission or withdrawal.

But navigating life using such false solutions causes part of us to remain stuck at that young age. So today, we are still harboring these wrong conclusions and resisting the unpleasant feelings attached with them, unnecessarily defending ourselves against ghosts from our childhood.

Here's a list of seven self-sabotaging behaviors that point out where we're not living in alignment with our deeper self, or Higher Self. These are the ways we behave when we hold untruthful ideas in our system along with old unprocessed pain. And each of them will attract more disharmony to us.

Seven self-sabotaging behaviors
- Won't ask for help
- Can't accept praise
- Isolate when hurt
- Always say "yes" to everything
- Put our own needs on hold
- Procrastinate on important tasks
- Try to be perfect

Sound familiar? If so, it's time to turn around and search for their roots, inside. For these behaviors are blinking lights telling us we're not fully living in truth. And when we're not able to be fully authentic, we're also not fully living in the present. Because part of us has gotten stuck in childhood hurts from the past.

It's time to heal ourselves by uncovering the true cause of our disharmonies. For our inner obstacles won't remove themselves. And this world needs more light.

Adapted in part from Pathwork Guide Lecture #15: Influence Between the Spiritual World and the Material World.

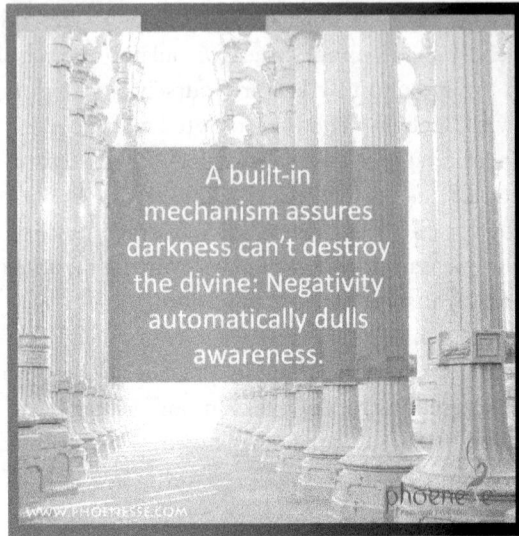

A built-in mechanism assures darkness can't destroy the divine: Negativity automatically dulls awareness.

Essay 13

Closing the gaps in our awareness

For many, there's a gap between what we say we want in life—fulfillment, satisfaction, success, happiness, peace—and what we're actually getting out of life—confusion, frustration, tension, exhaustion. Why is there this gap? And really, why bother trying to close the gap if, in the end, it seems like darkness will keep winning anyways?

In Chapter 10 of *After the Ego*, the Pathwork Guide explains that, no, ultimately darkness will not destroy us all. Although temporarily it can do a nice job of spoiling our picnic. The reason that darkness can't win in the long run is simply this: The greater our darkness, or negativity, the lower our awareness.

Consider the fact that if consciousness was allowed to expand—if people were able to wake up—and self-purification was not a necessary, simultaneous part of that process, then evil could indeed destroy the divine. So there's a built-in mechanism to assure that never happens: Negativity automatically dulls awareness.

In other words, opting to remain in the dark about our own negativity closes off our ability to perceive what's going on in and around us. As a result, blindness, deafness, dumbness and numbness set in. And these don't just happen in our bodies. They're happening inside us. In fact, as is always the case, our outer experience is just a reflection of what's going on within.

When we are steeped in negativity:

- We can't hear our wiser Higher Self voice—also known as guidance or intuiation—speaking to us
- It's a struggle to speak our own truth
- We're disconnected from our own feelings, so our own immature behavior is confusing to us
- We can't see how we are contributing to our struggles
- We can't see what others are doing with their negativity to deceive us or harm us

In such a limited state, we are not only quite ignorant, we are also quite powerless. For we are cut off from the center of our being where divine light always shines and all of life is in connection. The only way to come out of our darkened state is through our consistent effort to get to know ourselves.

Know thyself

Developmentally speaking, humans are in the state of consciousness where there is at least some self-awareness. This means we realize we can affect others with our decisions and behaviors. It also means we're at the point of taking self-responsibility. After all, humans don't operate according to instincts but rather according to our own choices.

For example, we can use our free will to express ourselves. And we tend to do so in whatever way aligns with our current level of development. Clearly, for humans, these levels are all over the map. We're all made of both goodness and darkness, and it's just a question of which part is in the lead in each moment. Most of us are somewhere in the middle. But we're all souls that are not yet fully purified.

When we're lower in spiritual development, the untapped potency of our consciousness will be protected by our lack of awareness. For if we were aware of how much power we have to create while we are still swimming in negativity, we would cause more harm than we already do.

Instead, our own negativity mires us in disharmony. Our unpleasant life experiences then become our medicine. If we face into them and unwind them, we'll start healing. That's what starts closing the gap.

Then, as we clear away our negativity—by clearing away our faults—more and more power will be available to us. For the more inner housecleaning we do, the more we live in truth. And living in truth is synonymous with living in peace and harmony. And these of course lead to having happy, fulfilling and satisfying lives.

The question is: How do we clear away our negativity and close this gap?

The four big God-blockers

There are four big God-blockers we need to find and clean up. The first three are pride, self-will and fear. The fourth is shame. Here's how they fit together.

There is a certain layer in our psyche between our physical body and our divine spark, or Higher Self. And the ego—with all its vanity, pride, fear and ambition—exists in this layer. It is in this layer that our longing for love transposes into a longing *to receive* love. This ego layer believes there's nothing better than receiving love without taking any risk that we'll get hurt. So for the ego, remaining aloof and detached is a highly desirable state.

This is the origin of pride, which essentially says "I am better" and "I am separate." With these sentiments tucked under our belt, we don't believe we can ever be loved, accepted, seen and respected the way we want. Actually, we're right about this, because love can't come to those who hold themselves back and won't give.

This leads to the untrue belief that we are not lovable. And this causes us to feel unhealthy shame that there is something wrong with us: We're not good enough, we're not lovable, we don't matter.

This wrong thinking leads us to use our self-will to demand love and respect. We'll force others both overtly, using aggression, and covertly, using submission. But love can't come this way, which is why none of our strategies ever work. This causes us to withhold ourselves even more.

Then fear says "I'll never get it!" "It" is essentially love, but this often spreads out to include all the things we have swapped out for love, hoping *these things* will bring us the fulfillment we now crave. In our growing fear that we'll never get our needs met, tension and anxiety build.

In truth, if we had no shortcomings, we would have no fear. And it's fear that makes us so miserable. This same fear blinds us to how joyful life can be. But using the tools that the Pathwork Guide is giving us, we have the ability to break the chains of fear.

Introducing guilt and shame

Part of us, deep in our belly, has known all along that none of our wrong beliefs are in truth. Such wrong beliefs include: we aren't good enough, we are not lovable, or we don't matter. And from that gap between our current beliefs and our deep inner truth, guilt arises. This is a false guilt, for if it were authentic guilt for something we had done wrong, the answer would be genuine remorse. Instead, we're left with gnawing guilt that eats at us relentlessly from the inside.

Similarly, if our shame were the right kind, the answer would be repentance. It is this kind of healthy shame that motivates us to do self-healing work.

The wrong kind of shame leads us further into darkness because it makes us want to hide. And this won't help us at all in untangling these twisted threads.

Overcoming darkness

When we expand our awareness, we are letting in more spiritual light. But this spiritual light cannot come to us from outside ourselves; it can only arise from within. This light, however, cannot penetrate our pride. For pride is to spiritual light what a concrete wall is to physical light. This is how pride acts to dim the light of our awareness and wisdom.

So we must be on the lookout for pride. Pride is the feeling that we're special, either because we're better than others or less than others. For feeling less than is just the flip side of feeling better than. And since pride is always an element in our triad of faults, if we find pride, we should also search for fear and self-will. And when we find them all, we'll discover shame and guilt are also nearby.

With all four God-Blockers present, we will be living inside a tangled web of confusion that creates big gaps in our awareness. Because the light cannot get through. This is what's behind the darkness we must work so hard to over-come. And while darkness will not win in the end, it sure can make us miserable in the meantime.

When we reveal ourselves honestly, we are performing an act of humility. And becoming humble is very healing.

WWW.PHOENESSE.COM

phoenesse

Essay 14

What's hiding beneath our stories?

I'd like to share a secret with you. When I am sitting across from someone as their Helper, and the Worker is telling me their story, I don't really care how the story ends. Because I am not listening to hear their story. I am listening to hear where they are stuck. For that's where an untruth is buried. Then we head in the direction of the obstruction and the work proceeds from there. If the Worker goes all the way through with transforming this piece, the story will now have a different ending anyway.

Sure, there are times when a person needs to talk and just have someone listen to them. It can be very healing to feel seen and heard, especially when we have a history of feeling ignored or neglected. But there's usually more value in getting help with unwinding our difficulty. And we can only do that by getting to the true root of our problems.

The importance of aligning with spiritual laws

To unravel our problems, we must come to see where and how we are not in truth. For when we align with an untruth, we are not in alignment with divine laws. And it is only by living our lives in alignment with God's divine laws that we will find happiness. In the end, God's desire is for us all to find happiness.

If we don't believe this is true, a good place to start may be to look at our God Image. This is our mistaken beliefs about God based on our impressions of our parents. Doing this work can help us see how we are currently using our free will in a way that goes against God's will and God's divine laws. In short, we're somehow not in truth and we don't yet know that. But such untruth is what's underneath feeling unhappy.

This is why it is so important to talk openly about ourselves with qualified people who can help us. We need to share our stories to find out what's underneath them. *What's the truth? What am I not aware of?* In our own Higher Self, we already know the answers to these questions. But the truth is currently hidden from us by our own layers of darkness.

As long as we continue to keep things buried inside us, we'll remain blind. For everything will appear out of proportion to us. We'll tend to exaggerate one thing and underestimate something else. But someone detached from our situation may be able to see things in the right light.

The Law of Brotherhood and Sisterhood

There is a spiritual law at work when we open up to someone else, whether that person is a friend, a family loved one, a therapist, coach or a spiritual counselor. It's called the Law of Brotherhood and Sisterhood, and it kicks in the moment we are willing to reveal ourselves honestly to someone. Because in that moment of letting ourselves become vulnerable, we are taking a risk and performing an act of humility. And becoming humble—as opposed to prideful—is very healing.

In fact, one of the most harmful things we do to ourselves is to try to appear more perfect than we are. But the moment we show another person what's really going on inside us, we will instantly feel relief. For having our insides match our outsides is a relief our soul has been crying for, even if the other person doesn't give us a single bit of advice.

When we act against divine laws, we are the ones who suffer for it. But when we are able to humbly reveal ourselves to someone else, we will suddenly feel better. This is the Law of Brotherhood and Sisterhood at work. In effect, what we are saying is, "Right now, I don't want to try to appear any better than I actually am. I want to reveal myself. I'm not trying to get love and respect that I don't think are due me because of the things I'm ashamed of."

Of course, we're wrong in thinking that we're not due love and respect. For every living creature is due love and respect. But since we have a distorted view of things, we are harboring the wrong kind of shame. And this unhealthy shame causes us to hide, violating the Law of Brotherhood and Sisterhood. We wind up suffering with feelings of loneliness, and so we go on pretending. We side with the wrong kind of shame, which closes us up, instead of leaning into the right kind of shame, which motivates us to change.

Notice how even a quality like shame can be held in the right light and have a positive aspect to it. All our feelings, including anger, work this way. Felt and aired in the right way, they are God-given expressions. But acted out in the wrong way, they lead to more pain and suffering.

Turning to others for help

When we become ready to uncover our inner darkness and step into the light, we will be guided to find someone who can help us. And then *we* are the ones who have to do the talking. No one can do this for us. Yes, our self-created problems may back us so far into a corner that we'll feel we *must* open-up to save ourselves. But still, it's our choice to take this step.

We have the option to refuse to be helped—to refuse to change—and instead go deeper into our corner. We might even resent that we feel we've been pushed into a corner. But we can also choose to come out of our hiding place. We can open our eyes, as well as our mouths, and discover that this is what will liberate us.

How to help

The role of being a healer can come about through whatever modality trains a person to help others. The key ingredient is that the healer clears away enough of their own negativity that they can hear and follow guidance from their own Higher Self. For our work as healers is to help someone uncover their own inner truth. And we can't help someone discover places in themselves that we've haven't yet explored in ourselves.

As healers and Helpers, we are able to provide guidance to others because at the level of the Higher Self, we are all already connected. So when we're listening to someone's story, we're tuning our inner listening ears to hear what sounds off. For when we are sitting in truth ourselves, we can learn to pick out truth from untruth in others. The Higher Self, after all, is the home of our truth-teller.

By listening within, a skilled healer or Helper—some kind of trained coach, counselor or therapist—can hear the guidance needed to help someone clear away their inner obstacles. That's what's blocking them from knowing their own truth. In fact, it's actually a person's Higher Self that hires someone else to help them see what they can't currently see in themselves. The work of cleaning up our Lower Self, then, is always an act of our Higher Self.

Following the call to heal

The way out of the Lower Self is to give. We must come to see that it's not true that we can fulfill our longing for love by only demanding love and not giving it. This boils down to wanting to cheat life. We want to get the goodies and not give fully. In our desire to get our way, we set limits, and we strategize; we calculate, and we only extend ourselves if we think it will get us love. And when that doesn't work—and it can't work—we become bitter.

Due to the way we've been approaching life, we may feel that life is constantly testing us. And in a way it is. For when we are going about things in the wrong way, life will show us that it's time to try living another way.

In many ways, we are like children; we don't know what's good for us. But if we are facing difficult hardships and we become willing to try a different route, God's helpers—who are constantly around us—will guide and inspire us to situations where we'll have the opportunity to receive help.

Now here's the catch: We must use our own free will to decide whether we want to learn from them. Are we ready to open our eyes and see the deeper significance of what's happening? Or do we want to ignore this call? And make no mistake, we are being called. It's our choice whether we pay attention and summon the courage to follow this call.

Revealing ourselves releases our shame

The Pathwork Guide teaches that it is actually better to tell a lie to others than to keep blindly lying to ourselves. For when we tell a lie, we know we are lying. But when we blindly create disharmony in our lives without seeing our part, we are lying to ourselves, but we don't know it. The way out is to uncover where the untruth resides inside us, just behind a blind spot.

Nestled in our stories, then, are our blind spots.

To deal with what we consciously know about and are hiding is comparatively easy. The deeper work—the more difficult work—is to unveil the unconscious currents that lie beneath them, in our blind spots. And we simply cannot do this level of work alone. We also can't do it without the courage to bring into the open what we already are aware of. But most of us carry as much in our unconscious as we do in our conscious mind. And the unconscious material is a little more complicated to find.

The place to start is by becoming open enough to talk with someone else about everything we know about. Especially the things that disturb us. For we need to lift away the shame that is blocking our way. Without this step, we can't reach the more hidden motives and emotions. And as long as we aren't willing to dive into our own unconscious and see what we're hiding, we can't say we know ourselves very well.

Letting go of our stories

When I went through training to become a Pathwork Helper, I learned a tremendous amount about the human psyche and how to help people heal. One thing I never forgot is this: Don't hold people to their history. For our work as healers and Helpers is to guide people through the process of self-discovery and self-transformation.

We do this by facilitating the process of deep healing, looking at every and any disharmony in life so we can unwind and enlighten whatever darkness it is holding. This is what allows a person to unfold and blossom in entirely new ways.

There is no way to avoid exploring our past, because it holds the keys to unlocking our struggles. Our history is our story of what happened—and keeps happening—to us. So we can use our stories to tell others about our past so they can help us heal.

But also notice our tendency to become overly attached to our stories. To use them to build cases against others. This is how the Lower Self works, creating wedges between us and others that always serve separation instead of connection.

As we do our healing work, we must work with our stories, and then also become willing to let go of our stories. We must allow ourselves to evolve. For our stories matter, and they also don't matter. This is an example of what it looks like to live well in duality.

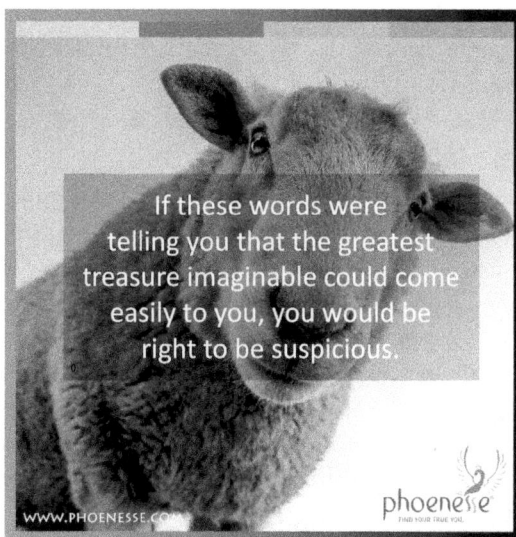

If these words were telling you that the greatest treasure imaginable could come easily to you, you would be right to be suspicious.

phoenesse

WWW.PHOENESSE.COM

Essay 15

Suffering? It's time
to search for images

"Here is a room full of people, and not one person is completely happy. There is not one person who would not want some kind of change—perhaps not even a pronounced change, a conscious 'I want this instead of that.' You may feel an unhappiness, unrest, disharmony, fear, insecurity, loneliness, yearn-ing. All of you, my friends, including those who will read these words, have the power to change this if you want to."

– Pathwork® Guide Lecture #40: More on Image-Finding: A Summary

Here on Earth, there are definite periods of time, and they are measured alike for everyone. A year is a year, a month is a month, and a day is a day, the same for all of us. Likewise for distance and directions. Up is always up, left is not right, and down is down. But in the Spirit World, it doesn't work that way.

Consider that on a clear day, an airplane pilot doesn't need instruments to tell them whether they are going up or down. But when flying through out-er space, beyond the Earth's field of gravity, an astronaut can't tell if they're ascending or descending. In fact, it will feel like you're going up when you're actually going down. Why is this significant?

Because when we travel in outer space, we are approaching the laws of the Spirit World. And they work in a way that's quite similar to spiritual development: Only by going down can we go up.

Progress feels like going backwards

It's only by exploring the deepest reaches of our own unconscious mind that we can ascend in the true sense. We must uncover the faulty wrong impressions that we've managed to form over the course of many lifetimes. Because only by finding them and correcting them can we understand ourselves, including everything that's happened and continues to happen in our lives.

As we work to dissolve these hidden misunderstandings, it will temporarily seem like we are going backwards. Yes, it's nearly unavoidable that as we search to discover the truth of who we are, we will experience depression. And when this happens, it may be helpful to think about the analogy between exploring space and exploring ourselves.

We have to descend into our wild and wooly unconscious in order to reach new heights of freedom and clarity. For if we do the work of self-purification while we are still here in our human bodies, it's possible to perceive far more truth than we now know.

Purification: What does this mean?

What does this word "purification" mean? It means we cleanse ourselves of all our attitudes and inner currents that are not in keeping with divine laws. For it's our distorted attitudes and faulty currents that cause our suffering. They are responsible for life seemingly not going our way. And so it's in our best interest to figure out just where and how we are violating divine laws. Because we suffer the consequences regardless of whether we're violating them on purpose or doing so unconsciously.

Generally speaking, people who are interested in self-development know right from wrong. So our work is not about whether or not to commit a crime. Because anyone reading these words is already living within human law. But what we can't yet control is our emotions. We don't yet understand what's be-hind them, and we aren't aware of how much they are influencing our life.

Is there really no justice?

The problem we're facing is that we doubt there is really any justice. For while we're doing our best to be good and decent people, we're still enduring so much suffering. And yet we look around and see others whose ethical standards are far below ours, and they seem to be better off.

What's the reason for this? Where's the justice in this? *Where is God in this?*

Here's what's happening: There are things that have gotten lodged in our unconscious that we react to by drawing conclusions. These conclusions form hard, rigid knots in our psyche. The Pathwork Guide refers to these rigid forms as "images."

So at a young age, our life made a certain impression on us, and from these impressions we have drawn general conclusions about life. It's like we took a picture of "how I believe the world is," and then put it on the shelf in our mind. We do this to tell ourselves how to navigate life so we can avoid ever experiencing such difficult feelings again. Then we forget we did this.

These images cause chain reactions to happen within our soul. Eventually, this leads to them controlling and directing how our life goes. And this happens even though—actually *because*—we are no longer aware them. This particular spiritual path is deeply concerned with digging out the wrong images that we're harboring in the unconscious parts of our soul. For without exception—allowing for a very few pure spirits who have come to Earth on a mission to help out humanity—we all have buried images.

Accepting in the right way

There is a tendency, especially among people who are devoutly religious, to feel we must accept any difficulty. That doing so is a sign of humility. But this is only true to the extent we can accept that we have been violating a spiritual law. If this is the case, then accepting the difficulty means that we recognize that *we're the ones responsible for our own misery.* This is the definition of true humility.

To be truly humble we cannot be totally passive. For being completely passive has as much to do with humility as being out-and-out rebellious. True humility has both active and passive parts. The passive part of true humility is about accepting our temporary state of suffering. We understand that somehow, in some way—which we may not yet fully understand—it's self-inflicted.

At the same time, when we are truly humble, we will be actively engaged in working to overcome the problem. We are willing to fight our way through our inner misunderstandings and to take self-responsibility for our suffering, in the most direct way we can. This is a good example of how the active and passive forces work together in harmony.

So we can't sit, with our hands in our laps, and wait for things to change. Instead, we have to work to change ourselves from the inside out. By doing this, we have the power to change whatever mishaps are happening in our lives. We can, in fact, completely change how our life is going.

But we can't do this by changing things on the outside, or by only changing our actions. We can only change our lives for good by changing the inner causes of our problems, which are our wrong conclusions about life. In short, we have to clean up our images.

Watch out for guilt

It is entirely possible for us to change our lives by understanding what is bringing us all our suffering. Only then will we be able to reeducate our emotions, dissolve our images, and start creating new fluid, flexible forms that align with divine laws. Sounds wonderful, right? It is. And yet this doesn't come cheap.

To truly master our life, though, is worth every bit of effort and every sort of sacrifice. Further, if we're serious about doing this, we will be given help. That doesn't mean God is going to fix things for us. But God has given each of us free will, and if we apply ourselves, we have the ability to find out what our wrong images are, and then change them.

A very important part of this process will be to have the right kind of humility. This is the kind that accepts the unhappiness we've been producing, but doesn't become angry with ourselves because we're not perfect. We need to truly accept that, at this moment, we're not perfect. And we must also vigorously work to understand why not.

Yes, we might know in our heads that we're fallible humans. But in our emotions, we may not yet know this. For in our emotions, we may want to be perfect. And when we discover an imperfection we hadn't noticed before, we might then revolt against seeing this.

A common symptom of such an inner revolt is guilt. When we start to look for our hidden wrong conclusions about life, called images—the things that are causing our suffering and all the repetitive patterns running through our lives— we are not going to be thrilled with what we find. It's helpful to anticipate that coming across these inner misconceptions will at first feel unpleasant. But feeling guilt when we encounter them will get us absolutely nowhere.

If we find ourselves feeling guilty, then we are rejecting the state we're in right now. We are essentially unwilling to accept ourselves as we are. We might even confuse feeling guilty with humility and repentance.

So here's a heads up about what to expect in the process of understanding our feelings: We may feel an unpleasant reaction *before* we become aware of what the recognition actually is. It's important to push on and formulate our feelings into clear, concise thoughts. This is major part of our work on this path. And if we do this, we'll see that what we feel guilty about is that we have made a mistake.

Why do we feel guilty about this? Because we want to be more perfect than we are. We want to be more highly evolved. We can't accept that somewhere inside us, we're ignorant, or we're selfish, or we want to find the easy way out. If we can steer our way through this, it will help our development process immensely.

Some advice about finding images

First, we need to face facts: This work is hard. And these teachings aren't trying to make it easy. If these words were telling you that the greatest treasure imaginable could come easily to you, you would be right to be suspicious. What can be said is that doing this work is, by far, the most rewarding thing you can ever do.

Nothing in this world can offer you as great a power as the feeling of security that can come from surging ahead on this road. But in the early stages, you won't have a sense of this. For starting out, the work involves gathering a huge amount of self-information from lots of little buckets. Every time we face any disharmony in life, we'll need to experience our emotions by letting them come all the way to surface. And then we'll need to articulate what we're feeling, using concise words.

It doesn't help to have a vague idea of what we're experiencing. It also doesn't help to keep pushing uncomfortable feelings to the side and covering them up. But if we take a close look at what comes up, we'll start to uncover things we've never been aware of. These things may surprise us.

And for some time, these isolated bits of information will seem disconnected. As such, we won't know what to do with them. We might even feel dismay: "How is it helpful to find out I actually feel this way, when I thought I had completely different motives? What am I supposed to do with this?"

Friends, don't give up and don't lose heart. Finding these pieces of information will turn out to be extremely useful. Although in the beginning, they may not seem to add up to much. Keep searching. Keep digging. And also know this: We can't get all the way through our work by ourselves. It's not possible. But for everyone who is willing, ways to receive help will always be found.

If we keep going, we will see that all our isolated pieces of information will start to connect. We will recognize how the chain reactions create vicious circles in us: One reaction leads to another reaction until the circle closes, and we feel stuck. Seeing these in action represents a giant step forward. The clouds will soon part and we'll understand things about ourselves and our lives, quite possibly for the first time.

Once we see the bare structure, we'll find it easier to keep going and fill in the details. Eventually we will see how the overall plan is currently working to create conflicts. Note, it will take time to grasp it all and to see our part.

Seeing vicious circles in black and white

It can't be stressed too much that when we find some aspect of our vicious circles, we must write down what we find. Otherwise, our learnings can dissolve once again and slip back under the waterline of our conscious awareness. But once we uncover them, we can start meditating on how these wrong conclusions have colored our lives.

Truly, nothing creates more powerfully than our images. And what they create is misery. Because there are hidden desires embedded in our images that go in the opposite direction of the conscious desires we cherish the most. Sorry to break it to you, but the hidden image-desires always win out over our conscious desires. For what's tucked away in our unconscious always overrules what we consciously think we want, no matter how much we may want it.

Here's how it works: Our images operate by silently drawing circumstances to us that correspond to them. For they are highly charged. So they draw both people and situations to us. It's not hard to realize, then, that it's our wrong conclusions that are responsible for the problems we are facing in life.

What can help us find our way through our struggles is to keep a list of our problems and conflicts in front of us, written down in black and white. For we need to find the common denominator in all our conflicts. We won't yet know what caused them, so we need to search to connect the dots of our conflicts.

With our list in hand, we may be puzzled to discover that some of our problems are recurring. Sure, they show up in different forms, but we start to notice there's a theme, or repetitive pattern. This is our first clue that we're dealing with an image. Note, some problems in life may occur just once, and therefore don't seem related to an image. But don't be too quick to judge.

This is a painstaking process, and it could be beneficial to enlist the aid of others, perhaps with a small group of people who all want to uncover their own images. The goal? To find where the choice-point lies. Where's the off-ramp for our vicious circle? To find this, we must find the hidden belief that is not in truth.

What to look for

Once we've identified a wrong conclusion and can see it clearly with our mind, we have to investigate our life. We need to see how our image has been influencing the way we behave in life, making the image seem to be true. Then we can start to turn things around. For example, we may want to consider, in theory at first, what the opposite attitude might be.

Once we can start to see a way out, we can't just leap to this new approach in our emotions. But we can start to see, right in the moment that our image is playing out, how our image dovetails with our life experiences. Then, by con-

74

sciously re-experiencing all the emotions that arise, we can discover what the right conclusion would be.

Having a more truthful perspective will shift how we show up in life. By doing this daily and meditating on what we're finding, our emotions are eventually going to change. So we can't stop at just changing our thinking. What matters is that our emotions change.

Also realize that our wrong conclusions, or images, are linked with our faults. We might already be aware of our faults, but we may not yet see how they are playing into our images. In fact, our images may contain an entire nucleus of faults. That said, don't go looking for faults when searching for images. For our unconscious does not like a moralizing attitude.

For now, just work to see the bare structure of the image. As you go along, it will become more and more obvious how your faults fit into this puzzle.

How all images are alike

There are a few things that all images have in common. One is the element of fear. Across the board, humans are generally afraid of being hurt, and we are also afraid of things happening against our will. Such fear exists because we have pride and self-will: "I want everything my way!" To avoid being hurt and/or feeling the pain of not getting our way, we build defenses.

We mistakenly believe that if we take a certain defensive approach, we can avoid the things we fear so much in life: disappointment, pain and suffering. Our error is that we fail to realize that by creating defenses, not only do we not avoid suffering, we actually make it worse.

To our Little-L Lower Self—the ignorant part of our personality that is immature and childish—these protective measures seem like a good and logical idea. But we created our defense mechanisms at the same time as when we built our image. When we were just kids! This makes the whole thing faulty. It's time to think all this through from a different angle.

Not only could we not avoid pain, but in the long run we brought way more pain onto ourselves than if we hadn't constructed the defenses that go along with our image.

It's important to consider our image from this viewpoint: "Why did I build it? What was happening at the time? What was I trying to protect myself from? How did that work out? And how might life go better for me now, if I didn't have my ineffective protective defenses?"

In a nutshell, here is the inescapable answer to our many questions: There's no surefire way to ward off pain. It's simply not possible to go through life without some measure of pain. We all know this. After all, no ordinary human being is pure. So we cannot avoid experiencing pain, at least to some degree.

But if we accept life—which can be painful at times—and always work to understand how we are calling it forth, then we meet it voluntarily. When we go about life like this, not only do we encounter less pain, the pain we can't avoid won't hurt half as bad.

Here then is a very helpful lens for looking at life: "What was I trying to avoid? How well did I succeed?"

"There are now several thoughts in this room: 'Why should it be possible to purify only in this way? There are many people who do not know anything about images, yet they also develop.' True, my friends, but in the last analysis it always comes back to this: No matter what period of history, what part of the earth you live in, no matter what names are chosen, the idea always remains the same: To find how you deviate in your unconscious from your conscious mind."

– Pathwork® Guide Lecture #40: More on Image-Finding: A Summary

Adapted from Pathwork Lecture #39: Image-Finding, and Lecture #40: More on Image-Finding: A Summary.

We can no longer bury our heads in the sand—along with our immaturity and images—and hope things will just all work out well in the end.

WWW.PHOENESSE.COM

phoenesse

Essay 16

Four hard lessons about immaturity and images

Everyone behaves immaturely from time to time. It's a normal part of being human. Not natural, maybe, but normal. Because, for one thing, every adult has to go through childhood before becoming a grown-up. For another thing, every childhood offers difficult experiences. And for a third thing, every person attempts to avoid the hard feelings those difficult experiences created.

So everyone grows up with immaturity stuck somewhere inside. Because avoided pain from childhood gets stuck inside us.

Lesson #1 about immaturity
We all have this

The first thing to know about immaturity is that we all have it. By understanding this, we crack open the door to compassion. For while everyone's problems show up differently in the world, underneath, we're all fighting the same dragons. With the rare exception of a prophet, we all come to Earth with inner issues. And the reason we are here is to heal them.

Our issues come with two parts. As already mentioned, there is immature behavior. The reason we act immaturely is that a part of our psyche gets stuck at the young age in which we experience wounding. As a result, we harbor immature feelings that didn't get a chance to mature. And when they are triggered, we act them out.

The second part of the equation is a wrong belief, which is now attached to these immature feelings. Because at a very young age, we start to draw conclusions about how life works. The Pathwork Guide calls these beliefs "images." It's like we took a picture of "how I believe the world is," and then put it on the shelf in our mind. We do this to tell ourselves how to navigate life so we can avoid ever experiencing such difficult feelings again.

The big problem with images

The big problem is that some of our conclusions about life—which we formed at a young age—are wrong. They are misunderstandings that follow the limited logic of a child. For example, if a child witnesses violence at home and is not able to do anything to stop it, the child might draw a conclusion about themselves, like "I'm a coward, because I can't protect someone I love."

To a child, painful feelings are akin to death. So rather than feeling the pain of being terrified and helpless, the child might conclude "I'm a coward." And then the child cuts off those painful feelings. Later, the child will see all future events in life through the lens of "I'm a coward." This belief and the painful feelings associated with it are now lodged in the person's unconscious.

From there, our emerging adult logic no longer pushes back on this wrong conclusion. Because the belief operates at a level that is out of our awareness. We don't think to challenge the premise it's built upon because we are no longer fully aware of it. Which is why we don't pause and say, "Wait a minute, what else was I going to do at that age? I was only a child. I really was helpless. And terrified. And that was painful. But that doesn't mean I'm a coward."

Note, images are almost always created in previous lifetimes and carried forward into this one. Our childhood experiences, in fact, are specifically designed to bring them to the surface in this lifetime, so we can heal them. When a painful experience happens that is not related to an image, a child can usually express the pain and move on. But with images, everything gets stuck.

Lesson #2 about images
They hide in plain sight

When we uncover one of our images, or wrong conclusions about life, it won't be *entirely* foreign to us. In fact, it will be more like seeing a relief map rise up out of the water. And then we'll suddenly see, in stark relief, what's been driving us our whole life. *This* is what we really believe is true.

For images make us act as though our mistaken conclusions are a fact. And we all do this. Have you ever reacted to a situation far beyond what the situation called for? When have you misread a situation so badly that you lost your mind for a minute and behaved like a child? If you don't think you have ever done so, then you don't know yourself very well.

How images cause "emotional reactions"

It's not really that we've completely forgotten about this hidden misunderstanding, or about the experiences that led us to develop it. It's just that our wrong conclusions are no longer in our conscious awareness. Until, that is, they rise up to the surface and reach out and slap someone, either literally or figuratively.

It's almost like something comes over us. And, in fact, it does. A split-off immature fragment of ourselves can become triggered, setting off what the Pathwork Guide calls an "emotional reaction." These can show up without warning, and we literally go into a trance and act out.

The tragedy of living in a trance

Whenever we're in a trance, we overlay the entire person of our parents—or whoever hurt us when we were little—onto the person standing before us now. And again, we all do this. For example, our co-workers are often stand-ins for our family of origin. This means we experience their behaviors through the distorted lens of how we felt our parents, siblings or other relatives treated us.

And the people we form intimate relationships with are going to be dead ringers for one or both of our parents. In the way we attract them and react to them, that is. The hard part, as we do our work of healing, is to tease the slides apart so we can start seeing the person standing in front of us in their true reality. In current-day reality.

Note, it's our reaction that's now distorted. Whatever pain we experienced as a child was real. But our emotional reactions become stuck in us. And they will remain there until we unwind them and release them.

Lesson #3 about images
When we act from an image, we are not in reality

There is a term called "transference" that is important to understand. And it is often confused with the term "projection." Here is an excerpt from a chapter of *Living Light,* in which the Pathwork Guide responds to a question about the difference between the transference and projection:

"Transference is what happens when we harbor certain feelings we aren't aware of towards one or both of our parents. We then go about life directing these same unresolved, conflicted and often contradictory feelings on other people. Our demand is that they fix their problems so we won't have to feel this way.

"…Projection, on the other hand, is when we have certain traits in ourselves that we can't quite accept, so we shy away from looking at them. But when they show up in someone else, look out, because *there*, they will irk the bejesus out of us.

"In other words, we project what we can't accept in ourselves onto other people, and then react toward them the way we truly react toward ourselves… Both, however, are nothing but mirrors for what are actually aspects in ourselves."

An emotional reaction that hit home

In my own life, I had a big emotional reaction a few years ago that still has me shaking my head. I had moved to a small town in Western New York to be with my then-boyfriend, now-husband, and I went to the local library to get a library card. There was a question on the form asking if I lived in the town or village, and I said I didn't know. So the librarian asked what it said on our mortgage. And that simple, innocent question surfaced a whole cascading waterfall of buried feelings. In short, I was launched into an emotional reaction.

For many days, I processed my way through all that was coming up. It had to do with the fact that I was not on the mortgage, and due to Scott's wounding around his divorce, I wasn't sure I ever would be. My biggest inner reaction came from the recurring phrase that went through my mind: "Another woman got here first and there is no room for me."

An alternate tape that my mind played said, "Another woman got here first and sucked all the air out of the room." This was my experience of childhood, with my mother taking up all the oxygen in the room, so none was left for me. I was the lone girl with two older brothers.

I shared in my memoir, *Walker*, about walking through the doors of AA over 30 years ago. I heard them talking about low self-esteem, and I thought, "I don't have low self-esteem. I have *no* self-esteem. I don't feel I deserve to take up the space that my own body occupies."

I needed to see that whatever had happened between my now-husband and his former wife looked like a re-creation to me. But I was not actually being threatened or hurt personally. Nothing that had happened in his first marriage was about me. But my view of things made me feel, in an immature part of myself, like I was under attack.

The rewards of doing the work

As I write about this now, there is no more sting about any parts of this story. I have been doing my work. But the pain that surfaced during the days just after my visit to the local library was intense. Further, the conclusions I had drawn about not having a space in the world really colored the way I showed up in life. And it was only by seeing all this and releasing those old feelings that I found my way to the other side.

What I didn't do was act out. I didn't blow up at anyone. I didn't make a snotty comment. And I didn't lash out at Scott. Because I have been doing my own personal healing work for a long time, and I know what the territory looks like. I know it's very hard to cross through these rough places. And I also know that I can do so without acting immaturely.

It's not that our work is to squash down our reactions. But we must learn to navigate choppy waters while, at the same time, limit the impact our process has on other people. In my situation, I was in a relationship with a man who has also done a lot of deep healing work. He knew I was going through something difficult and that I would stick with it until I came out the other side.

When I was ready, I was able to share with him what the journey had been about. Interestingly, I found I could express myself best using little hand-drawn cartoons. For a lot of this wounding happened at a very young age.

Embedded in my process was a communication with Scott about how his hesitancy to fully commit to our relationship was affecting me. But that's different from blaming him for my reaction. Scott chimes in here to add that by doing my work, he saw that I truly was the person he wanted to wholeheartedly commit to. And so we both received what we truly wanted.

Lesson #4 about images
They cause us to act against our own best interest

The last thing to understand about images is that they never do us any favors. Because they are not in truth. The result is they cause us to act in ways that are not in alignment with the truth of who we are, or the truth of the situation.

Let's underscore "they cause us to act in ways." It is our own images that cause us to show up in life acting in ways that make them seem to be true. For example, without getting through my piece that surfaced, I may have started to resent Scott for keeping me at arm's length. I may have started pressuring him to commit. I may have stomped around the house, angry that I didn't feel I had an equal place to that of his former wife. And any of those things could have cost me my place.

As one can imagine, when we're in a snit about something old, we don't tend to make a lot of sense. But our errant behavior may easily push the hidden buttons of the other person, creating a much bigger mountain than the original mole hill warranted. Because people react to us based on how we behave. And we all behave in ways that are driven by deeply buried old stuck feelings and beliefs that are no longer a match for reality.

The worst part is, the way our immature feelings and buried images affect our actual current-day reality, it makes us believe our own wrong conclusions were right. And the wheel keeps turning.

Immaturity and images alter our reality

Immature feelings are always very old. And at the same time, they are very young. They are part of the Lower Self that some call the Little-L Lower Self. This is the part of us stuck in childhood that hopes to avoid feeling the feelings we couldn't handle back then. (Or at least we thought we couldn't handle, believing as children do that feeling pain is the same as dying.)

This part of ourselves doesn't yet realize that there is now an adult version of ourselves available to help us walk through hard things. That we can now safely release that old pain, and we can mature.

We know images are an aspect of the Lower Self because they are not in truth. And we know that the existence of untruth is connected with every disharmony in life. In other words, when there is conflict, there is also a misunderstanding. And since images are basically buried misunderstandings, it makes sense that they're involved many of our conflicts in life.

And they are not going to go away on their own. A person can have a luxurious, well-crafted life built on hard work and talent. And an emotional reaction can show up at any time and take us to our knees. None of us can afford to ignore our images.

Experiences are intensifying

Here's something else we need to realize. Things are amping up right now. Collectively, the world is experiencing an influx of energy that is helping to shimmy our images to the surface. For that's the only way we're going to see them and heal them.

This influx, then, is coming to help us heal. We can no longer bury our heads in the sand—along with our immaturity and images—and hope things will just all work out well in the end. For there is a Lower Self script running in the background of every person's life. And if Lower Self is directing our show, the ending will always be sad.

Many people go through many lifetimes stuck in old patterns. These ways of reacting and behaving become deep, well-worn grooves. And the longer we take to course-correct, the harder it becomes to change direction. When it comes to personal healing, then, sooner is far better than later.

Over time, if we are truly doing our personal healing work, maturity becomes our steady state. Then if immature feelings arise, we have a clear indication that we're no longer in true reality. We're in an emotional reaction and we have another piece of work to do.

We can heal

No question, images are at the root of much of our work. The Pathwork Guide gave four lectures in a row on images, to underscore the importance of this topic. Once we start to uncover our images, they will stitch together many of the strange behaviors and attitudes that have been showing up throughout our life.

It will start to make sense, for example, that someone with unhealed childhood wounds and a conclusion that they are a coward, will later become a bully. After all, such a person unconsciously believes they must prove—to themselves and others—that they are fearless, strong, invincible.

These days, it's popular to see bullies as villains. But bullies are not the bad people of the world. They are simply people with wounds. Just like you and me.

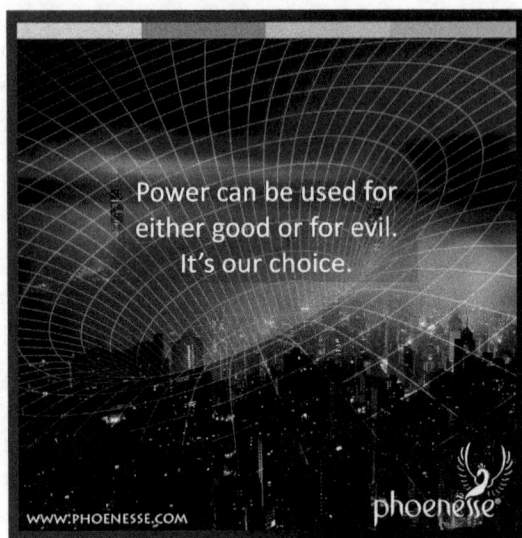

Power can be used for either good or for evil. It's our choice.

WWW.PHOENESSE.COM

phoenesse

Essay 17

Why did God make war?

According to the Pathwork Guide, if only a small percentage of the people on Earth—like 10% of the world population, and perhaps not even that many—started doing their inner spiritual work, wars would no longer exist. For the more we finish the wars that are waging within nearly every human soul, we more we will all tilt in the direction of goodness. Because the outpouring of light—the creation of positive energetic forms—would be that dramatic.

Keep in mind that by being in a human body, we're already standing at a crossroads, so to speak. Which is exactly the point of this world of matter. It came into existence through influences—longings, really—from both light and dark spheres. And that positions us, more or less, in the middle of things. Meaning, we get to choose: Which are we going to let influence us the most, the higher spheres or the lower spheres?

By choosing where and how we want to align ourselves—by exercising our free will—we have the chance to develop much faster. For example, the Guide goes on to say that a person who is consciously doing their personal work of spiritual development can accomplish in one lifetime what might otherwise take twenty.

Why friction is our best friend

We can likely all agree that we live in a world filled with people at very different levels of development. This causes friction, because all these different levels of development create misunderstandings. The friction, then, hands us our work, which is to sort through our difficulties and resolve them. Instead, due to our blindness, we often stay locked in conflict.

Yet this friction is exactly the key to developing faster. Because conflicts are what bring our own weaknesses to the surface. For unbeknownst to us, hidden in our psyche—in the unconscious part of our mind—there are conflicting trends. One part wants to go this way, and the other that way. Worse yet, we're not even aware this is going on!

All this makes being human quite difficult. So then why couldn't all this have been avoided? Why can't we just live with people who hail from the same spiritual spheres as us? Well, once upon a time, we did. To understand why we left a place of peace and harmony only to arrive into this difficult dimension, we'll need to understand the bigger story of creation.

What it takes to create

Behind all of life there is a great living force that many refer to as God. (Please fill in any word for God that you like. This force is made up of both an active principle and a receptive principle. When we see life, or God, wearing his active face, we see God creating. People living in the West are most familiar with seeing this active, masculine side of God. Examples of God's creations include an infinite number of divine laws, as well as an infinite number of spiritual beings.

When we see God's receptive face, we witness the slow evolution of life. In her feminine form, God allows an organic building process. This is the flow of life, and it's the side of God seen more often in the East. In order for this universe—with all of its laws and other beings—to come into existence, both the active and the receptive forces must be involved.

The divine substance of this living force is a radiant fluid, and each creature contains some of this divine stream. This is what it means to say we are each made in the image of God: We each contain some divine essence, but to a lesser degree than God.

Following the urge for union

When we eventually reach the highest degree of development possible, the male and female aspects of divinity will once again be re-united and combined into one. For at that point, there will be no more disunity or division. The reason we have men and women as separate entities on Earth is a result of the splitting that happened during the Fall. In short, each spirit being was split into two halves, one mostly masculine and the other mostly feminine.

Our innate urge to find the right partner springs from this longing to reunite with our other part, the half we've gotten separated from. Sometimes we'll go through incarnations when we'll be able to join with our true double, or counterpart. And embedded in the happiness that such a reunion entails, therein lies a duty for us to fulfill something.

We'll also have to go through other incarnations without our counterpart. And in that lies fulfillment of different sort. But that doesn't mean we need to lead a life of celibacy. There will be others with whom we can create a meaningful life, be happy, and fulfill other duties, possibly even paying off some karma. No matter how we learn it, if we learn to love—if we learn to connect our loving heart with our sexuality, with whomever we love, however we love—we come a step closer to God. And that's a path that always leads to our own freedom and fulfillment.

Yet the question remains: Why did God create all these beings? After all, God must have realized that misery could result from this.

Why did God create spiritual beings?

The creation of spiritual beings stems from the reality that God is love. Simply put, love must share, for that is the nature of love. Further, each being has been created with free will. And yes, with this free will we have the ability to bring misery into existence. The hope was that we'd have the wisdom to not abuse our power, and therefore to always continue living within the boundaries of divine law.

If we did that, we would know eternal bliss. If not, well, that's why we're all here.

The beings who were part of the Fall—that's us—took the opportunity to understand even better the amazing perfection of divine laws. For that's what we'll come to realize once we've all gone through this valley of death. In the end, we'll be even more godlike than before. But let's not get ahead of ourselves.

For now, we must endure a temporary misery that we've brought onto ourselves through our own wrong decisions. But take heart, for this self-inflicted misery is nothing compared with the eternal happiness waiting for us, once we get all the way back home.

What takes away our harmony?

Long before our material world came into being, there were many, many worlds: worlds of total happiness and harmony, of infinite beauty and possibilities. In those worlds, our creative divine aspects could continue to unfold. In those worlds, our divine substance was not covered over with a foreign layer of un-godlike matter.

These dark, foreign layers are what rob us of our unity—with ourselves, with others and with God—and it's our task here in this world to free ourselves from them. We might call these dark layers our Lower Self, with the divine substance or divine spark at our core being our Higher Self.

To be clear, this light that rests at the core of each human being is godlike, but that does not make us God. That said, only this divine substance, once purified and free of darkness, is able to unite with God. If our desire is to become part of the Oneness—to once again be at one with God—we must become like God. For no substance that is not like God can unite with God.

Exercising our power to choose

To be given the same aspects as God means we had to be given free will. And having free choice means we have the possibility to go against divine law. When we steer clear of that, freely and correctly choosing not to abuse our power, we win the jackpot: love, wisdom, courage, serenity, and other fine qualities such as these.

If we choose to go another route, then we will become caught in a web of spiritual laws. These laws, which God had the good sense to create before making each of us, provide for the possibility of returning to God if and when we misuse our God-given powers of choice. They work in cycles, which always have to close. Ultimately, everything that turns away from God and divine law will return.

For the farther away we are from God, the more misery we experience. But it's this misery itself that gives us the incentive we need to come back into alignment with divine law. If we look, we can see this law at work in our lives, in everything from the big situations to even the smallest incidents.

Here, the idea might arise that God really should not have given everyone free will. Because then the Fall could not have happened. Or, at a minimum, God should have stepped in when things started going downhill. But such a view is ridiculously shortsighted. For happiness only exists when we are in union. And to be in union—eventually with everyone, including God—we all must be cut from the same cloth. In other words, our free will must always remain intact.

The origin of our dark layers

How, then, did these foreign layers come into existence, covering up our original inner light? Well, for a long, long time we all lived in a state of bliss, although such worlds are forgotten and unimaginable to us now. And we were invited to freely choose to stay there and live within divine law, or to go against it. Eventually, one particular spirit fell to the temptation to act against divine law.

Note, not only is acting against divine law the same as acting against God, it's also acting against our own best interest. And to this day, that's exactly what our Lower Self does: it acts against our own best interest.

How did this fall into temptation come about? Imagine, if you will, that you possess an incredible power. And you know that if you use this power the wrong way, it might not go well for you. As long as you don't exercise this power the wrong way, all is well. And still you become remarkably curious about what would happen if you did use it the wrong way. Over time, it becomes more and more tempting to try this out. The stronger the temptation becomes, the less you can come up with reasons to not try it out.

You don't even plan to keep using this dangerous power. But you feel you must try it out, at least a little bit. Just to find out what would happen. Sure, you see your friends trying it, and then getting swept away by it. Yes, you understand that this is really not a good idea. But your better judgment dissolves under the growing weight of how tempted you are. And then, once you try it, it's not possible to resist being swept away by it yourself.

Falling is just like that.

Here's an example that might hit more close to home. Let's say we're tempted to try something that's addictive. We don't plan on succumbing entirely to it, for we know, as everyone does, it could ruin our lives in every respect. And yet we think we can try it, just once, and see what it's like. But slowly, after some time, we find that we can't escape any more. We're caught, and now it's really hard to go back.

The long, slow slide into darkness

Once that first spirit gave into temptation, something new was set into motion, and it couldn't be changed any more. The spirit understood that this would be the case. But after falling, he no longer wished to remember that he once knew this. And in truth, it's no different for any of us now.

The end result? A gradual change.

In fact, that long, slow slide toward the dark side—sinking from harmony into disharmony—happened just as gradually as our long, slow journey of personal healing must occur. Whether we're going forward or backward—evolving or de-evolving—it can never happen suddenly. All the principles that held true long ago during the Fall, when everything opposed divine law, are exactly the same today.

When that one spirit fell first, he generated a power that ran in the opposite direction from divine law. It was still the same power, just used in a different way. By using this power, that spirit could then start to influence others. And little by little, that's exactly what he did.

To be fair, not all spirits fell for his charm. And hence a division was created between those who fell and those who stayed true to God. For those who fell, the "Fall of the Angels" was now underway. And in this process, each divine aspect became twisted into its opposite nature.

So, harmony turned into disharmony, and beauty changed to ugliness. Wisdom rolled over into blindness and love became fear, hatred and egotism. Union became separation. The more the pull of temptation went on, the further wholeness split, until evil had come fully into existence.

Living in like-minded spheres

Here on Earth, which is a material world, we think of thoughts and feelings as having no form. They're abstract. But in other worlds—what we might call spiritual worlds—everything in our psyche has form. There, spirits automatically create the spheres they live in as a byproduct of their state of mind. So then only spirits with the same level of development can share a world. This might make living together easier in some ways, but it slows down an individual's development.

Imagine living in a world where your thoughts and feelings, opinions and goals, all come together to create your world. If you are highly developed, you'll be surrounded by beauty and light. Fallen spirits, however, will live in a world that's dark and ugly.

In an effort to help fallen spirits graduate from dark spheres to light ones, a great plan was put into operation. Through this plan, many in-between worlds came into existence, which offer varying degrees of harmony and disharmony. Fallen spirits would find themselves living in these spheres, according to their state of development, as they worked their way back to the light.

Our material world is one of these in-between worlds.

There are other worlds that are more disharmonious than Earth. Many know of them as Hell. They reflect the state of mind of the fallen beings living there. In fact, they came into existence as a direct result of those beings. But Hell isn't just a one single sphere. Just as there are many spheres in the divine world, or so-called Heaven, Hell also has more than one address.

After all, when the Fall happened, not all who participated in it sank to the same level. The degree of disharmony and evil we brought onto ourselves varied by individual. As such, different spheres came into being in the world of darkness. And always, they corresponded to the fallen being's state of mind.

So no one has ever been *sent* to Hell. Rather, we arrived there because it was a match for our own state of mind.

Why we live in a state of disharmony

Remember, every divine aspect had turned into its opposite during the Fall. And if we now find ourselves living in some level of disharmony, then we have not yet reached complete purification of our soiled soul. What this means is that some characteristics of the Fall must still be going on inside us, at least to some degree.

We can uncover them by searching within to find our faults. As we do this, we also want to find the original divine aspect. What is the God-given essence that wants to once again shine through us? For no fault could ever come into existence all by itself; all faults are a distortion of something that was, once upon a time, a divine gift. If we look, we can always find the divine aspect in all our faults.

Once we are able to recognize this, it will be much easier to purify our faults. At the same time, we won't become so hopeless about finding ourselves which, starting out, means finding our faults. This perspective can help us lose any sense of inferiority we are feeling about ourselves.

But in order to find these hidden gems, we must first take a good hard look at our faults. We must face ourselves as we are right now.

Who creates?

It's not quite right to say that God created heaven and earth. More correctly, God created the divine spiritual laws that govern the universe, and God is involved in the creation of all spiritual beings. God also created various forces and powers that are distributed in such a way that every living spirit can use these powers by exercising their free choice.

Remember, we are each created in the image of God. So not only do we have free will, we also have the ability to create. One expression of our creative power is all these various worlds or spheres coming into existence.

This sphere we live in, our planet called Earth, came into existence gradually. And it doesn't matter whether we say that God created this world, or that it was created by the longings of both fallen and pure spirits. For it's really one and the same thing. The bottom line is that God continually creates through each one of us, and God also creates through spiritual laws. We, however, cannot create anything without using the power that God has created and given to us. And that power can be used for either good or for evil. It's our choice.

We can add light or create more conflict

Using the life force, or creative power, that's at our disposal, we can direct it into whatever channel we wish. This means we have the ability to create harmonious worlds of beauty, or ugly worlds filled with conflict and pain. In fact, we're creating worlds all the time. Every day, every hour, we're building the world we live in.

Yes indeed, this material world we live in is still being created.

Earth is an expression of our state of mind, and in this regard we're all the same: we are all part good and part bad, part lightness and part darkness. But as long as we do not fight to transform our Lower Selves—with our faults, our immature reactions, our stubborn rebelliousness and the like—we will remain enslaved to our own inner darkness. And the outer expression of this conflicted state is, among other things, war.

Yet once we reach the stage when we learn to control ourselves—when we become aware of what's happening in our psyche, or state of mind, and stop acting out our inner conflicts—then wars between people will stop. For it's our own dark layers that roll up to create wars on Earth.

To realize this, is to become enlightened. And that involves waking up to who we really are.

"It is only through the long road of self-knowledge and self-recognition that the answers will gradually make a whole, the answers that you yourself have to find."
– Pathwork® Guide Lecture #24 Questions & Answers

A spiritual hymn by a Brazilian healer and teacher known as Godmother Baixinha:

Message

Why did God make war
If we are all brothers and sisters?
We must pray that
God forgives everyone
Who says they are with God
But really are fooling themselves

Adapted from Pathwork Guide Lecture #20: God: The Creation, and Pathwork Lecture #23: Questions and Answers

On a
spiritual path,
we're a trailblazer
working our way through
an unexplored jungle.

WWW.PHOENESSE.COM   phoenesse

Essay 18

It's a jungle in there:
Hacking our way around a spiritual path

To seek God is perhaps the most satisfying thing we can do. To find God, though, takes time. Yet seeking and finding are the only way to become free from our inner chains. And so we each must embark on a spiritual path.

What exactly does this mean, to be "on a spiritual path?"

For starters, it doesn't mean we walk along a road that's already there for us. No, when we decide to go this way, there isn't a path yet. We have to make it. As such, we're really then a trailblazer working our way through an unexplored jungle.

Along we must go, hacking our way through wild shrubbery and under-growth, setting down one foot after another and making slow, steady progress. We must basically pick our way through the tangled landscape that now exists in our psyche.

In this self-created jungle, we are constantly building new forms by way of our behaviors and actions, our thoughts and feelings. So in every typical human soul, there will be such a jungle. That doesn't mean we're bad people. It merely means we're full of confusion, error and lack of awareness. We are out of alignment with divine law, and we don't know it.

It's this ignorance that creates a wilderness we have to thrash our way through. And the final goal of all this effort? To find God.

Our personal hills and valleys

Because we're stubborn and have various prejudices, we create conflicts— both inside us and in our outer lives. On our spiritual path, these will appear as rocks and boulders, as well as high mountains we will need to traverse to dissolve.

We'll have to make our way through our faults, which will show up as thorny shrubs and poisonous plants. Now, instead of going around them or turning back, we'll need to pick our way through them.

There will also be rivers to cross, where we must re-channel wild, raging waters. These are our out-of-control emotions that are running amok because we don't understand where they've come from or what they're really about. We'll have to jump over gullies, which are our fears of life, as well as our fears of pain and disappointment.

In fact, what we'll find is that to fully master life, we have to jump into the unknown. For the only way to lose our fears is to go through them. We can't keep turning away from our self-made gullies, which wouldn't even exist to begin with if we were able to understand life and take it as it comes. Indeed, it's only after we become willing to leap that we'll discover there wasn't really any gully.

This jungle is for real

This jungle analogy isn't just an analogy. These forms do, in fact, exist in our psyche. And when we set off on our spiritual path, we will need to find our way through such difficulties. For they actually do exist within us, in our subtle matter.

To go on this spiritual path is not easy. It's a long climb up the steep side of a mountain, where the cliffs are often hidden in shadows and covered in darkness. At times, when we've had a small victory and the sun comes out, we'll get to rest for a while. The scenery will be brighter and a little more friendly.

Then off we'll go again, ready to tackle the next bit. Sometimes we won't be able to see the goal for a very long time. We may know what it is, but we will still be a long way from having a direct glimpse of it.

In fact, for quite a long time while we're at the beginning of our path, it will probably feel as though we're going around and around in circles. Because we'll keep seeing the same scenery, over and over, as though we haven't moved from where we started.

The arc of a spiritual path

If we don't understand what's going on, this can be very discouraging. What's happening is that on a spiritual path, we are moving along on a spiral. And it's inevitable that we must start out this way. For all our errors and ignorances, faults and wrong conclusions roll up to create a giant vicious circle in our soul.

What happens is that each of our individual faults interacts with all our other faults, creating a mess of chain reactions. To break out of it, we'll need to separate our faults into individual buckets. By concentrating on one after the other, we'll be able to find the links of cause and effect in our personal vicious circle. We can't possibly understand the whole complicated circle completely after just one pass.

Going up?

After the first round, we'll need to start again. But each time we start, we will gain a little more traction in understanding how our negative qualities are working together. Then we will stop experiencing our faults as these one-off events, and rather start to see them in our mind as a whole circle. Until we have this broader perspective, we'll need to keep repeating the rounds.

At the beginning, this might seem like nonsense, like we're getting nowhere. But that's not true! And in fact, without going through this necessary part on the path, we can't reach the light and become free. So the circle we're spinning on is actually a spiral that gradually leads us upwards.

Going up feels better than going down

The path to self-awareness, then, does not follow a straight line. Not even a little. It actually goes up and down in spirals. It can happen that we are on a downward curve but are actually a step higher than during our last upward curve. It's goofy like that.

And even though going up on our last self-development roller coaster ride was lower, on the whole, than our current downward motion, it probably felt better. Because heading up feels better than heading down. There's a certain elation and freedom we feel going up—"Oh, now I see what's been going on!"— that's not there on the downward curve.

But the work we've already done on our spiritual path has helped us work our way up to a new level. Then down we go again, running into whatever conflicts we haven't yet resolved. These conflicts, of course, bother us. We feel unsettled, restless and fearful, until we work them out and understand them.

At that point, we have fit them into the bigger picture, or into at least as much of it as we can now see. And from here we're on the upward curve, enjoying the clearer air that naturally comes from pushing out the edges of truth a little further.

And then down we go once again, diving into the darkness where confusion and error abound. These are what cut us off from the flow of the divine stream. But in our confusion, we mix things up, saying things like, "This is depressing. I keep experiencing things I don't like! And *that's* why I am cut off from the divine flow."

Why unpleasantness is good for us

The big trouble at this point is that we're half right, which is always a dangerous situation. Yes, we're experiencing unpleasantness. But this is only a reflection of something inside us waiting to be dug out. The unpleasantness is an unavoidable effect of a cause we ourselves have set into motion.

It's our inner problems—which are just waiting to be solved—that cut us off. But we become surrounded by this world of manifestation, and it frankly makes a strong impression on us. We've tasted the feeling of true reality before, but now it's gone. Or at least it seems to be gone because we're disconnected from it.

Actually, we need this disconnection because it calls us to battle—to lean into our faults. For that's the only way to attain victory again. And every blessed victory means another upward curve.

But while we are riding through the rough patches, it's natural that we won't feel good, and we also won't feel God. For we won't yet resonate with the truth. And we can't force this to happen with our will. What we *can* do, and should do, during difficult times is to think clearly about what we're discovering. We can sift through our findings in light of what we now know.

For these are the times when it's hard to pray. It's hard to keep the faith.

Who wants to be happy?

Deep down, we all have a desire to be happy, and to make others happy. But at times like this, when we feel so disconnected, it's hard to feel happy. For happiness is a byproduct of feeling unified and connected. So the idea of "secluded happiness" is not really possible.

It's our inner walls of separation that must crumble, which is exactly what we're so afraid of. What we fail to realize is that when we keep shoring up our walls of separation, we defeat the purpose of living. Further, we scuttle our own self-development, which we also both desire and fear. In short, becoming happy means losing our separateness.

How does one go about losing their separateness? By doing the very thing that seems like the hardest thing to do. For many, this means giving up pride and going through what feels like tremendous shame. Yes, this is what it takes to let go of our walls and become happy.

What to pray for

And let's be clear, God wants us to be happy. We have a long history of misunderstanding this, and instead believe that being godly means being unhappy and severe. Somehow godliness has gotten mixed up with martyrdom. All of humanity has gotten a dose of this wrong idea.

Friends, feeling happy is not a reason to feel guilty. And yet praying to become happy doesn't work. What we need to pray for is the strength and ability to remove whatever obstacles we've placed between ourselves and happiness. Between ourselves and God.

To get where we want to go, we'll have to go through the jungle of our unhappiness that we've inflicted on ourselves with our wrong thinking and errors.

And what will we get for all this effort? The clear light of peace, the joy of harmony, the beauty of living in freedom. It is in this spirit that we offer our prayers, asking God for help in making it through all the ups and downs of our healing work.

Adapted from Pathwork Guide Lecture #36: Prayer.

Finding unity—being able to hold opposites—is the true magic behind living in peace. So, finding our inner sovereignty is only half the story.

WWW.PHOENESSE.COM

phoenesse

Essay 19

What's behind all the resistance?

One of my favorite things about the Pathwork teachings is how they illuminate topics from many different angles. This is incredibly insightful, yet it can also make things seem complicated. But the reality is, people *are* complicated. And therefore the solutions to our bigger problems are seldom simple. With that in mind, let's look at resistance, and consider it from a few different perspectives.

We can begin with some wisdom from one the biggest thinkers of our time, Albert Einstein, who supposedly said, "We can't solve problems by using the same kind of thinking we used when we created them." [Editor's Note: This quote may be misattributed to Einstein. In that case, a good back-up source could be the Pathwork Guide, who said pretty much the same thing.]

The kind of thinking that generally leads to conflict comes from the dualistic perspective of the ego. It says, in short, "Either I'm right and you're wrong, or you're right and I am wrong. And I am going to win." That, in fact, is the basic perspective of the part of us that faces out to the world.

This Outer Self, if you will, is the part of us we have direct access to. We could liken it to our hands and feet: If we want to have something or to get somewhere, all we have to do is move them and ta-da, problem solved.

How half-truths trip up the ego

Holding the whole truth, then, requires a greater capacity than the ego has. Not only is the ego unable to support all sides of a situation, it also doesn't have truthteller as part of its job description. Meaning, although we may know many things that are true, our ego does not have a deep inner knowing about what's the truth. That's why it can easily be misled by half-truths.

Half-truths, in fact, are the worst. They are confusing, deceptive, and can be easily misused to effectively perpetuate untruth. So they can trip up an untethered ego fairly easily, especially if our ego is not actively aligning with that greater part of ourselves, our Higher Self.

Enter…resistance.

When we don't know what to think, what to believe, or who we can trust—when we don't know what the truth is—we are forced to think only of ourselves. Then we latch onto our limited ego even harder and try to understand complex situations without the benefit of deep inner guidance. In the end, left to our incomplete and overwhelmed ego self, we just don't know. The result? We fall back into "it's either me or you" thinking, and we resist.

Our lopsided relationship with opposites

One of the Pathwork Guide's most powerful teachings is that everything, no matter how negative, has an original essence that is good. Going along with this is the matching reality that everything good—including every truth—can be twisted and distorted. And because this is what we humans do, it usually is.

For example, what might be the positive essence of resistance or rebellion? How about standing up for ourselves and being willing to fight to right a wrong. We must find the place deep in ourselves where we choose the light, where we are willing to fight for ourselves.

Some might call this claiming our "inner sovereignty." And at some point, this is what we all must do. For life is all about discovering and asserting the truth of who we are. It's about shining from our core, where we're longing for freedom and wholeness.

But hold on, because sovereignty is only half the story. If we want to align with the truth at the center of our being, we must allow our sovereignty to co-exist with its opposite. For at this level of our being, we can't experience anything without also making peace with its opposite.

"The opposite of a fact is falsehood, but the opposite of one profound truth may very well be another profound truth."
– Niels Bohr

Reaching wide to hold the whole truth

What is the profound opposite of Inner Sovereignty? That would be things like sacrifice…surrender…compliance...obedience. It's the ability to give of ourselves so completely that we align with something greater than ourselves: We align with all that is. Because at this deeper level, we understand we're not alone. In fact, at this level, we're all already in connection.

Whereas in our limited Outer Self, it's "either me or you," in our deeper being, or Higher Self, it's: "I'll fight for myself, and I'll fight just as hard for you." And it's also: "If I hurt you, I hurt myself." So, we must start to behave in ways that care for all concerned. For when we are living more and more from our Higher Self—when we are becoming spiritually awake—we must act like it.

Any conflict, then, that we're experiencing on the outer level of our being can only be resolved when we drop into the deeper level of ourselves. That's the brilliance we're all looking for. And we won't ever find it if we keep searching only on the surface, working with the same limited part of ourselves that created the conflict.

Creating the perfect blend

If we want to live in peace and freedom, we must find a new vehicle, one that can get us where we all want to go. And the ego simply isn't equipped for this ride. What the ego can do, however—and eventually must do—is wake up and learn to surrender to the deeper self within. This is the way to connect with the source of all that is. And that's the way—the only way—that everyone can truly win.

"For all truly beautiful and meaningful experiences emerge from a perfect balance between our volitional outer ego and our non-volitional inner self."
– *Blinded by Fear*, Chapter 7: How Fear of Releasing the Little Ego Spoils Happiness

But keep in mind, there is a vast area we must travel across before we can let go of our Outer Self and live from our Higher Self. For we must work our way through all the twists and turns of our Lower Self. We must face all our unhelpful resistance by learning to fight to become more whole.

Indeed, before we can reach the promised land, we'll have to clear away the many obstacles that litter this in-between space. And one thing we all must explore is our rebellious reaction to authority. For this causes us to resist, even when resistance doesn't serve our highest good. And yet it's a deeply embedded part of the human condition.

Our rebellious relationship with authority

This spiritual path, as outlined by the Pathwork Guide, shows us how all our outer problems are connected with inner conflicts. Sure as a magnet attracts a nail to itself, our tangled emotional landscape will have us tripping over outer events that have been drawn to us by to our hidden inner untruth. And one place where many stumble relates to resistance to authority.

Our problems trace back to childhood, where our very first conflict in life was dealing with someone—likely a parent or guardian, and later a teacher—who said "no" to us. Since they were always denying us this-or-that wish, they seemed hostile to us. No matter how much love and affection we also got, and no matter how appropriate their boundaries were, this was our first hurdle in life. And we didn't like it.

Fast forward to adulthood, and many of us still harbor the same hidden reaction to authority now as we did back then. Of course, for some, this hurdle has become a steppingstone toward maturity. But for others, where strong reactions remain lodged in the unconscious, the grown-up person will retain a childish reaction toward any and all authority. In fact, such a person will react negatively toward authority, even if it's administered in a perfect way!

But of course, since people tend to be imperfect, authority is often meted out in an imperfect way. And so a barrier is set up between the child-now-adult and the authority, who is seen as the awful grown-up. Again, even if the child was loved, this conflict exists. Because on one hand the child wants the love of the parent, and on the other hand the child resists and rebels against being told, by the authority, what it can't have or can't do.

Two unhealthy reactions to authority

No doubt about it, a child feels authority is bad. It's a hostile force—an enemy—that locks us behind bars and makes us feel frustrated. The child then has but one desire: to grow up and be free. But then the child does grow up, and the face of authority merely changes. Now instead of being a parent or a teacher, it's an employer, a police officer, the government, or society. Whoever a person feels dependent upon, that's now the jailer.

So now the conflicts still show up, they're just in a different form. And our options are: Openly rebel against any restrictions, or face the fear of not belonging, not being accepted, not being loved. This is what sits unresolved in the unconscious layers of many people. And it can't be resolved as long as we're not willing to look at it more closely.

There are essentially two ways that people respond to this hidden conflict, and most people are some mix of these two opposite reactions. One will revolt and rebel against authority while the other will attempt to sidle up to authority.

But since neither of these reactions is in truth, neither approach will lead to peace. The only way to unwind all this is to find the original reaction that still lies lodged in our old, unfelt emotions.

For indeed, an acceptable and effective kind of authority does exist, even if it's imperfect. Most, in our logical minds, even agree that some authority is necessary. But as long as we blindly react from this place of inner turmoil, we won't be able to recognize good and proper authority, even when it's standing right in front of us.

Which authority can we trust?

What we must come to realize, as we do the work required to unwind our inner authority issues, is that there is a genuine higher authority nested in the center of our being. And if we are able to contact our core—by clearing away our inner Lower Self obstacles and by using our healthy reasoning abilities— then we can develop the ability to discern what's in everyone's best interest. And we will be able to know this intuitively, not intellectually.

Why do you think Jesus had so many people in authority coming after him? Because Jesus often associated himself with people who were considered lowly, such as common criminals and prostitutes. What those people felt was that Jesus understood them, so they didn't rebel against him. They felt not only his genuine goodness, but also that Jesus understood the reasons why they were the way they were.

He wasn't standing there judging them, but rather he was there *with* them, regardless of the fact that he didn't agree with their wrong attitudes or actions. He could actually laugh with them. And at the same time, he could laugh at the pompous kind of authority that was so proud of itself and its laws.

The kind of authority we want to be striving for is the kind Jesus showed us. We can be *with* a person who is revolting, resisting or rebelling, and at the same time, we can also realize that somewhere, somehow, this same struggle is going on inside of us. *How are we also reacting in some way against authority?* For we can better understand another person's attitude if we also better understand our own. Then we can build common ground.

Moving from duality to unity

We don't need to be the judge and jury. Instead, we can extend our hands to each other and find a way to walk together into a fresh new world in which we all, somehow, figure out how to get along. If we want to be part of the solution, we must be willing to walk through hard places.

The first part of our healing work involves dissolving our hidden childhood conflicts. But the main point, which is the second part of our self-discovery process, is to move from a state of disconnection and isolation—from the ego-centered world of duality—into union with all that is.

If we're willing to go deeper into ourselves, this is what we must eventually discover: That all wounds can be healed, and all conflict can be resolved, *if we are willing to look and work more deeply.* This is the way for all of us to work together and learn to live in peace.

Adapted in part from Pathwork Guide Lecture #46: Authority.

Like colorful mandalas, we're each a unique design, yet we're all making the same journey inward.

Essay 20

Feeling lost?
Here's how to find yourself

At one time or another, most of us have felt lost. We feel like we've gone missing. What we're really missing is our own inner light. And what we're lost in is the illusion of duality. But telling someone they are lost in illusion will not help them one iota in becoming found. What we need for finding ourselves is a map.

The basic shape of the map of the psyche is a mandala. In general, a mandala represents a spiritual journey. Starting from the outside, we travel through the layers to reach the inner core. Of course, there as many mandala designs as there are people. So in a sense, we are each a unique colorful mandala, created with a very specific design. Yet in the end, we are all alike in that we are making the same journey inward.

And where are we all heading? What's the destination? To find the light at the center of our soul. This is the human journey, created by the human condition. In other words, our goal is to reach our core and let our particular light shine. Some traditions call this reaching for enlightenment. But to get there, we'll need to overcome a few obstacles along the way.

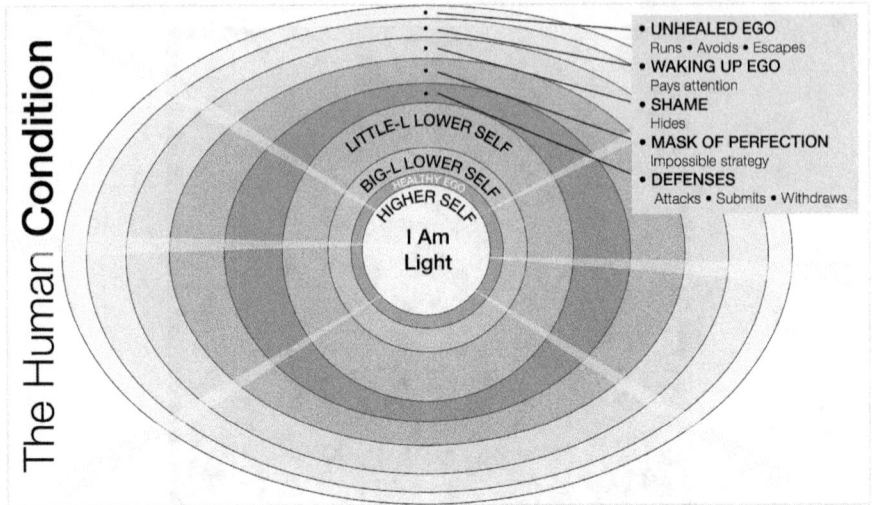

The Human Condition

- **UNHEALED EGO** Runs • Avoids • Escapes
- **WAKING UP EGO** Pays attention
- **SHAME** Hides
- **MASK OF PERFECTION** Impossible strategy
- **DEFENSES** Attacks • Submits • Withdraws

LITTLE-L LOWER SELF
BIG-L LOWER SELF
HEALTHY EGO
HIGHER SELF
I Am Light

Unhealed ego: Denies, avoids, escapes (addictions) > **Waking up ego:** Starts paying attention > **Shame:** Feel need to hide > **Mask of perfection:** Ineffective strategy to get love > **Defenses (Mask):** Attacks • Submits • Withdraws > **Little-L lower self:** "I can't" > **Big-L lower self:** "I won't" > **Healthy ego:** Surrenders > **Higher Self:** I am light

What must we face?

Here's the set-up. We all come into the world totally helpless, making it perfectly natural that babies can only receive. And if we could just stop there, things might end up OK. But in fact, it's not just that children are wired to *only* receive. They also want to receive all the time, in the very best way, and to always have their way. And this, friends, is impossible.

For one thing, all children have parents or guardians who are imperfect. Even the most well-meaning parents are simply not capable of giving 100% pure love. Second, this world has limits, so having good boundaries is important. Which means children can't have their way all the time.

Introducing the reality of life on planet Earth.

Since this is a world built on a foundation of duality, this means there are both good and bad forces here. So good parenting must involve setting boundaries. Then, as we grow up, we must each learn the difference between what's good and what's bad. And it isn't always obvious. You could even say the human experience is all about learning to discern and make better choices.

Right from the start, we are set up for struggle. No one gets it right.

Fast forward a few decades, and now we're adults. And yet we're languishing. The only way out of this quagmire is for humanity to come to understand why we are here. What is the point of being human? How do we turn things around?

Living in the land of hiding

In the Spirit World, where spiritual language is quite different from our human language, they have a name for this sphere we call Earth. The name implies that Earth is a sphere of disconnection, a dimension of fragmented awareness. That there are holes in our awareness. And these interruptions create missing links in our awareness of what's happening in our lives. These gaps, then, often mislead us and distort our understanding of reality.

All of us are blind to certain things. And the thing we are most unaware of is the landscape of our own inner selves. And that's why we've lost ourselves.

For one thing, we often don't know the true depth of our magnificent Higher Self. So we don't deeply know how much we each matter. We also don't yet realize our positive essential qualities and may still be acting them out in a distorted way. Further, we don't yet see that we have everything we need, deep inside. That we're enough.

Becoming vulnerable and imperfect

One thing we'll need to work on is becoming vulnerable. We must learn to let people see us—including letting us see our own selves—even if at first what we'll find are our Lower Self faults. But our faults are nothing more than aspects we are here to convert back to their underlying goodness. We can even consider asking our close friends or family members to help us see our faults, so we can work with them. (Trust me, they already see them, and might appreciate a chance to help us see them as well.)

To get to these darker, denser Lower-Self layers, we'll also need to see how pretending to be perfect is actually part of the problem. The root of perfectionism stems from our desire to be approved of and loved. Our mistaken belief is that if we're perfect, then we'll have everything. In truth, it never works that way.

First, on this dualistic plane, perfection doesn't exist. Remember, good is always a package deal with bad. Second, what we'll learn is that being vulnerable and real will take us much further on our path. Trying to be perfect will only keep us chasing our tail. And judging ourselves for our imperfections only hampers our progress.

The two stages of healing

There are two stages we must travel through on a spiritual path of healing. In the first stage, we're clearing away our inner obstacles. This includes a long list of negativity such as our rebelliousness, destructiveness, resistance and defiance. We've also got buried misunderstandings to unearth and frozen blocks of energy to release. There's much work to do.

The part of ourselves that orchestrates the healing process is our ego. In fact, what we need to develop is an ego that is strong enough to eventually let go of itself.

Unhealthy letting go into addiction

Holding back, holding on and not letting go are classic moves of an ego that hasn't yet cleared away our Lower Self obstacles. Such an unhealthy ego refuses to give up control, believing that letting go means death for the ego. In reality, letting go is the intended design of the ego.

But we must learn to let go in the right way. The idea is let go into our own deep connection with the truth, including the truth of who we are. This is not a one-time event, but something we must practice doing over and over until dying into the truth of each moment is our natural movement. This how we truly learn to live.

What happens if the ego tries to let go without first doing the work of self-realization? It will let go in an unhealthy way. This is the fundamental reason for addictions. On any spiritual path of self-enlightenment, we must first clear up our addictions before we can make any true progress. For they are an escape from doing the work of healing, and not a path to freedom.

Addictions are traps that keeps us locked out of our own divinity. As such, additions will never, ever get us to where we truly want to go.

Interestingly, people with addictions often partner with people who won't let go, who won't give up ego control. With such an unhealthy ego, there will also be a tendency to alternate between these two wrong extremes. For left to its own devices, the ego doesn't have many levers it can pull. But addiction and codependency are definitely not the right levers to be playing with.

The right way to let go

In the second stage of our healing work, the ego must actively work to surrender and align with the guidance that flows from within. Whereas we need others to help us with the first stage—for our lack of awareness prevents us from seeing ourselves in truth—we must do the second stage by ourselves.

"If we want to learn to trust God, we will need to travel through some interim self-created states of mind. But as so often happens, we are hoping we can avoid what we ourselves have created, including pain, confusion, emptiness and fear. Nonetheless, these are the things we're going to need to embrace so we can come to understand them on our way to dissolving them…

"Often the thing that limits our wish fulfillment is our insistence that fulfillment can only come in one specific way. But if we let the creative process have some rope and margin, we'll experience that it by far surpasses what we hoped for or could visualize. Our ego mind can hardly conceive of the richness of the universe. We need to learn to empty ourselves in the moment so the divine can reveal itself to us. This is what it means to "let God"…

"The key to creating an open energy system is letting go into trust. But we can't get there in one giant step. We must lay down some intermediate links, without skipping steps along the way. These links will build a bridge to having genuine, positive expectations about life free from pressure, anxiety and doubt. We'll develop a deep faith in a kind and caring universe where we can have the very best, in every possible way. What a valuable key."

– *Pearls*, Chapter 17: Discovering the Key to Letting Go & Letting God

Getting unstuck

The reason so many people are languishing today is that we're stuck. And this, folks, is the human condition. For everyone has a Lower Self that is stuck in some way, as well as being numb, rigid and unchanging. Such qualities are what the Lower Self uses to build inner walls that create our self-made prisons.

"This is one of the very best reasons to embark upon a spiritual path: to gain personal freedom from the chains of our inner distortions. For it's when we won't take responsibility for our own issues that we lock ourselves in chains. And then we claim someone else holds the key. That's how we cut off our own freedom.

"What we must realize is that there's a fair and natural price we must pay for liberty. It's self-responsibility. And the more we avoid it, the higher the toll becomes…It's our desire to dodge self-responsibility that results in our lack of understanding, our lopsided discernment and our inability to weigh the good from the bad. So it's our attempts to escape and deceive ourselves that keep us stuck."

– *Spiritual Laws*, Chapter 17: Being Affected

Over time, we will resolve what's blocking our light. To do this, we must:

- Drop our defenses
- Develop the right kind of selfish
- Overcome our hate, spite and greed
- Uncover and dispense with half-truths
- Stop hiding and keeping secrets
- Let go of control
- Move from me versus you, to me and you
- Tackle our "no" to life
- Release the wrong kind of shame

The **Way Out**

An overview of the work of healing

Action	Follow through
Something triggers an **emotional reaction**	Bring reason to our emotions to discover the cause
Come out of **blame** and being a **victim**	Take responsibility for seeing cause and effect in you
Pray & meditate to see the truth	Use mature ego to connect with Higher Self
Find the **image**	Clearly express the statement of the belief
Release **residual pain**	Feel the pain of unmet needs
Find the **duality**	See the misconception and open to seeing reality
Feel and unwind the **forcing current**	Or find the collapse into hopelessness
Recognize **faults**	Reveal the triad of pride, fear and self-will
Connect with **negative pleasure**	Discover the pleasure in being destructive
Transform **negative intention**	Find where you need to give
Search for a **no-current**	Find faulty thinking that undermines fulfillment
Uncover **real needs**	Pray and meditate to connect with your longing
Impress soul substance with new **awareness**	Re-educate the inner child with the truth
Pray for healing	Let divine energy fill and heal the wound

"As we do the work of self-finding, we steadily march our way toward personal freedom. And while ultimately we all are capable of enjoying total freedom, our freedom will start out limited since we must journey through the results of what we have created. Indeed, we can't skip past hardship now when our past actions and attitudes have been based on illusion and are therefore destructive.

"But buck up, for we do possess the complete freedom to now choose the attitudes that lead us to our self-produced fate. When we see that all our hurdles have been of our own making—a direct result of our inner distortions—we have the information we need to prevent recycling the same, and maybe worse, experiences. In this way, our stumbling blocks become our steppingstones."

– *Spiritual Laws*, Chapter 24: Creating

Therapy versus a spiritual path

The work of personal healing is largely what people are doing in all the various forms of therapy available today. A key difference between therapy and a spiritual path is that therapy is usually a limited-time treatment for dealing with a particular life problem. A spiritual path, on the other hand, deals with any and all disharmonies in life. Because all our problems in life are pointing us toward our inner work.

Both, however, are valid and effective vehicles for working through the first stage of our personal healing work. And we're never too old to start. After all, there is no other reason for the human experience than transforming our negativity and getting to know our true selves.

Guidance for getting started

"Let us all become very still, and I will say the words, and inside of you try to go along with these words: Be still and know I am God, the ultimate power. Listen to this power within, to this presence and to these intentions. I am God, everyone is God. God is all, in everything that lives and moves, that breathes and knows, that feels and is.

"God in me has the power to make the separated little ego know the ultimate power to integrate this ego. I have the possibility to feel all my feelings— to deal with and handle all my feelings. This possibility is there in me, and I know this potentiality can be realized the moment I know it. And I now choose to know I can be alive; Yes, I have the strength to be weak and vulnerable.

"I can accept my numbness now, my insecurities, my feeling state and my nonfeeling state. And I can listen into this state and wait. I can be still and feel into me. Also, I can be still and hear my superior intelligence, the God intelligence, instruct me. If I try, I can establish this contact.

"I will pay the price by giving the best I have and am to life. I will live my life honestly in wanting to give the best. For then I will be able to receive the best without cringing. I do not fear to invest the best of myself into life."

– The Pathwork® Guide Q&A #201

Key Aspects of
the Spiritual Journey

Unity

All is one.

The Fall

Use our free will to experience negative aspects of divine qualities; Descent into dark spheres caused masculine-feminine split along with inner splits and fractures in psyche.

The Plan of Salvation

The plan that gives us a path for escaping the darkness and returning to God, if we choose; Now we can save ourselves.

~Incarnation~

We take on a task to heal a certain aspect of our negativity in this lifetime.

Transference

Main soul split is transferred onto parents.

Mask Self: Defenses

Shame

Outer layer of our mask that wants to hide our inner distortions from ourselves and others.

Idealized Self-Image

Mask of perfection is designed to compensate for missing self-esteem and bring love: "If I am perfect, then I will be loved."

Defenses

We choose a strategy for avoiding pain and getting our way: Aggression, Submission or Withdrawal.

Little-L Lower Self: "I can't"

Needs Not Met

Child wants 100% perfect, exclusive love and to always have its way; Due to the nature of reality, this results in feelings of rejection and frustration that make the child feel inferior.

Images

Wrong conclusions about self, others and life are generalized and go into the unconscious.

Blocks

Resistance to painful feelings creates frozen blocks of energy and consciousness, which are held in the psyche and show up in the body.

Big-L Lower Self: "I won't"

Inner Critic

Internalized voice of parents becomes cruel to self.

Faults

Lower Self uses various faulty ways to overcome its fear of humiliation (fear) and feelings of inferiority (pride); It wants to win and won't let others off the hook (self-will).

Negative Pleasure

Pleasure current has gotten attached to pain during childhood; Life force is later activated through destructiveness.

Negative Intention

Lower Self resists giving or giving in; Uses images to justify this; Stays stuck and therefore stays in separation.

No-Current

Hidden faulty belief says No to fulfillment, making Yes-current frantic and ineffective.

Vicious Circles

Negative patterns are continually recreated, resulting in pain, hate, shame, guilt and self-punishment.

Higher Self: "I am not alone"

~Purification~

We must bring all this into conscious awareness; Call on God to help correct wrong thinking, release unfelt pain, re-educate the inner child, and visualize a new reality based on truth; We must find our hidden No to life and transform it.

~Transformation~

Activate the greater consciousness within.

Unity

Continually, consciously surrender to God within; Experience self as one with all.

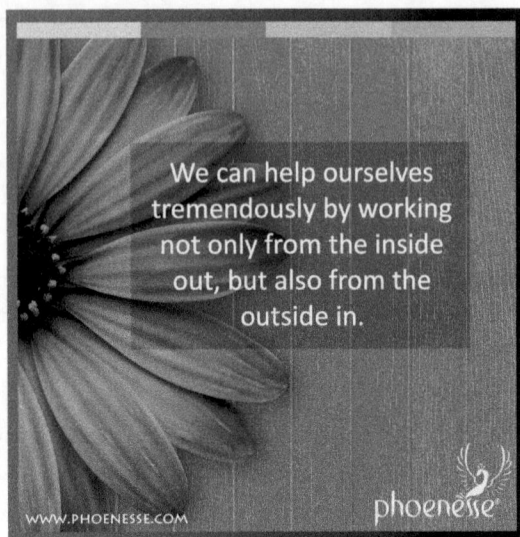

We can help ourselves tremendously by working not only from the inside out, but also from the outside in.

WWW.PHOENESSE.COM

phoenesse

Essay 21

Healing from every angle, in body, mind and spirit

Although the roots of our problems can be found in our psyche, they branch out into our body, mind and spirit, and create problems there. What's important to realize is that we can help ourselves tremendously by working not only from the inside out—by examining the contents of our psyche—but also, from the outside in. And we can do this from many different angles.

Working from the outside in

Consider the topic of order and disorder. The Pathwork Guide tells us that the Spirit World of God is an orderly one. Yet when we look around us, we often see outer disorder or chaos. This always reflects a state of inner disorder and disharmony. And these stem from the places inside where we're not yet aligning with truth.

But we don't have to wait until our insides are neat and tidy before we straighten up our surroundings. In fact, it can help us create more order inside if the environment we live and work in is clean and uncluttered. We can literally feel more squared away inside by organizing our spaces.

"As we heal and become more whole, we will see the spiritual principle of orderliness surfacing in our lives. When order is not evident, that gives us a lot of information about where we stand, inwardly. For the spiritually unified person is also going to be an orderly person."
– *Spiritual Laws*, Chapter 16: Mutuality

The part of us making the effort to clean up the physical space around us—as well as inside our physical bodies—is our ego. This is the part of ourselves we have direct access to. So when we need to develop better self-discipline, this is the part we are working to strengthen.

Three things need to move

The only way out is to let in the light of truth as we actively work to free ourselves. And we must do this in three key areas:
- The ego moves the mind to uncover inner wrong conclusions
- The ego moves feelings to release old stuck pain
- The ego moves the body to restore balance between activity and rest

Moving our mind

Human beings are fragmented. We all arrive here that way. If we had the vision to see back through time, we could trace our fracturing back through previous lifetimes. For the work of healing does not stop at the end of a life.

Yet knowing about previous lives, says the Pathwork Guide, is not necessary. Because everything we need to know to heal ourselves can be found in *this* lifetime. If information from a previous lifetime would be helpful for us, it will surface from within. In other words, we can trust that our childhood experiences in this lifetime will show us *plenty* about our inner issues.

One way to explore these issues is meditation. In meditation, we are working to empty our mind. But as we become still, what we will first see—what we won't be able to avoid—is the clutter and chaos currently present. And it's by paying attention to what's currently happening in our thoughts, feelings and behaviors that we can sort ourselves out.

The Pathwork Guide suggests doing a daily review, in which we jot notes each evening about what we noticed that day. Over time, if we keep our notes brief, we will start to see patterns. These patterns are the rigid structures we want to break up so we can restore ourselves to fluidity and flexibility.

And the part of ourselves orchestrating this clean-up effort? The ego.

"Anywhere we feel hopeless and have fear, we must also have an idea of finiteness that our mind has locked onto. As a result, we are locking out the great power that is here for all who are ready to honestly receive it…

"We must start to puncture this closed circuit. Note, we can't just immediately dissolve our mind, because we need it to live. But by puncturing our mind, the flow of new consciousness and energy can work its way into it. Any place it has not been punctured, we stay locked inside its narrow confines, which our spirit is quickly outgrowing.

"On the other hand, our mind must become neutral. It must rest and not hold onto fixed opinions. This is what will allow us to be receptive to the great new force that is now sweeping the inner universe of all consciousness."

– *After the Ego*, Chapter 12: Creating from Emptiness

Moving our emotions

We uncover our inner truth by first clearing away the frozen difficult feelings, which are blocks of unfelt pain. After a certain amount of work has been done to clear away the old pain and the associated misunderstandings of the Little-L Lower Self, we will find another part of the Lower Self: the Big-L Lower Self. And this part says a great big "No!" towards life.

This part is responsible for digging in our heals, even when saying "no" goes against our own best interest. It's our rebelliousness and resistance toward life that rolls up into defiance. And it doesn't care who gets hurt along the way, including our own selves.

Once again, we'll need to repeat this process and find the untruth that is pinning this "no" into place. We also need to realize that this part of ourselves is highly charged. We're on fire when we're aligned with our Big-L Lower Self.

It is hate and anger and self-righteousness and pride and self-will, all fired up and charging against our own Higher Self. Our goal is to restore all this life force—giving us the same aliveness in a version that feels good—by returning it to its original positive face.

When we have something negative hidden in our psyche, we are not only hiding it from ourselves, but we also want to hide it from others. This is what's often going on behind shyness, which is an out-picturing of our inner desire to keep something from being seen. Alternatively, we might hide an untruth behind our brashness.

Here's an important truth we must all come to realize: We need to have both a healthy "yes" and a healthy "no" in life. This is what we use to create strong, safe boundaries. Without both, we'll allow what we shouldn't and push away what we should allow. And we won't know which is which if we aren't in connection with our own Higher Self.

"Obviously then, if we want to move on down our spiritual path, we must directly concern ourselves with what hurts. We have to look at the suffering we endured as children and have gone on to defend ourselves against feeling. We need to allow ourselves to express our until-now unfelt feelings. And then we'll have the realization—the felt reality—that denying the original hurt is what compels us to recreate it in our lives, again and again. And every time we recreate the denied painful experience, we rub salt in the wound. Now it's time to feel things in a new, intentional way that is done safely, and which leads to finally healing what hurts."

– *Bones*, Chapter 2: The Importance of Feeling All Our Feelings, Including Fear

Moving our bodies

Our bodies are the vessels that hold our spiritual beings. If, in our emotions, we are tight because we're holding back old unfelt pain, we'll experience that tension in our bodies. This is why, on a spiritual path, we need to move our bodies. We want to free up the stuck energy that's held frozen in our physical being.

Also, over time, the negativity in our psyche will eventually show up on the physical level in the form of sickness in our body. Illness, then, is a sign pointing to something in us that is out of alignment with truth. So, as always, to find the source of our troubles, that's where we must look: inside ourselves.

Consider that when the body gets hurt, it immediately begins to try to heal itself. For example, if we damage our skin, our blood starts to clot and white blood cells travel to the area to start the healing process. Bones too automatically start to mend themselves. At the same time, we also typically reach out to people in the health care community to help us heal.

Those who are healers—both medical doctors and nurses, as well as more holistic healthcare providers—must be trained to identify our physical problems and offer remedies that can help us recover. All around the world, there are medical communities filled with people who are willing to try to help us.

Healing at the level of our psyche works much the same. Our hidden stuck feelings and mistaken beliefs will continually surface difficult situations so that we identify the true cause of the disturbance and heal it. As with the body, this is a natural process that happens for our benefit, even if we don't like it.

Pay attention to the clues

Too often, regarding physical illness, we fail to use our egos to find the hidden causes. Yet everything is always connected. And our body, mind and spirit are always offering us so much information—so many clues to follow—for inquiring within and investigating further.

In the Pathwork Q&As, people asked questions related to physical issues. This Q&A about vision speaks to the deeper meaning behind a physical eye-related condition:

QUESTION: A few months ago, a doctor told me I have a problem with my eyes which I have had since I was a child. I take in very little information with my eyes but somehow by using my brain, I deduce the rest of the information and end up with 20/20 vision. This has affected my ability to read well and has apparently influenced me to study science.

Another effect has been the overtaxing of my brain in using it for seeing rather than for other things. I also have a lot of tension in my body and tiredness. I realize I'm telling this story backwards, in Pathwork terms—the cart before the horse. I would like you to comment on this and its relevance to my life task.

ANSWER from the Pathwork Guide: I will comment on it in larger terms. There are other life manifestations in your development in which you have, in what you call the past, had a contrary overemphasis. Integration and evolution is a constant back and forth, a balancing factor of finding new levels of balance where the scale has to go once more in this direction and once more in the other direction.

There was for a considerable time—over lifetimes—an under-emphasis of an essentially very good and well-developed brain, where there was a laziness there. That has created the need to create a new balance in which you have given yourself this impediment in order to use your brain more.

Now the time has come, however, where re-creation of the balance system on the higher level can occur. You can then integrate the deductive brain functioning—the good intellect with the deeper intuitive faculties of inner and outer vision in the receptive centers. Your conscious emphasis on this will help you.

You can then tune into yourself, in which you can perhaps glean both these tendencies in you—the one from way in the past where there was a desire to not use your brain, to be lazy in your thinking, which then has created the overemphasis. You may really be able to connect with this feeling, and then subsequently connect with the feeling how you can now create more integration with the brain function you have succeeded in developing well, and now bring in the visionary function.

Now, I could also say to you, by putting it from the other side, that each of the parts that lags behind at any given period implies an unwillingness to accept and face certain things in self and life. And that is quite obvious. I do not believe you have, at this point, too much difficulty in understanding this, at least theoretically and, to quite a degree, specifically and personally.

As you now make more recognitions about yourself—when you overcome resistance, when you see more of what you did not want to see – you can then understand quite clearly how either of the two approaches – either the brain (the deduction, reason, the understanding) or the vision—could be used in a constructive way or in an exclusive way that makes deeper insight impossible. Both abilities can be used positively or they can be abused. Is that clear?

QUESTION: Yes. When you speak of vision are you speaking of vision through the eyes only?

ANSWER: No, the inner vision.

– Pathwork® Guide Q&A #241 on Body & Health/Vision

"Here's something interesting to ponder: the active principle in distortion—as murderous and harmful as it might be—is never able to cause as much damage as the receptive, passive principle in distortion. So the lowliest attribute on the bad-ways-to-be scale of humanity is not to be hateful, it is to be lazy. Inertia—including laziness, apathy and unwillingness—is the freezing of the flow of divine energy. In inertia, the radiant matter hardens and thickens, being blocked and deadened...

"Inertia doesn't take action in defense of good. Instead, laziness and inaction support selfishness and lack of engagement, keeping things stagnant and not growing; change is thwarted. Even if activity swings a bit wide in the opposite direction, it at least prevents us from being lulled into the ever-present temptation to stop."

– *Gems*, Chapter 9: Why Lazy is the Worst Way to Be

We will uncover far more light through curiosity than by judging ourselves or others.

WWW.PHOENESSE.COM

phoenêsse

Essay 22

The tricky thing
about self-responsibility

If we simmered all the teachings from the Pathwork Guide for a year, reducing and reducing and reducing them, they would all boil down to this: self-responsibility. Yet this notion that something *in us* is at the heart of all our disturbances can easily go sideways.

One problem lies with the issue of awareness. We're simply not aware of what we're not aware of. And as long as we lack awareness of the origin of our conflicts in life, we can't see how we could possibly be responsible for them. Here lies the crux of the challenge of being human.

In her excellent book *Left Neglected,* neuroscientist Lisa Genova tells a story about Sarah, a woman in her 30's who suffers a brain injury. What's fascinating is that the injury steals the woman's awareness of everything on her left side. So she must retrain her mind to perceive the world as a whole.

At one point in the story, her husband is visiting her in the hospital. She asks him to tell her everything he sees in the room. He names the bed, sink, chair, door, window. Then she asks him to say what's on the other side of the room, the side he can't see. He's confused. There isn't another side. But that's her experience now. She has no awareness of one side of life, which is every-thing on the left.

You could say our unconscious is, in effect, everything on the left. It's the part of life we can't see. As such, we don't even know where to turn to start looking for it. Most people are unaware it even exists.

Pitfalls to realizing we're responsible

When we start to catch on that we, ourselves, are responsible, we're at a ma-jor milestone. Yet it's possible to misunderstand this as well. First, many think the idea of self-responsibility eliminates God. So either there is a God and that's who directs our lives, and if suffering is involved we just have to take it on the chin. Or we turn to atheism and believe there is no God.

But this is a false choice. In truth, we will only find self-responsibility to be a burden if we feel guilty every time we uncover an inner error. But once we get past this by accepting ourselves as we are right now—without getting angry or rebellious, or feeling the wrong kind of shame or guilt—then self-responsibility will become a doorway to freedom.

There's no false security in the world that can match the true strength we gain from seeing what's caused our discontent, our worries, our unhappiness, and our problems. It doesn't matter what kind of false security we've tried: relationships with others, concepts, distorted ideas about God. True strength and freedom start arriving the moment we start understanding our own causes and their effects.

Yet as crucial as self-responsibility is for our development, most of us want to avoid it in some way. Even though we also revolt against having our freedom curtailed! The only way to resolve this conflict is to find out how and why we have limited our own freedom. How have we given up self-responsibility in order to opt for an easier way to go through life?

Although it looks different for everyone—since we're made up of differ-ing qualities, faults and currents—pretty much everyone has a desire to escape self-responsibility. And the more we run from it, the more shackled we become. Then we strain against the chains, kicking and screaming at the world, and feel-ing it is all so unjust. We'll even wallow in self-pity, while we stop doing the very thing that breaks the chains: take on self-responsibility.

Steps to freedom

The key to becoming free lies in self-responsibility. First, we must find out: a) "Where am I causing myself suffering?" And then b) "How is it in my power to change this?" Second, we must find out about our fear of getting hurt. We must come to see how this fear is what causes all of our misery. Our excessive fear makes us act like a person who is so afraid of death they commit suicide. That's basically what our images are doing. We're so afraid of being hurt that we create these rigid forms in our soul. These forms, and the defenses they launch, bring far more needless hurt to us than would happen without them.

The reason we must accept hurt is not because God is giving it to us. It's because we have given it to ourselves. And that doesn't mean we should now revolt against ourselves or the wise divine laws that structure life this way. What we need to accept is that we are imperfect, and depending on the extent of our imperfections, we will suffer. And the more we are willing to work towards purifying ourselves, the less suffering we will experience.

There are many requirements for doing this self-healing work, and one of them is to not expect miracles overnight. We can learn a lot by meeting our pain, and by accepting it for as long as we're in this stage of our development. The more we can relax into the process of finding and eliminating the causes inside of us, the faster we'll get over these obstacles.

Going about the process in a slow and persistent way will help us have the right attitude about pain. Once we accept pain—which we can do in a healthy way, and not by struggling against it or by masochistically making more of it than necessary—then pain will finally cease. Because when we accept pain, we go through it, and it dissolves. And it's only by going through something that we can reach beyond it. It's by going down, into the depths of our soul, that we rise up.

Self-responsibility is not self-judgment

Back to self-responsibility, the only way to truly unwind our difficulties in life is to look for where they truly originate. And always, that place is inside us. The way forward then is to unwind our hidden untruth and release the old un-felt pain associated with it. This is what we've been running from for eons. It's time we start to see the whole truth.

But this is exactly where things become tricky. For the moment we catch on that we are responsible for our troubles, we turn on ourselves and start to judge ourselves as being bad or wrong. After all, we're compelled by the illusion of duality to split everything into good or bad, right or wrong.

Yet as the Pathwork Guide teaches, the unconscious does not respond well to a moralizing attitude. So if we're hoping to give up the untruthful secrets behind our struggles, we'll need to find another approach.

What's a better approach?

The best way to move ahead is to become curious. *What could I possibly be hiding that I have not been willing to see?* We must see where we have been in distortion, where we have acted from our faults, and then correct our course. We must allow ourselves to feel remorse for any pain we have caused by what we have done, or not done, due to error.

But as we step into self-responsibility, we must not slip into moralizing guilt or shame. For we will uncover far more light through curiosity than by judging ourselves or others.

"True remorse has nothing to do with either guilt or shame. With remorse, we are simply recognizing where we fall short. These are our faults and impurities, our shortcomings and limitations. We're admitting that there are parts of us that violate spiritual law. We feel regret and are willing to admit the truth about our destructiveness. We recognize that it's a useless waste of energy and hurts others and ourselves. And we sincerely want to change."

– *Pearls*, Chapter 17: Discovering the Key to Letting Go & Letting God

Truth is a solid foundation

If we build our house on sand, it might last for a while. But eventually things will start to crumble and collapse. We may even have forgotten we decided long ago to build on sand. But that doesn't change the reality of the situation.

In the end, anything not built on a solid foundation of truth is bound to eventually collapse. It must. So it can be rebuilt the right way.

The era that's now arriving is going to further shake whatever is not sound, whatever has been built on sand. We must collectively come to realize that the only way to get to the other side of our challenges is by stepping through the doorway of self-responsibility. And that's exactly what the Pathwork Guide is showing us how to do.

When we live in
a state of contraction,
it's impossible to float.
We're like a swimmer who
is scrunched up into a
tight little ball.
The result?
We sink.

WWW.PHOENESSE.COM

phoenesse

Essay 23

How to swim with life,
by evolving and resolving our splits

In this dimension, or sphere, we call Earth, we are surrounded by things that are split. One such split is our two theories about how we came into being. Was it through evolution, as the scientific world says? That humans evolved from animals which evolved from fish which came up through amphibians and reptiles, taking billions of years to arrive where we are today? Or was it more the way some religious people claim? That God created each species, including humans, more or less separately?

When asked about this, the Pathwork Guide's answer was clear: "The way of evolution is correct." We are each gradually growing and developing through stages, through lifetimes and perhaps even through different life forms. And the fundamental reason for all these developmental processes? To resolve our splits and return ourselves to wholeness.

Why are we split?

Where did all these splits come from? They originated during the Fall, when created beings who were disloyal to God—including you and me—split into many fragments. For prior to the Fall, our souls were in a state of unity. It was after the Fall that a plurality came into existence. When this splitting happened, it's not just that one being—a dual being—was split into female and male halves. But as the Fall went on, our splits multiplied and multiplied.

This wasn't a sudden thing. In fact, the process of the Fall happened very, very slowly. Similarly, the process of evolution is slow and gradual, and so must be our process of healing and reunifying ourselves. At this point in time, we could say that the more split we are, the lower is our level of development. The more we progress in our development, the more mature—and more whole— we become.

So our work is to reunite our fragmented souls, and restore ourselves to wholeness. And we can only do this by finding and fixing our splits.

Where does God fit in?

As we proceed on our spiritual path, doing our work of self-knowing, it can be confusing where God fits into all this. What, for example, is the difference between contacting God and connecting with the divine forces within, which we can also call our true self or Higher Self? Actually, these are one and the same thing. Here's why:

It will help if we can appreciate that God is both personal and impersonal. That God is inspiration as well as spiritual law. Now, when we say God is personal, this does not mean that God is a personality. For God is not a person who lives at a certain address in heaven. Rather, God is highly personal, and we can experience God in a very personal way.

The best place to look for and find God, then, is within. For the only way we can experience God personally is by experiencing God inside ourselves. That said, we can see evidence of God outside ourselves when we enjoy the beauty of nature or see the wisdom that science has collected. But we will only be able to see these things if we first experience God within us.

Here's the most important thing to understand. To have a deep inner connection with God, we must be in truth. Because God is truth. This means we must remove all our inner obstacles, including our false beliefs and any unpleasant emotions that are stuck inside us. For they are always based on untruth. In other words, we must clean our inner house by facing ourselves fearlessly and with complete candor. And we must stop avoiding and escaping ourselves.

When God manifests through us as spirit, we have the option of whether we will be inspired by the truth of God, which comes through our Higher Self, or the distorted truth, which comes through our Lower Self. If we give in to our Lower Self blindness and allow our distortions to manifest, then there will be conflict and disharmony. If we follow the more difficult path of rising above our Lower Self, then we can ask for inspiration of the highest truth to help us dissolve our blind spots. For they are what cause the gaps in our awareness that create disharmonies.

So we can use our conscious thinking to mold the life force—which is God as spiritual law, and as creativity—and create life experiences that align with truth. Or not. It's fine either way for God. After all, God has given us free will and we are able to do as we wish. Plus, we've been given all the time in the world to make our way home. But the journey will be far less fun for us if we keep allowing untruth to guide our days.

Having more consciousness is good

The creative spirit of God penetrates everything that is. Humans have more of this consciousness than animals, who have more of it than plants, who have more than minerals, and so on. As we expand ourselves more and more, we keep gathering more and more of this creative spirit. This allows us to think more clearly, make better decisions, use good discernment, examine, select and choose. Also, we have a conscience because our nature is the same as that of God, only to a lesser degree.

And our essential nature is not altered in the least when we behave negatively because we have become alienated from the truth of who we are. It just means we act blindly, from untruth, and mold our life in a negative way. But our very nature remains unchanged. We always have the potential for purifying our psyche and living our life in alignment with our God-shaped center.

Our splits cause self-alienation

This feeling of alienation results from our lack of awareness of what's going on inside, in our inner reality. But we can learn to tune into ourselves and these more sensitive, deep inner layers. We do this by making a deliberate and yet relaxed effort to feel into what's behind our difficulties in life. What's the inner cause for our outer problems?

Because all our unhappiness and sadness, all our unfulfillment and emptiness, all our suffering and frustration—all these things—stem from the fact that we're no longer connecting with their causes, which lie within us. Whatever we are experiencing, we are somehow producing.

It's not just that we have errors and misconceptions, and destructive behavior patterns and feelings. For indeed, those things do exist and will lead to unpleasant experiences. But that's not really the worst of it. The really bad thing is something we may not yet understand: That when we want something on one level, but we don't have it, then on another level of our being we are denying it. Because we are split.

Why our splits tear us apart

When we don't realize that we are somehow denying ourselves what we're also consciously wishing for, we create great pain for ourselves. For we are pulling ourselves in opposite directions. Then if we happen to close in on what we want, we unconsciously shrink away from it in terror. This makes us feel very frustrated. The results are both confusing and frightening, and this makes us feel hopeless about life.

When our souls are moving in two opposite directions like this, we literally feel like we're being torn apart. The fact that we don't understand what's happening adds more tension to the pot. The more hopeless it all appears to be, the more we strive and grasp for what we want.

All this tense motion, even if it seems like it's going in the right direction, defeats the goal. For tension, which comes from twisting up our hopelessness with our doubt and sense of urgency, works against the smooth movement of being in the flow. All this twisting and grasping and despairing creates real pain. Just becoming aware that there are these divided parts inside can bring a moment of blessed relief.

Let's look at this more closely. For it's going to be impossible to feel at home in ourselves as long as we're not aware of this hidden layer that says no to what we're so strenuously saying yes to on the surface.

Uncovering our tendency to blame

We can start by making room in our mind for the possibility that something inside us is pulling in the opposite direction from where we say we want to go. Go ahead and give yourself some encouragement, strengthening your will to find this part of yourself. We may even need to remind ourselves of this principle from time to time. For even after making some progress on our path, we tend to forget we have these opposing parts.

When that happens, and we find ourselves feeling unhappy, we automatically look around for something or someone else to blame. And the minute we do this, we cause further damage. Because the more we blame, the harder it is to stop this blaming pattern of behavior.

What's more, right behind our blame comes a bunch of other destructive attitudes. These include stubbornness, blind resistance, and a desire to punish whoever we think is responsible for our unhappiness. Often, we'll resort to some sort of deliberate self-destruction as a way to punish them. *Take that!*

This is a common pattern that most of us do, at least to some degree. And it becomes more poisonous and damaging when we're not aware we're doing it and we rationalize our blame.

Whenever we are feeling unhappy, the first thing we need to do is look for that side of ourselves that says "no," for whatever reason. Then look for how we're blaming others, even if it's only a little, and perhaps only done in secret. We can explore our feelings and search for where we're building a case against something or someone else. Maybe we're even building a case against life, at large.

Then consider that no matter how wrong others might be, they can't be responsible for our suffering. No matter how things appear on the outside, we must have matching pieces inside us. And it's by seeing these inner pieces that things can start to shift.

Note, sometimes we don't blame anyone else, but instead we overly blame ourselves. But self-blame is really just a disguise for violently hating and blaming others. It holds a vindictive streak that's less direct but still destructive. So self-blame will also keep us from lifting up our head and finding a better way.

The process for moving ahead

If we really want to find the cause of our suffering, and if we truly want to remove these causes, we must start by wanting to see where we say "no" to what we want most. Admittedly, starting out, this may seem impossible. Yet this is what we must do.

The way forward involves questioning our emotions. Why do we feel what we feel? It may help to work with a coach, counselor, therapist or other trained professional to get to the bottom of what we're feeling. And then we must look at how our feelings are playing out in our lives. How do our feelings make us act in ways that are contrary to what we imagine we want so much?

Free-flowing feelings really do exist. But we must be in harmony with the laws of life for them to affect us. We must be in truth. Often, though, we deny the truth, including the fact that we somehow say "no" to life. Then we turn around and blame others for our struggles, and then deny that we are blaming, to boot. In all these ways, we are violating the laws of life.

As a result, our feelings no longer flow freely. So when we feel into them, we're likely to find a knot. Chances are, we can sense the tightness of this knot somewhere in our body. When we feel into this knot—by breathing into the tension in the body—we will feel the tension that prevents the free-flowing feeling of life.

The spiritual laws of life are in truth. And they ask us to search out all the causes inside us, which are all the places we're not in keeping with divine laws. For that's where these laws really are: inside us.

Let's go for a swim

In doing our work of healing, we must start to pay attention to these inner soul movements. We do this by tuning into our inner atmosphere. When we become quiet and listen into ourselves, we will feel it. We must come to know what is moving in us and motivating us, even though it may be very subtle. Now realize that this is what's emanating from us and affecting everything around us.

What we will start to notice is a complex series of chain reactions that produce contradictory feelings and thoughts. One idea will overlap another, yet they're all mysteriously connected. Once we start connecting our own causes with their effects, we'll start to move in harmony with life. It will be like we are swimming with life.

Like a swimmer, we will float on the water of life, letting it carry us. Yet we will move and we won't be passive. For if we are totally passive, the water can't support us for very long. At the same time, if we're too active—thrashing around, moving tensely and anxiously—we won't enjoy swimming, and it won't be safe. Then the water will control us instead of supporting us.

The best way to swim is to move smoothly in a relaxed, rhythmic, confident way. We can feel confident in the power of the water to carry us, and also confident in our ability to move with purpose and grace. The more relaxed we are and the more harmonious our movements are, the easier it will be to move through the water. Then our movements will become effortless and self-perpetuating. We can enjoy a pleasurable and secure relationship between our body and the water.

When a person is swimming, there is a wonderful balance between the passive forces and the active forces. And it's this balance that determines the harmony of the relationship between the human body and the body of water. In such a state of harmony, we feel a justified trust that the water will carry us. And yet we don't deny that we have some responsibilities and must participate in the act of swimming. Even in the act of floating.

The way to be in life

Swimming is analogous to how we want to navigate the universe. Our ego needs to be active, in a relaxed and healthy way. We don't want to throw away the ego or think we don't need to participate in the act of living. But at the same time, we can allow ourselves to float on life forces, fully trusting them to be there in supporting us.

When we embark on this spiritual path, we will have the sensation that we are being carried by life. This floating movement is a byproduct that comes from facing our inner difficulties directly and discovering the true cause of our suffering. As we go along, we will develop a more firm and therefore more healthy ego, and allow the universal force to establish itself in us.

As we walk this path, we will float as though we are carried, yet we will actively participate and be self-determining. This will unfold in a way that will be both strong and relaxed. And this, friends, is a truly wonderful way of being. Really, it is *the* way of being.

There is nothing else like it, or that can replace it. There is no substitute solution we can search for or hope for that can equal this feeling—of our own power, our own strength—that comes from connecting with what's inside us that's causing our negative experiences. For only then can we resolve the problem that is causing us to have unpleasant experiences.

STEP ONE: Deciding to search within

Searching for causes within is not an easy step to take. And you're not alone in approaching this path and then resisting finding the causes inside. If things go well, this feeling will subside as you push onward. But every beginner clings to the hope that we can find the cause of our suffering outside of ourselves. What we fail to realize is that even if this were possible, nothing would be gained by it.

Because then we still couldn't change our fate, since we can't change others. What stops us is often a blind fear of finding out we aren't perfect. And due to our pride, we want to overlook this. On we go, struggling to pin the fault on something or someone else.

The biggest step we can take is this: To say, "With all my heart, I want to see the cause that's inside me." The more we cultivate this thought with deep prayer, the more something opens up inside. This opening is the hope and the salvation we've been searching for. And sooner or later, the willingness to search for inner causes is the step we all have to take. (See a Deep Prayer for healing, Appendix B.)

STEP TWO: Tackling our pride

Once we've taken the first step, our work is not done. Now we must go on and take another step. At first, this one may seem harder than the first one, but really it's not. Take a breath and consider that these struggles we're facing are illusions. And in a similar way, any fear we have about finding the cause of our unhappiness within is an illusion.

As someone who has done this healing work for decades, I can attest that finding a cause within brings relief. It makes us feel safe and more confident in life. The only thing stopping us is our pride. Pride, in fact, is exactly what makes this next step seem so hard.

Pride is one part of a three-part constellation. The other two parts are fear and self-will. And you can confidently bet your last dollar, when you get to the basic cause of why you deny the thing you most wish for, these three basic faults will be involved. They're the evils of humanity, if you will, and *everyone* must learn how to deal with them.

STEP THREE: Facing our fear

Why is fear considered a fault? One, because it's built on a lack of trust. Two, it arises from our hate. To whatever degree we are unhappy about our own self—about our character—fear will exist. Said another way, if we truly love ourselves, we have no fear. It's our self-disliking that leads us to fear the many processes of life, including fear of death, fear of pleasure, fear of letting go, fear of change, fear of living with the unknown, and fear of being imperfect. We also fear ourselves. And yet all this fear is an illusion.

Nonetheless, we can't overcome our fear unless and until we have gone through it. So having stared our pride in the face and decided we're ready to see what's really going on inside us, now we have to face our fear. Agreed, this is not easy to do. We shy away from this step even more than from the step where we decide to find the cause of suffering inside.

After all, many of us put all our energy into avoiding whatever it is we fear. And yet the results of doing this, as we stand here today, are disappointing. Because we're following the way of error. We're cramping up against whatever it is we fear. And the more we cramp, the more we alienate ourselves from the center of our soul. And that's the place from which everything good flows.

When we live in such a state of contraction, it's impossible to float. We're like a swimmer who is scrunched up into a tight little ball. The result? We sink. Yet that's how we're going through life.

Fears prevent the flow of life

The constrictions caused by our fears create all sorts of knots in us, on the physical, mental and emotional levels. And these knots are what cause the disconnections in us. Most notably, they disconnect us from our Higher Self, or divine center, which is the source of all wisdom and all sense of well-being.

Our inner God-shaped center is where life flows forth from, and where we will find our ultimate happiness. But we can only uncover this inner well of life force by facing into our illusions. We must challenge them, test them, and penetrate them. For only by penetrating the illusion can we find out the truth.

And what is the truth? That we can have what we want, including pleasure, fulfillment, a meaningful life, success in whatever way we want, the realization of our potentials, love, health and companionship. In other words, we can live in connection with the real processes of life.

But none of this can happen when we are in fear. It's impossible. And so we must meet our fears.

The real challenge is: How do we do this? How are we supposed to get past our fears? Let's ask another question. Are we still expecting some nice authority to come along and take them away, from the outside? And if that did happen, would that really reassure us, for good? Could that really solve anything?

In a word, no. The only genuine assurance comes from knowing our own capacity to meet our fear and deal with it. That we can do so realistically and in a smart way. And we can only do this by going through our fears, never by avoiding them.

It's important to be specific

Start by making a list of your fears. Then look at your fears. In what way are they caused by pride? To what extent do they come from having a rigid, unyielding self-will, that refuses to change and flow with life?

We can't meet a fear if we don't yet know what the fear is. And still, we need to meet our fears. This is painstaking work, and it needs to be specific. It doesn't work to gloss over our fears in a general way. We need to name our fears and think them through.

Once we've done this, the next step will be possible. We need to look our fear squarely in the face. And granted, this may require a bit of courage. But the self-respect and self-liking that come from having the integrity to look at what's there are more important than anything. Everything, in fact, depends on this.

For when we think our fears are untouchable ghosts, we fear our fears even more. And that's how we breed terror in ourselves.

Little by little, our life will evolve

Our goal is to unify these terribly painful splits inside us. And the way to do this is by mending the cause of the split. We must see how we fear the thing we want. Before we can face our fears squarely, we much face into our pride squarely. For we so desperately want to believe we are perfect that we fear falling off our self-made pedestal.

Good news, many fears will vanish just by giving up our pride. Because by doing so, we see how unfair it is to blame life or other people, when the real cause of our problem lies inside us. This is always the case, no matter how wrong or imperfect someone else may also be. But when we deny that that there's any error inside us, we are the one being unfair. Meaning, we're not in truth. That's why pride makes it impossible to resolve our fear.

Once we start reversing our old habitual pattern of blaming and avoiding what we fear, something remarkable will begin to happen. Little by little, accompanied by quite a bit of stumbling, our soul substance will start to change. Our inner climate will shift. The old stuck way will lose its binding power. Just by seeing ourselves in the grip of it, it will loosen.

We'll still sense this level on which we are anxious, tortured, numb, hopeless and twisted in pain. But we'll start to feel another level of reality, underneath this current one. There is another state *beyond* the unpleasant one we're on. The ego-centered level we're on—where we alternate between twisted anxiety and hopelessness, on the one hand, and feeling numb and lifeless on the other—is not the only level of reality there is.

We've gotten so lost in this unpleasant back and forth that we aren't aware there could be another *inner* state. At first, we'll just get glimpses of this other state. As we keep going, it will be become more frequent. Gradually, over time, a new way of being will evolve from our current tortured state. But for a time, we'll experience them simultaneously.

Don't let the shift be a surprise

The feelings associated with this new level of reality are of immense safety and peacefulness. We'll have a sense of vibrancy and well-being, and we will feel deeply alive. There will be a flowing feeling of utter confidence. Like we're being carried along by life, while at the same time knowing we have the power to navigate life in the best way possible.

For a while, we'll function at these two levels at the same time. The upside of this is that it brings our splits fully into focus. Eventually, the new way of being in true reality, which at first will be a vague feeling deep inside, will become our steady state. And the old feelings of hopelessness will recur more and more rarely.

This experience of two very distinct levels of reality happening simultaneously should be expected. Don't let it come as a surprise. Let it greet you, confirming you are indeed going on the right path. You are heading the right way. Even though there is still anguish and depression, perhaps along with wracking anxiety, there will also be a feeling of deep peace and contentment. When you see the former for what it is, it will no longer have so much power over you.

Expect these states to fluctuate, to alternate. For this path is not a straight line. You'll gain new ground, then lose what you found. Occasionally, you'll wonder if what you experienced was real. We have to battle our way through these periods where we feel thrown back into an old state before the new one has fully taken hold.

But every battle matters. They are milestones we're crossing that make it possible to attain a new way of living that's secure and permanent. As we grow, we'll get lost less and less often. Until one day, self-realization will be ours. Then happiness will be our new normal. That's the promise of what it means to evolve and resolve our splits.

These words carry a healing force that can strengthen and enlighten us, if we open to their deep meaning. But if we close ourselves to them, we cannot feel them, and in turn, they cannot reach inside us to help us.

So the question is: Are you ready to learn how to swim with life?

Adapted from Pathwork Guide Lecture #160: Conciliation of the Inner Split, and *The Path to the Real Self*, Chapter 3: God, Man and the Universe, by Eva Pierrakos.

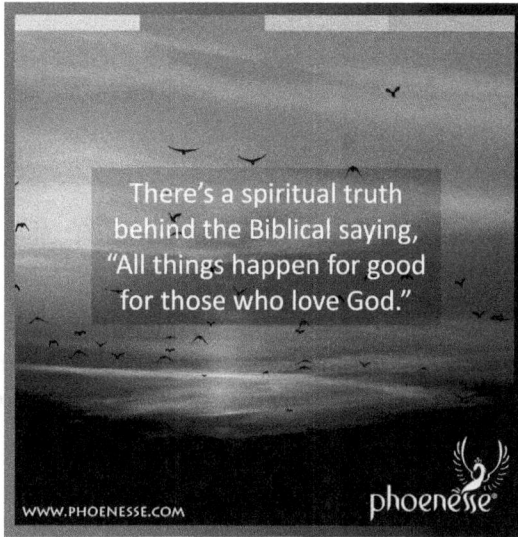

There's a spiritual truth behind the Biblical saying, "All things happen for good for those who love God."

WWW.PHOENESSE.COM

phoenesse

Essay 24

Playing the long game

The first time I picked up a Pathwork lecture, I knew I had found something special. The year was 1997, and by then, this material had already been around for a few decades.* What I didn't realize then was that the Pathwork Guide was playing the long game. And at the time, I didn't yet understand that I, too, would now be playing the long game.

Pathwork lectures are deep but dense

Starting out, I found the Pathwork lectures to be hard to get through. The sentences were long. The paragraphs were long. The lectures were long. The list of lectures was long. Even after I got rolling, the years it took to make noticeable progress were long.

But the concepts were deep. Deep enough to make a real difference. And the wisdom was profound. Profound enough to change my whole perspective about life.

It is our nature, however, as human beings, to want the quick fix. We want instant gratification and immediate results. For this is how the Lower Self rolls. Yet, as the Pathwork Guide teaches, the Lower Self is the part God wants us to work on—to heal and transform. And God, it turns out, is really playing the long game.

The best game in town

Earth is a stop along the way in our journey to return home to God. It's a halfway point, if you will, made up of souls who are not all that bad and not yet all that good. For we must already have at least some connection with our Higher Self to earn a ticket to Earth. But we also have a Lower Self that needs some clean-up.

For me, starting in 1997, I would spend a lot of effort and resources participating in various Pathwork groups, workshops, retreats and healing sessions to clear away the darkness that was hiding in my Lower Self. I read lecture after lecture after lecture, and I dove deep into my psyche. I uncovered things I never imagined were in there. I found my way out of my darkness. It was hard work, but I don't regret a single minute of it. I'd do it all again in a heartbeat.

Why? Because I can now look back and see the value of playing the long game. I understand that there's actually no other reason for playing this game we call life. We're in it to win our freedom from all the difficulties we create for ourselves.

Launching myself into the game

Fast forward a few decades and it's now the end of 2013. I've been a Pathwork Helper for a few years, so I've done some teaching at Sevenoaks Retreat Center, led a Pathwork group and held individual Pathwork sessions. My youngest son is graduating from high school the next Spring, and I've been ready to leave my corporate job for some time.

During the second half of 2013, I launched into a project of cleaning up and organizing all the Pathwork Q&As. That whole time, I was following a flow of guidance and energy that was racing through me like water through a firehose.

Nearing the end of the task, I sensed I had gotten a green light to leave my corporate job. And so I leapt. I shared at length about what unfolded over the coming months and years in my memoir, *Walker*. It included creating a website to make the Q&As available to anyone in the world and putting my favorite Q&As into a single book called *Keywords:* Answers to Key Questions Asked of the Pathwork Guide.

It included writing many books—now at 19!—and creating 120 podcasts to make the Pathwork Guide's teachings easier to access. And it included the creation of a high-level overview and dozens of writings that attempt to help a person get their arms around these teachings. Because when I started out—did

I mention?—accessing the Pathwork teachings wasn't easy. I would have loved having access to the content I've been creating.

It's now been nine years, and what a gift this journey has been. None of it has gone the way I imagined it might. And yet each time I finished another project with the Pathwork Guide material, I have felt great satisfaction. For working with the wisdom in these teachings is nourishing and fulfilling.

The grand plan for the Pathwork teachings

At one point, the Guide said Pathwork was never intended to be very big. It wasn't until I created the book *After the Ego* that I understood why. The original teachings were designed to reach a limited number of people. These people would be guided in doing their own personal healing work, anchoring enough light on the planet for the whole world to move into the coming era.

And my task with these teachings, starting in 2013, has been to unpack them so more people can access them. For they are a map we can use for navigating this next part of our collective journey. The Pathwork lectures have been playing the long game.

Back-up plans can be better

Here's one thing I've learned along the way. The Spirit World has plans. They also have back-up plans. And they have back-up plans for their back-up plans. There is no end to their back-up plans. And here's something else that's fascinating. The deep back-up plans can be far better than the low-hanging fruit of the first plan.

The spiritual teaching here is this. When we hang in there, especially when plans go sideways—and maybe even fall apart—that's when the game really gets interesting. That's when we see the hand of God sweep in and make things happen that take our breath away. For there's a spiritual truth behind the Biblical saying, "All things happen for good for those who love God."

When we are working on clearing away the obstacles and darkness of our Lower Self, we are completely in alignment with why God has invited us to come here to Earth. In other words, we're working to heal ourselves and this is what reveals our love for God, for goodness, for what's right.

And when we are doing *that*, there's no obstacle in our way that God won't help us move. There's no mountain before us that God won't help us climb. There's no end to what God will do to help us win our freedom. For God is playing the long game. And when we are on God's team, God is fighting right there next to us.

Taking the more direct path

People, this is not an easy path to walk. But before I found the Pathwork teachings, I tried living life another way. *My way.* And I can tell you for sure, that other way was just as hard. More importantly, it didn't bring me to the light. It didn't help me heal my deep wounds. And it didn't bring me peace. Instead, it led me further and further into the tangles of my own Lower Self.

I invite you to consider going another way. Because here is a secret that's important to know: We are all heading in the same direction; we are all trying to get home. And there is no easy way to reach the mountaintop. These teach-ings from the Pathwork Guide are going to take you straight up the steepest side. But that also makes these teachings the most direct way to get where you ultimately want to go.

If you're like me and you want to stop going in circles, this is the way to go. If you are reading these words, you have what it takes to play the long game.

Let's go this way together. Let's go home.

*Pathwork lectures were given monthly from March of 1957 to January of 1979 by Eva Pierrakos. Over those 22 years, Eva only missed giving one lecture and that was the day her cat, Psyche, died.

The biggest problem we face in a marriage is stopping short.

WWW.PHOENESSE.COM

phoenesse

Essay 25

The key to a happy marriage? Honesty

When my husband, Scott, and I met, we immediately had a common connection through our love for the Pathwork Guide. And indeed, in our marriage, it is the tools of this spiritual path that keep us walking straight together. For as the Pathwork Guide points out, the key thing that is missing in most marriages is honesty. And this spiritual path, more than anything else, is about learning to be honest—with ourselves and with others.

It's not just that learning to be honest in a marriage is a good idea. For that's the case with all of life. But in a marriage, honesty is the necessary ingredient for keeping the union alive. In fact, the Pathwork Guide calls relationships a "path within a path."

Meaning, a spiritual path is about bringing all our dark bits—our faults and our flaws, our shortcomings and our misunderstandings—into the light. For this is the only way to transform them back to their original free-flowing state. And relationships, by their very nature, are going to bring all our darkness to the surface.

See the connection?

Get curious

The biggest problem we face in a marriage is stopping short. What so often happens is that we know a superficial amount of stuff about our partner and we think that's all there is. When this happens—when we no longer search for more depth, more intimacy, more understanding—the spark dies out.

There is actually a name for this spark. It is eros. And it's part of the three-legged stool of relationship. The other two parts are love and sex. And while eros is responsible for launching us into a relationship, it never has to end. More to the point, if we want to keep our marriage alive, eros must not end. For each of the three—eros, love and sex—plays an important part in a successful marriage.

"Eros has carried us to the edge of the beginning by boosting us in the tail with some much-needed oomph. But after this point, our willingness to continue to plumb the depths of the other or to reveal riskier aspects of our inner landscape is what determines if eros will become a bridge to love. And that's basically up to us. How badly do we want to learn to love? This, and only this, is what's needed to keep the eros alive within our love.

This is how we find the other and allow ourselves continually to be found. There is no end. Every soul is limitless and eternal. A whole lifetime could never suffice to know another soul. Never will there come a point when we know all there is to know. Never will there come a time when we are known entirely. Our souls are alive, and nothing that lives remains unchanging. We can always reveal even deeper layers, which already exist.

We're constantly changing, renewing and moving. As such, marriage can be a marvelous journey of discovery and adventure, as it is supposed to be. We can forever find new vistas, instead of falling flat as soon as the first momentum of eros fades. We need to use its thrust to push us over our walls, and then soldier on further under our own steam. That's how we can bring eros into true love in marriage."

– *The Pull*, Chapter 6: The Forces of Love, Eros and Sex

The fountain of love

Human beings are complex. Not only are our bodies amazing, living machines, our psyches are a vast pool made up of various moving parts. The part we are most familiar with is our ego. This is the part of ourselves that we have direct control over. Our ego decides and takes action. It moves inward or outward. It's the control center, if you will, of our entire being.

That said, the ego is rather limited in what it can and cannot do. And one thing the ego cannot do is love. For *this*, the ego must surrender into the part of us the Pathwork Guide calls our Higher Self. We must learn to let go. Of course, it's not safe for the ego to let go if we still have a lot of dark Lower Self bits cluttering the way. But for now, let's just focus on why the ego should care about learning to let go so we can love.

It's because, in a word, loving brings renewal. Each time we see some rigid block in ourselves—something we've been blind to before—we have the chance to restore ourselves to our peaceful, free-flowing condition. We have a chance to find more love. It is this kind of self-transformation that opens the tap and allows the healing, replenishing force of divine love to flow through us. The ego simply does not come equipped with such a faucet.

"Another state that replenishes us is mutual love. When we let go through intense, healthy self-forgetting, we dip into the vast sea of beauty and universal power. This happens when we accept and merge with another "sphere," or person. By melting into another being, we make ourselves compatible with the universal life force, and have an experience that fills every level of our being: mental, physical, emotional and spiritual. Therefore, a loving sexual connection is the most complete spiritual experience we can have.

By partaking of our Real Self, we are nourished by this creative substance in all its splendor. By letting go, the ego becomes temporarily immersed, resulting in a temporary release of its duties. But it reemerges stronger and better than before! The ego actually becomes wiser and more flexible, and filled up with pleasure. Once it has dipped into this heavenly ocean, the ego will be forever changed.

The ego not only is incredibly enriched, but its capacity to surrender and remain submerged in bliss—to be in love and in truth—expands proportionately. This intense melding of the ego with another is the most effective way for us to forget and transcend ourselves."

– *After the Ego*, Chapter 4: How Unconscious Negativity Stops the Ego from Surrendering

The thing that stops this from happening is our withholding of ourselves from our partner. When we allow our fear of exposing our vulnerabilities and our inner hurt places to hold us back, then we are, in effect, giving up on honesty. In doing so, we are killing the very thing that wants to surface and enliven our relationship, and then we turn around and blame the other for our misery.

Friends, if we find ourselves stuck in a once promising but now dead marriage, it is our own unwillingness to reveal ourselves and search the depths of the other that is the cause.

Honestly connecting within

Since Scott and I were married in 2019, we have had many opportunities to hold the light for each other. And I can attest that over time, this becomes easier and easier to do. For once we get a taste of the freedom that lives on the other side of our dark places, we learn to welcome our struggles for the growth they allow. And it's only by continually growing that we can create more and more beauty in our lives and in our marriages.

As we each work to clear away our inner obstacles, we free up more and more inner light. Along with this light comes the inner guidance that helps us walk through life with ease and grace. So it is by listening within and hearing the voice of our Higher Self that we learn to live in peace and harmony.

Over our time together, Scott and I have come to realize something inter-esting. Before marriage, we were two individuals walking side by side. Then, when we stepped into marriage, something new was created: the union itself. And now we both have the task of keeping this new entity alive.

Although we are still two individuals, we now also work as a team. And often, when one of us receives a particular message from within that pertains to us a couple, the other doesn't receive the same message. This is by design. There are essentially four things this does:

1. It motivates us to pay attention to the messages we receive. Because if we understand that we may be the only one receiving this message, our inner listening really matters.

2. It encourages us to sort out the difference between what's inspiration and what's ego. Is this fresh, creative guidance, or a recycled thought from my ego mind? Remember, the ego also does not have creativity in its toolkit.

3. It pushes us to share our messages clearly with our partner. Often, we need to check things out with them in order to figure out what's what. If our partner doesn't feel the same inner resonance as we do, that's helpful informa-tion for guiding our journey together.

4. It guides us in learning to trust ourselves and our partner. The more we get it right, the more alive our relationship will be. The more we get it wrong, the more we will learn and grow. Either way, it's good.

Don't be afraid to grow. And don't be afraid of being fully alive. For it is by walking through our fear that we find the magic for keeping our marriage alive.

If we do this work of self-transformation, our many life stories will begin to have better endings.

WWW.PHOENESSE.COM

phoenesse

Essay 26

The story of our lives:
Why look within?

What does it mean to find yourself? What does it mean to find God? Turns out, this is the best Buy-One-Get-One deal ever. For according to the Pathwork Guide, these are basically the same thing. In other words, if we look within and manage to find ourselves—and therefore start to understand the story of our lives—we will have successfully figured out how to find God.

The reason we need to look within and "find ourselves" is that along the way, we've lost our connection to our own inner divine nature. This is our inner light, which the Pathwork Guide calls our Higher Self. In order to rediscover and reconnect with our Higher Self, we'll need to clear away whatever inner obstacles are blocking our inner light.

These temporary inner obstacles—which are the cause of so many unhappy endings in life—make up our own inner darkness. They are part of what the Guide calls our Lower Self. And they create nothing but conflict and disharmony in life. For they are always built on hidden untruths.

The only way we can find and transform these Lower Self aspects is by looking within. If we do this—if we do the hard work of transforming our dark Lower Self aspects back to their original bright, shiny Higher Self condition—our many life stories will begin to have better and better endings.

You know, it wasn't always this way. We haven't always had these layers of darkness. There was a time—long before the creation of this time-bound universe—when we were all free-flowing beings of light. And we were all living together in freedom and peace, in truth and connection, in joy and contentment.

So, what happened?

The story of creation

First, we have to back up a long, long way to tell this story, which begins by talking about God and creation. And second, know that any explanation like this must, by necessity, be a story. For we wouldn't have the ability to understand it otherwise.

There is a body of spiritual teachings given by a Swiss woman named Beatrice Brunner, in which a spiritual being named Lene often spoke. Regarding the being we call God, Lene said: "I am unable to give you any orientation, because you human beings lack the concepts to understand it. Even spirit beings in the world beyond have difficulties in comprehending and understanding the person of God."

The Pathwork Guide says we are closer to understanding God when we acknowledge we really don't understand God. Perhaps we can go with the Guide's description of God as being "life and life force." It's a bit vague, but then also broad enough to capture the essence of the one who enlivens and governs all things.

For now, let's consider there was a time when God was the only thing in existence. And that God's existence far exceeded—as it still does—the limits of our comprehension.

God lived in a spectacular ethereal world, and enjoyed a wonderful house framed by nature. There were mountains and streams, animals and minerals. Truly, God had it all—*God was it all*—and everything served God. Plus, God had the ability to develop it more.

The story of the firstborn

At some point, after an eternity of being alone, a desire arose in God to unfold further. In short, God had a desire to create a likeness—an image, if you will—of God's own self. Someone God could talk to and love. And so it was that a being we know by the name of Christ came into existence. God could do this because within God, every substance and every quality already existed.

The being of Christ, then, was God's only direct creation. God created Christ with every divine quality and attribute complete in total perfection. And for a really long time—like another entire eternity—it was just God and Christ living together in happiness and peace.

Although it's hard for us to imagine it, God does have a form. And the being that God first created has basically the same form, the same figure. Believe it or not, since both of them have form, both also wore clothes.

And so it was that the being created by God, Christ, was also clothed from God's own garments. Those garments were—and still are—made of the highest spiritual material that can possibly exist. It shines pure light and radiates a splendid variety of brilliant colors. A human could not look upon these robes without going blind. They are that full of life.

It was God's wish to only create one being in God's own image. And therefore it was God's will to call only one being God's own. As a result, Christ's love became completely united with God, and God meant everything to Christ. Yet this would not be the end of the story of God's creation.

For God also wished for creation to continue, saying to Christ, "You shall have siblings! And these siblings will all come forth from you." So just as Christ had come into being out of God, so too would all these brothers and sisters come forth from Christ.

Keep in mind, God and Christ were together talking about all this for an infinitely long time (with time, of course, being a decidedly human concept). For eons and eons, the two spoke together about how creation would further unfold, and how it would expand.

As God and Christ exchanged ideas, God kept encouraging Christ by saying, "You will be able to do everything. I will give you might and power. And everything that comes into being shall come through you. You will do this in my place." After all, God had given Christ a healthy share of God's precious knowledge.

The story of the Light-bearer

And so it was that over vast intervals of time, various princely brothers and sisters came into existence. The first being to come from Christ was given a name that means "light-bearer," or "bringer of light." For this being would inherit the most incredible radiance, glory and creative power from Christ.

As such, for a very long time—yes, another eternity—there were essentially three beings living together in an ethereal natural world. At that time, there was also a plant kingdom and an animal kingdom, although both to a somewhat limited extent.

Many, many more lifeforms would later be designed and formed by Christ. And then each would be given life by God. For God continued to always be the one who would bestow the breath of life. God is who makes life possible, by giving all of creation God's light.

Vast periods of time passed while God, Christ and the Light-bearer lived together in perfect peace under one roof, so to speak. God's house was large, and when Christ came along, it was expanded so that Christ could have his own quarters. Later, the Light-bearer came into being and new spaces were created.

It's just like here, with our families. We have a home, and then when children arrive they remain with us in our home. Until one day the time comes for more independence, and then it's time for the children to leave. Of course, all this talk of time is really quite misleading. Because for God, a thousand years feel like a day.

The story of becoming lost

Eventually, more brothers and sisters came as well. And God blessed all of this, with everything unfolding according to a great divine order. In this way, spiritual nature would keep on unfolding and expanding, with more and more angels being created. Later, the many couples that came into being through Christ were sent out to create heavenly nations.

Keep in mind that each being Christ created was perfect in at least one divine attribute, or divine ray of light. So the Plan of Creation was—and still is—that all of creation would keep growing and expanding. Each created being, then, would keep moving toward greater and greater perfection by developing all divine attributes within themselves.

Imagine the joy that Christ experienced through his first creation. Consider how great the love would have been. Not to mention all the other brothers and sisters that came into being, which gave the possibility of an endless unfolding. And all this was happening in accordance with God's will.

There was life, life, life and nothing but more amazing life.

Until one day, the Light-bearer decided he wanted to become the leader of it all. Despite all he had been given and despite all of his amazingness, Christ glowed even greater in perfection. Over time, the Light-bearer grew jealous of Christ, his brother and maker, and wanted to be King.

Which is why the Light-bearer set upon a mission to replace Christ—the one and only child of God—with himself.

The story of darkness

Once again, we must think of things in terms of time. And so for an incredibly long time, the Light-bearer went to work convincing many other created beings—called angels in that realm—to support him in his bid to become their King. If we are here, having a human experience, then at some time in the past we saw his point and agreed with him, at least to some extent.

Apparently, the Light-bearer was ridiculously charismatic. So it was not easy to resist his charms. But by offering our support to the Light-bearer, we not only turned our back on Christ, the born King, we also turned against the will of God. For we knew what God's will was—that Christ was made to be King—and we chose to go another way.

Eventually, it was this reality—that we willingly went against the will of God—that led to our inclusion in the Fall. And where did we fall to? We fell into darkness. This, friends, is how we have come to have darkness within our own beings.

The reality of God's will

Ok, so where are we going with this? Let's bring things back around to the topic of how finding God is roughly equivalent to looking within and finding ourselves. Because as we can now understand, God is the source of all life. And God is also the source of our inner light.

But then each of us went through the Fall, during which our inner light became covered over with layers of darkness. And now, any time we choose to align with our inner darkness instead of our inner light, we fall a little more. For by doing so, we continue to choose to go against the will of God.

This notion that we need to learn to align our will with God's will puts a lot of people off. Like, really off. *Why is that?*

For one thing, we think we know better than God what's best for us. But now let's reflect on where we have all come from—dwelling in a place of eternal harmony, dazzling light shows, and really awesome wardrobes—to the land we're living in now. *Do we really know what's best?*

It seems that perhaps that strategy of seeing and doing things God's way—which leads to deep contentment, inner fulfillment and enduring love—might not be so bad.

The reality of spiritual laws

To align with God's will means we align with God's spiritual laws. For God and God's law are really the same thing. The spiritual laws we are talking about are the laws of justice that were set into place 2000 years ago. And they work to guide us in making better choices. They do this by making the consequences of our choices that go against God's will unpleasant, if not downright painful.

In other words, if we align with God's spiritual laws, we will eventually come to bliss. If we go against them—and we have free will to do so—we will create more struggle for ourselves. Eventually—according to these laws—it will be our own pain and suffering that will motivate us to course-correct and try things another way: God's way.

The place we get snagged is that many of us—*most* of us?—have a confused understanding about God. This is caused, in part, by what the Pathwork Guide calls our God Image. What happens is that we take our negative reaction toward one or both of our parents—our greatest authority as a child—and hang it on God.

After all, most of us learn growing up that God is the ultimate authority. Then we overlay our struggle with our parents onto God, conflating and confusing the two. When this is the case—when we have a difficult human reaction that we unknowingly cast onto God—we tend to see God as some kind of vengeful disciplinarian. And so we rebel.

As a result, we don't trust God. *Because how can we?* Especially when we think so little and so wrongly of God. This is a serious problem. For we are never going to come around to adopting God's laws as long as we think God's way is the wrong way.

So our work must be to look within and sort ourselves out. We must find out where we are not in truth. And we must discover for ourselves what the truth really is. Both about ourselves and about God.

The reality of free will

There's another piece of this *How did we get here?* puzzle to factor in. And that's free will. Recall that when that very first being was created, God made Christ in God's own image. Well, a key thing to know about God is that God has free will. To make a being in God's image then, and to go on creating all other beings from *that* being, means everybody gets free will.

Long story short, without free will, we wouldn't be compatible with God. Which is why God will never ask us to do anything against our own will. Further, without free will, we wouldn't be able to live in Christ's Kingdom. Remember, that's where we were all living before the Fall. And that's where we're trying to get back to.

During the Fall, all divine qualities became twisted into their opposites. Regarding free will, this became distorted into domination. Namely, we were cast into darkness and were now under the complete rule of the Prince of Darkness, the former Light-bearer. So the primary reason for Christ's mission in incarnating as Jesus was to restore our free will.

It is now our work—through the use of our own free will—to fully restore our inner light. We do this by uncovering our hidden darkness, which is typically hidden from our own awareness but not so hard for others to see. That's why we need the help of others to go through the painstaking process of transforming our Lower Self aspects back into their original Higher Self form.

This is the only way to return home. We must go inside. For as Jesus taught us, that's where heaven is.

To align our will with God's will means we are ultimately to become incredibly happy. But God does not force us to live such a joyful existence. Case in point, if we want to keep using our will another way, we can keep coming here and living on Earth instead.

Earth, if you think about it, is not a punishment. It's an opportunity to change and grow. By the time we arrive here, we have worked our way up from whatever level of darkness we landed in after the Fall. Because note, not everyone fell to the same depth.

Once we start coming to Earth, we have already gained some access to our inner light, or Higher Self. At the same time, if we're here—unless we are a saint—we also have some Lower Self aspects to work on. We have some inner housecleaning to do.

The reality of our reactions

A good way to see where our work is, is to look at our inner reactions during our interactions with others. The Pathwork Guide calls these our emotional reactions. *What sets us off?*

One thing that can trigger our resistance is the mere mention of words like "God" and "Christ". Because humans—through our inevitable human nature—have introduced so many wrong associations with these names.

For this writing, I actually thought about changing "God" to "Creator". But then that could be misleading. For isn't Christ also an amazing creator? For that matter, *aren't we all?*

The answer to this last question is critical to our understanding of the story of our life. Because yes—yes, yes, yes!—we are all amazing creators. After all, we are all made in the image of God. And so we must all, by our very nature, have the ability to create.

If the life stories we are creating for ourselves are not pleasant ones, we must find the inner darkness—the Lower Self aspects—hiding in our own psyche. This is why, if we want to craft a different life story, we must become willing to look within.

And how about "Christ"? *Where do we even start?* I thought about changing the name "Christ" to "Robin," a name used in English for both men and women, as well as for a lovely bird living in nature. It is clear that Christ must have been endowed with both active and receptive principles in order to create everything. For both aspects are always needed in every creation. And Christ is also a genius when it comes to creating nature.

In the end, some things are better left alone.

Oh, and the Light-bearer. Many people know of this being by various other names, including Lucifer, Satan, and the Prince of Darkness. These are all true and correct names for us to know him by. But what's also important for us know about him—to truly and deeply understand—is this: Just like the rest of us, under all his layers of distortion and therefore darkness, the Light-bearer's potential for restoring his magnificence remains.

The reality of returning home

Fortunately for all of us, Christ's mission in coming to Earth was successful; it totally restored our free will. This is true for every human who ever lived and ever will live, regardless of whether we've heard of Jesus or believe in Christ. It was such an incredibly big deal!

It opened the doors to heaven so that if we do our personal healing work—if we make ourselves once again compatible with God's Spirit World—then we can get back to it. But this is not a one-and-done deal. We can't just say we believe and we're home.

For it's simply not possible to become compatible with God and God's Spirit World without doing deep soul cleansing work. Further, it's not possible to align ourselves with something we aren't able to trust.

And here's where everything comes back home to looking within and finding ourselves. Because until we clear away our inner darkness—our inner Lower Self obstacles—we are not trustworthy people. After all, our lives are being built on untruths. And as long as we cannot trust ourselves, we will not trust God.

In reality, God and our highest good are one. For God and our inner light are the same. To be clear, we are not God, but *we are all of God*. And no one wants more goodness for us than God does. What God really wants is for us to learn to stand on our own two feet.

And Christ? Christ has never stopped loving each one of us. Just as a parent still loves a misbehaving child. What's more, Christ—with the help of the beings not part of the Fall—has never stopped guiding us in our return home. In fact, working together with God, Christ orchestrated the creation of this world we live in, to make our return possible.

Consider, too, that the Story of the Prodigal Son tells the story of a passage Christ had to go through. For Christ had to come to accept that one day Christ's beloved brother, the Light-bearer, would return as well. And like all the rest of us, the Light-bearer—after learning to realign his will with God's will—is going to be welcomed home with great joy.

The story of our life

Ultimately, the story of our life is always up to us. Which way do we want to align? Which way are we going to turn? When will we learn? Who can we trust? Where should we take action? *How* should we act? What do we need to accept?

For our life, as we experience it, is nothing more and nothing less than an out-picturing of what's going on inside ourselves. Said another way, the story of our life always reflects the state of our psyche. And our blindness to seeing how we're creating our own life story is just a reflection of our unwillingness to look within and make the inner connections.

Every conflict we face with our brothers and sisters points to our inner work. Every disharmony signals an inner untruth. All bad attitudes are blinking arrows. Each day is a chance to choose another way.

Look at the story of your life. And then turn and look within.

Adapted, in part, from a lecture by spirit-teacher Lene, received in German through the medium Beatrice Brunner during the meditation week in Waldhaus Flims, Switzerland, September 19, 1982: *The Spiritual World*, Issue 3, May/June 2022 (in English).

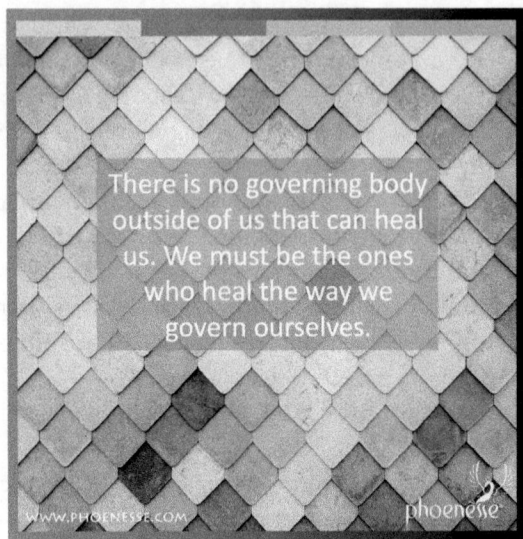

There is no governing body outside of us that can heal us. We must be the ones who heal the way we govern ourselves.

WWW.PHOENESSE.COM

phoenesse

Essay 27

How to heal a country

"May all of you find here or there a little key, a clarification, a helpful hint so as to shed light on your way, in your struggle to reach the light of truth, to understand your life in relationship to the universe, to understand yourself and therefore life."

– Pathwork® Guide Q&A #132

I once heard someone say that the most ideal form of government is a benevolent dictator. If there were such a thing as a perfect parent, maybe that's what they would be like. A "perfect" parent, however, would need to be well-balanced within, and then also well-balanced with their partner. But getting this just right takes many lifetimes. Most of us parents don't get everything right.

As for the dictator style of governing—such as we find in a monarchy and in feudalism—according to the Pathwork Guide, it is one of the less evolved forms. And it only works when you have a leader who is fairly evolved. So it's really prone to eventually involving a dictator who becomes crooked with the rules. Because, *I'm in charge, so the rules don't apply to me!* Once such a leader gains power, the rest of us won't fare well.

Historically, such dictatorial disasters have led humans to develop more equalizing forms of government, namely communism and socialism. But these too go off the rails when—as it inevitably turns out—not everyone makes the same effort.

Which brings us to democracy. Or in the case of the United States, capitalistic democracy. This style of political system offers us the most freedom. But such a valuable incentive comes with a price. The price is that a democracy requires the highest level of responsibility—for all involved—in order to work. Most especially, it asks for more from the leaders.

The outer reflects the inner

Before we look more deeply at this situation, let's touch on where these various political systems come from to begin with. If you're familiar with the many powerful teachings from the Pathwork Guide, it won't surprise you to hear that these three primary political systems—the three main ways we govern ourselves—arise from inside of us.

Why is this so? Because everything does. The Guide frequently said that our perception of the world is backwards—or inside out—from how it actually is. In reality, the world around us is always an out-picturing of what's inside us. The outside is a mirror of the inside. Our world reflects the collective contents of our psyche. For the micro rolls up to create the macro.

That's exactly why the world we're living in seems to be falling apart. For people are fractured and fragmented within. This is the human condition. The goal of life, then, is to work on putting ourselves back together. But if we are not willing to look inward and sort ourselves out, our outer world is going to keep shaking and possibly collapse. Then we will know crisis both within ourselves and in our outer lives.

What's happening is we are dropping the ball on the two things a democracy demands most from each of us: self-responsibility and compassion. These are the two things we each must be working toward. And they are not easy to come by.

Growing up and waking up

Consider that for thousands and thousands of years, people have been slowly growing. Over time, we gradually develop and evolve. Which is why our styles of political systems have been changing over time. Like it or not, we always keep rolling forward.

Occasionally, as we roll with change, we must go through times of transition. That is what's happening now. For we are now entering into a new era. A new epoch, actually. This is the last development phase for humanity. We are now fully entering adulthood. (Note, this next phase could take millions of years to get through. It's really up to us.)

One of the ways life changes when we become adults is that more is now expected of us. For one thing, we must learn to stand on our own two feet. For most of us, this means we will trip, stumble and perhaps fall, possibly quite a few times. Because it takes us a minute to get our bearings. Along the way, we may follow a few dead ends.

It's like this for most children who get ready to leave adolescence. And humanity, in general, is now stumbling its way into growing up, and waking up. We really have no idea what's coming. But we can see things are going to have to change.

Two parties, two big challenges

By now, many have tasted the freedom—and also the pitfalls—of finding our own partner, choosing our own job or career path, and settling into our own space. These are the fruits that so many generations worked so hard to gain. Such freedoms are what our evolution as humans has all been about!

Yet at the same time, our primary relationships are often rocky. People are unsatisfied at work. Many work long hours for not enough pay. Lots of children are growing up in poverty. Safe, affordable housing is hard for many to find. Healthcare is wonderful, but fewer and fewer can afford it.

Why are we bungling things so badly for so many?

There are two important things to understand about our two-party democratic system:
1. For democracy to be successful, people must develop *within themselves* the key positions of both parties.
2. A two-party democracy can easily trip over duality.

What are the two essential positions, or platforms, that a two-party system relies upon? In a nutshell, they are self-responsibility and compassion. Of course, there are tons of other factors and positions to also consider. But fundamentally, self-responsibility and compassion are the two main pillars of a democracy. Without both of them, the whole structure will tear itself apart and eventually collapse.

In the end, there will be more and more struggle for everyone, and less and less freedom.

Why we need compassion

Interestingly, self-responsibility is also one of the main themes of all the teachings from the Pathwork Guide. They all keep pointing us back to where the source of all our problems really lives. And it's always within us. This is why we must always keep turning the aim of our fingers around and searching for our part in every conflict. For no matter how wrong the other may be, if we are disturbed, we are also playing a part.

At the same time, there is a natural tendency to judge ourselves harshly whenever we discover something amiss within. *When we find we are in the wrong*. Each time we discover how the very thing we really hate *lives inside us*, the temptation is to turn our hatred toward ourselves.

Because once we see how our destructive outer life is truly an out-picturing of our inner destructiveness, we may turn our hate and judgement onto ourselves. We may want to turn around and destroy ourselves. This is why another main theme from the Pathwork Guide is self-compassion. As we do our work of self-discovery, we must not turn into our own worst enemy, making a difficult path even harder.

Compassion is not pity

The essence of democracy is the search for the common good. For at our core, we are all connected. This means that when I hurt someone else, I also in some way hurt myself. But when I help my brothers and sisters, I also help myself. Having compassion then is a strength, not a weakness.

In the Q&A on compassion versus pity, the Pathwork Guide explained that compassion is not the same as pity. What's the difference? The emotion of pity feels heavy, so it reduces our strength and the help we can give. When we are involved in pity, somewhere we are negatively involved within. Maybe we are projecting our fear that the fate someone else is suffering will land on us. Or we might have hidden guilt we're not in touch with.

It's actually not uncommon for us to feel a certain satisfaction at someone else's misfortune. Not only do we not have to deal with that same fate, but we like that someone else is being punished and going through difficulties. This doesn't really make sense, but it does contain a sort of backwards logic: "If other people are also going through hardships, then I must not be so bad. At least I'm not the only one suffering. This makes me glad that others are also suffering."

An inner reaction like this creates a shock and a guilt in our psyche that we completely repress. Then we overcompensate for this by feeling an unproductive pity that makes us weaker. We mistakenly believe our pity excuses us because it makes us suffer along with the other person. But we are doing so in a destructive way.

Our work is to discover the wrong thinking that lies behind this kind of unreasonable attitude. We start by noticing our genuine reactions, keeping in mind that we are all humans who have many unpurified emotions. Some are childish, others are selfish. Many are shortsighted. The goal is to learn how to accept them without condemning ourselves, condoning our off-base attitudes and justifying our behavior.

Our misguided perspectives will dissolve to whatever degree we really get to know them. Then our pity will transform into compassion, making it possible to give constructive help to people who are suffering. We can do this with our actions or just by communicating that we genuinely care about them.

No one wins

One of the tenets of looking within means we stop looking "out there" for someone else to blame. In truth, there is always plenty of blame to go around. After all, we are all human. But even after we identify how others are at fault, this never does the trick of resolving our problems. For it is only by finding the roots inside ourselves that we can effectively address them.

In the case of our two-party democracy, it's quite easy for things to go sideways. Because there is *always* error on both sides. So there is always someone else we can blame. As a result, both sides get to feel self-righteous when they correctly identify the fault in the other side. Then both sides lean into the faults of the other side. Yet neither side takes steps to work on their part.

This is the stalemate that is sinking America right now.

How duality can lead to destruction

Where does it come from, this drive our many leaders have to destroy the functioning of our government? It actually arises when we distort the fabric of duality. Hence, duality is the second big hiccup for a two-party democracy, due to the way it so easily hooks into the illusion of duality.

Briefly, duality is the situation where everything comes in pairs of opposites. Good comes with bad, day comes with night, pleasure comes with pain. Here's where we get lost: We believe we can live a better life by seeking only the "good" half and avoiding the "bad" half. The moment we start thinking this way, we leave reality and start living in illusion. The illusion is our misguided belief that this can work.

The only way out of this dilemma is by going in and through. The way forward then—and the *only* way out of duality—is by learning to make peace with both sides of every duality. We don't do this by embracing darkness, but rather by walking through it. In other words, we must face our inner darkness. This is the way to find the middle of the road of duality. What doesn't work is to plant a position and then spend the rest of our life defending it. Look at our government. Look around you. Ask yourself, *Is this working?*

154

Where we get stuck

There are two parts of ourselves that are inherently caught in duality. One is the part of ourselves that fragmented when we were young. This happened due to whatever pain we experienced. The other is our ego. For now, we're going to focus on the ego.

The ego is the part of ourselves that we have direct access to. So it's the part that takes the lead in cleaning up our inner house. It fills the bucket with water, finds the mop, adds the soap, and starts to scrub. We need to have a healthy ego if we want to heal ourselves.

But because the ego lives in duality, it will never be able to understand the awakened state. In the awakened state, we rest comfortably with opposites. But the ego cannot grasp this concept. Instead, the ego competes and tries to win at life. In its unhealed state, the ego will only look out for itself. Because, being stuck in duality, the ego believes this is a "me versus you" world, and not the "me and you" world it really is.

To be awake is to live unified within. This is the natural resting condition of our deeper, inner self, which the Pathwork Guide calls our Higher Self. In order for us to make peace with duality—and therefore to eventually leave this difficult dimension—we must learn to let go of our ego and live from our Higher Self.

But before we can do that, we must clear away all the obstacles dwelling in our Lower Self. Painting with broad brush strokes, our Lower Self is the repository of all our negativity, destructiveness, rebelliousness, and the like. Waking up, then, is a two-step process. First we must clean our inner house so we can find our Higher Self. And then we must let go of our ego and learn to live from a that deeper place within.

The power of the Higher Self

To the ego's way of seeing life, this is nuts. *We will never win if we do this.* But the truth is that the only way to "win" is to let go and discover our inner connection. This is our connection to the divine. And from here, true abundance can flow.

At this level, we are already all connected. From here, what best serves us also best serves everyone. There is enough for all of us. And not because we take from one person and give it to another.

In reality, there is no conflict at the level of the Higher Self. We can each follow the stream of goodness that flows from inside us and gradually come to live in peace and harmony. It is only at the level of the ego that we keep running into struggle and conflict, disharmony and seeming injustice.

The first step on our journey to the Oneness—to living together in peace and harmony—is to develop a strong ego. Because to do this work, we need an ego that is strong enough to let go of itself. For that's the only way for the ego to learn to listen to the voice of our Higher Self and follow the guidance that flows from within.

When an ego, however, becomes very strong, but doesn't know the next step is to let go, things can really go wrong. For the ego may know there is a greater power available, yet it doesn't know how to reach it. Instead, the ego may become obsessed with its own power. This is known as megalomania.

When this happens, the ego is not being guided by the Higher Self. Part of the problem is that the ego has not done the necessary work of clearing away untruthful negative obstacles in the psyche. It also hasn't learned to surrender itself. So then the power the ego craves—and then wields—becomes distorted and destructive. As such, the person gets a giant thrill from using their power to destroy things.

That pretty much sums up the condition of American politics today.

"It is the same process as, for instance, you know through all spiritual, religious and metaphysical teachings, that love is the key to the whole universe. Yet you have to admit to yourself first in what areas your heart does not know about this, where in your innermost self you feel hate where you would want to feel love."

– Pathwork® Guide Q&A #113

Shifting to balancing opposites

The shift that must happen is we must evolve from a world run by outer rules to one run by people ruled from within. This movement calls us to learn to balance opposites, which takes time and effort to master. This brings to mind some advice I was given when I was pregnant with my first child. A friend in my neighborhood held a baby shower for me, and the party game was for each mother in the room to write down their favorite piece of parenting advice. One stuck for life: Lots of love and lots of discipline.

The challenge of balancing these seemingly opposite qualities—in all areas of my life—became a guiding light for me. I didn't do this perfectly, of course. But I have always kept trying.

Here's another example of the opposites we must learn to balance: firmness and flexibility. Whereas the ego thinks of firmness as rigid, inflexible rules, in reality the truth is always also fluid and flexible. The way the Pathwork Guide explains it is this: In the Spirit World, the more structure something has, the more flexible it is. So, we must develop firmness—find solid ground to stand on—and also hold our positions with a certain softness.

The swinging pendulum of evolving

It's clear we're not ready to give up our laws and rules. We're not collectively developed enough for that. But perhaps we can look at our one-sided stance regarding any particular topic. Can we see how we are being rigid and one-sided in our position?

If so, our work may be about loosening our grip. What other perspectives are we not able to see? As the Pathwork Guide points out, a good attorney is able to defend both sides of any argument. This is a skill everyone can work to develop: the ability to see and understand all sides.

So at different times, we will need to work with both sides. Because the way of growth follows the path of a pendulum swinging widely from side to side. During each swing, we shift to the opposite side. Each time, we will approach the middle way a little more. Eventually, we will reach the point when we can see both sides clearly. That's when we truly have something of value to offer.

In short, we must do our own work before we are in position to help others. We simply can't give what we don't have. Said differently, until we have learned how to stay in the middle of the road, we will just keep trying to pull others into the ditch with us.

The folly of finger pointing

The current state of affairs is that our society is splitting down the middle, separating into two warring factions. Each side feels self-righteous about their position. But both sides are actually abusing the system.

"How do we manage to abuse and distort capitalistic democracy? One aspect is the abuse of power by a stronger few. These are the more willful individuals who impose disadvantages on those who can't or won't stand up for themselves. In truth, disadvantage will be the natural result for people who refuse to fend for themselves; they become parasites at the expense of others.

"But through the distortions in this system, those who exploit others becomes parasites themselves. They use the very ones who want to leach off others. Instead of working to help these people wake up and adopt more fair and appropriate ways of being, they play right into their hands. They end up validating the excuses of those who are lazy and cheating, who say it is an unfair world they live in and that they are victimized by the greedy. *Because they are.*

"So this system can be abused from both sides. Those clamoring for socialism can become more parasitic and blame the power structure for keeping them down. On the other extreme, those who are strong and diligent, who risk and invest, can justify their greed and drive for power by blaming the parasitic nature of those who are lazy. But abuse is abuse, regardless of how it dresses for the party."

—*Pearls*, Chapter 3: Exploring the Spiritual Nature of Political Systems

Working all sides

Everyone in both camps is called to develop self-responsibility. Because that is the task of being an adult. But in the camp of those who have the power, the scales are tipped so that more, not less, is required of them. For there is a spiritual law that goes: From those to whom more has been given, more is expected.

This is one of the choke points of democracy. When those who are leading and profiting won't take responsibility for checking their greed and managing their one-sided self-interest...when they refuse to look within and see how they are contributing to everyone's struggles...they create a crumbling system.

The other choke point is lack of compassion. For although we are all fundamentally equal, we are not all actually developed to the same extent. Some people have more work to do, while others are further along. And again, for those who are further along, there is an added responsibility to help those in need of a helping hand.

This is why we must add the core strength of compassion to our mix.

Try more, care more

Think of it like this. If we are a person who likes to hold our own feet to the fire—we are always striving to be better, have more, get on top—then we probably don't need to learn to try more. What we now need to learn is how to care more. We need to learn to look outside ourselves and be of service.

So then if there were two political parties called Try More and Care More, which side would we be on, at least for now? It may seem we belong on the Try More side, because that's our strength. But in fact, we need to sit on the Care More side for a time. We need to develop our ability to care more. Later, we may move back to the Try More side. But we will do so with less harshness and a more compassionate perspective.

Conversely, maybe we are a person who is forever self-sacrificing, and always putting others first. But if we haven't finished clearing up all our inner obstacles, then our work is now to Try More. We must learn to look within and stop ignoring our own faults. Remember, we can't give what we don't have.

Note, to try more doesn't mean to try harder. It means to try another way.

The real work is humbling

Every time we face a disharmony in life, we are being shown something that we can use to learn and grow. And let's face it, we will never reach the promised land—whatever that means to us—without making mistakes and course-correcting. This turns every conflict into a a chance to look within and make a change.

Without a doubt, this is going to be humbling. We're going to discover that we don't know everything and we're not always right. In fact, we *must* discover this. Because if we were already standing fully in truth, we would be living in peace.

Becoming humble is the antidote to pride. And pride, according to the Pathwork Guide, is one of our three primary faults, along with fear and self-will. It is only by seeing ourselves more clearly—by truly facing ourselves as we are right now—that we will get over this mountain.

"The truly wanting to get answers, to be in truth, is the key. If you truly want it and you formulate that desire and you become more specific in the de-sire, then you establish this contact with the divine self, with the cosmic truth within you."
– Pathwork® Guide Q&A #172

We have to want it

But wait, aren't there people who won't want to try more, or to care more? What are we to do with them? We help them as well. For we were all, at some point in the past, in that same boat. It takes many lifetimes before we fig-ure out that we must make an effort to get the good stuff. That there is always a price we must pay for what we want.

Indeed, many, many people go through many wasted lifetimes, not moving the ball forward by much. God allows this because this also serves a purpose. For eventually such a person may look at the arc of their many lives and realize they are getting nowhere. One day, they will turn around and start to do their own work of healing.

Changing the story

The history of our country is filled with stories of courage and inspiration, as well as challenge and destruction. All of our stories together have brought us to this moment in which we are living. During this time of transition, we have the chance to craft a better ending to our current story.

What we must find is the way to reconnect our fractured selves, to rejoin our wounded parts. To do this, all who are capable must learn to look within ourselves and heal the shattered fragments of our psyche. That's the only way to heal our fractured nation. There is no governing body outside of us that can heal us. We must be the ones who heal the way we govern ourselves.

We do this by individually searching within for compassion, and by learning self-responsibility. When we develop and integrate both of these inside ourselves, we bring something new and wonderful into the world. This is the only way out of this difficult dualistic dimension. We each must become able to see all sides.

"The answer always lies within the self. For if it were otherwise, man would indeed be lost. The fact that he has himself as a key, which makes it so accessible and so possible to stop fear and to stop uncertainty, that is the beauty and the truth of creation. It is possible to know yourself."
– Pathwork® Guide Q&A #130

We must reach and shake

The work of personal self-development goes by many names. The list includes: self-finding, self-knowing, self-transformation, self-actualization, self-discovery, self-awareness, self-realization, self-purification, self-healing. All of these point to the same process.

And this process is multi-faceted and complex. Over the course of 22 years, the Pathwork Guide gave roughly 250 lectures, each revealing another facet of this remarkable journey of being human. When he spoke about the same facet he had talked about previously, he illuminated it from a different angle. Each time, the Guide was giving us something new to see.

A few years ago, my husband and I began learning a second language, Portuguese. There is a word in Portuguese, "alcançar," that means both "to reach" and "to attain." Indeed, if we want to attain the jewels of self-knowledge—the true treasure of life—we must become willing to reach.

We are also going to need to shake. In fact, a lot of people are shaking on the inside these days. One of the Portuguese words that means "to shake" is "balançar," which also means "to balance." So to create a new balance, we are going to need to shake loose everything that no longer serves us. To do this, we'll need to find some trustworthy teachings to follow.

To this end, consider exploring the Pathwork Guide's teachings. I have organized and rewritten just over 140 Pathwork lectures—always with the Guide's inspiration and support—to make them easier to access. They are available in the various books published by Phoenesse, with chapters also available as podcasts by most podcast providers.

"I will answer your questions to the best of my ability, my dearest friends, and the answers may not always be on the level you expect. They may approach a different orientation, a new level, another angle, but that is then precisely what you need.

I ask all of you to tune deeply into yourselves, for every question and every answer being presented here can be an aid to all who are present, who can apply every single thing on some level, although the answers will be particularly designed to help the person where he is now.

Now, who would like to ask?"

– Pathwork® Guide Q&A #237

We must learn to lay the sword of truth on its side. Then we can spread truth the same way we spread butter. Smoothly, evenly and without slicing anyone.

WWW.PHOEN...E.COM

Essay 28

Learn to fight the right way, for the right thing

It's 1989 and I have been sober for about six months. Then, almost as if by magic, my career takes a sharp turn for the better as I transition from technical sales to working as a copywriter at an advertising agency. In that new role, I would learn some valuable lessons about what to fight for, what to fight against, and how to fight in the right way.

The ad agency I worked for focused on business-to-business advertising— one business advertising their goods to another business—working primarily with industrial companies. My clients included Johnson Yokogawa, maker of process control instruments, and Georgia Pacific, maker of pulp and paper goods. The owners of the agency had left their previous jobs as engineers to start this company.

Briefly, the agencies I worked for in the 1990s were organized into two main departments: creative advertising and public relations. On the advertising side, there was another subdivision. On one side were the account representatives who went out and met with the clients. On the other side was the creative team.

And the creatives were also split into two groups: copywriters and graphic designers or art directors. Of course, there were also project managers, finance people and human resources departments. The saying for ad agencies was: All our assets go down the elevator every day.

On my first assignment as a technical copywriter, the account representative was floored that the client only had one small edit for my copy. That was basically unheard of. Because receiving edits is part of the job for a copywriter. It's the feedback that helps get everything just right.

If you've ever read a good book, you've probably noticed the laundry list of people the author thanks at the end. *This book wouldn't be the same without your help.* And the editor usually gets one of the biggest shout-outs. Because good feedback is vital to doing good work.

The skill of giving good feedback

Over the years I worked as a copywriter, I interfaced with many engineers and scientists. My college major was chemistry, with a minor in business, so I could speak their language. One thing I noticed to be generally true about engineers and scientists is they are smart. Another thing I noticed—although I'd like to think I'm an exception—is they are not very good writers. Also, their people skills are not always great.

So as a copywriter, I often heard feedback like this: "This is terrible. Here are my edits." *Ouch.* First, copywriters are humans who have feelings. Insulting them is not going to make them want to engage in the editing process. Second, a creative person needs to stay engaged in the editing process. Because editing is part of the job.

Third, it often happened that a highly educated person would provide really awful editing suggestions. As in, taking their feedback as is would really ruin the piece. But the client is always right, which meant my job was now about fighting to salvage good work. This happened so much, I eventually moved to an in-house marketing communications position where I had more say.

I was reminded of this recently when I asked my husband, Scott, to edit an essay I had written. (Sharing here with his blessing.) I knew he would have valuable suggestions, because he too has studied the Pathwork Guide's teachings for decades. I especially wanted his input since this time I was referencing a spiritual teaching from another source.

Plus, he's smart. He has a master's degree in aerospace engineering and another master's from GE in mechanical engineering. And he's a good writer— yes, another exception—although his style is different from mine.

All this to say, I wasn't terribly surprised when he said, "This is terrible. Here are my edits." I explained to him the importance of developing a better filter so that I could receive his edits more gracefully. To clarify, having a good filter doesn't mean we fake being nice. It also doesn't mean we avoid having difficult conversations.

A good filter helps us navigate the rough terrain of difficult conversations. It smooths feathers and clears the way so that change can happen more easily. Having a good filter is about making an effort to heal instead of hurling unwelcome and unhelpful comments. It's an art that opens doors, and an important skill to practice.

After incorporating most of his suggestions—today, I get the final say about my writing—Scott said he thought the essay was really very good. And editing my next essay went much more smoothly. As a grateful author, this feels like a good moment to express my heartfelt thanks to Scott for offering such helpful feedback.

How to hold the sword of truth

One of the most well-known archangels is Saint Michael. And one of the more interesting things about St. Michael is that most—maybe all—of the images of him show him holding a sword. Which begs the question, *what does an angel in heaven need a sword for? What is St. Michael fighting?*

In fact, St. Michael is fighting the forces of darkness. And he is doing so on our behalf. Darkness is also what we need to be fighting. To be exact, we need to fight the darkness still in us. Fortunately, when we truly become ready to join in fighting darkness—instead of aligning with darkness—St. Michael will give us our own sword. This is the sword of truth.

For darkness always contains untruth. So our work is to uncover untruth wherever it lies—especially inside ourselves—along with the negative energy attached to it. And then we need to reorient ourselves to the truth. In short, we must learn how to *overcome* the darkness by learning the right way to fight it.

Note, overcoming is not the same thing as always needing to win. The drive to always win comes from a misguided understanding about how to prevail in this land of duality.

"Living in this land of duality, we are continually harboring arbitrary either/or concepts. Some of these, we may not even be aware of. One of the most common ones, which causes one of our greatest limitations, is an attitude we hold about being a winner versus a loser.

"In this way of looking at things, being a winner means being ruthless. We must be selfish, trampling and triumphing over others and belittling them. This leaves no room for being kind, considerate or sympathetic. Should such emotions be allowed, one would fear turning into a loser.

"Being a loser, then, means to be unselfish. We are then self-sacrificing, kind, good and considerate people. Some of us will adopt one alternative, and some the other. But everyone fears the consequences of being the opposite of what they are.

"Neither of these two choices is good. Neither is better or worse. Both have the same misconceptions built into them. And both lead to nothing but loneliness, resentment, self-pity, self-contempt and frustration.

"When two people come together in a relationship from these opposite teams, it will be fraught with great friction that will lead to the point of hopelessness. The winner will be fearing impulses of genuine affection as much as they fear weakness and any inner desire for dependency. For the loser, their concept of goodness is equated with total approval from others. This means they can't stand any form of criticism, whether it's justified or not.

"Both sides are basically resenting in the other what they are fearing and fighting in themselves, which is their hidden tendency to be like the opposite choice. Oh brother."

–*Finding Gold,* Chapter 8: Winner vs Loser: Interplay Between the Self and Creative Forces

As we start doing our personal development work, we will gradually unwind the twisted wiring in ourselves. And this will bring us into more and more clarity. Our confusion about what to believe—about what is the truth—will go away. But what can happen, as we start to see things more clearly, is we pick up the sword of truth and use it to stab people. After all, even though we're accessing more light, we still have darkness within us. Overcoming our own darkness is a long, slow process.

What we must learn to do is take this sword of truth and lay it over on its side. Then we can spread the same truth, but we can do it the way we spread butter onto bread. Smoothly, evenly and without slicing anyone.

Getting better is a co-creative process

Due to this need for getting good feedback, the art of writing is an inherently co-creative process. This doesn't mean the editor gets full credit for our work. They don't become the co-author. But we want to gratefully acknowledge their contribution.

In the end, writing well requires we have the humility to ask for and accept feedback. (And also have thick enough skin to receive feedback, however it comes.) We could extrapolate this sentiment to all of life. For, in a similar way, if we don't have the humility to ask others to help us see the error of our ways, we're not likely to live better.

As such, living in relationship with others can be considered a co-creative process. We are still the authors of our own lives. But if we want to make ourselves—and therefore our lives—better, we need to become willing to take in feedback and correct our ways. For that's the best way to grow and develop.

Finding our faults

The Pathwork Guide calls relationships a "path within a path." For by their very nature, relationships will tease all our darkness to the surface. This is a divine plan that—when used the right way—can help us work on transforming ourselves. If we lean into our relationships—if we use them to surface our faults—we can become better, faster.

In the teaching on finding our faults, the Pathwork Guide explains that one of the hardest parts of the fault-finding process can be simply identifying our own faults. Here's one way to go about it. Look for a pet fault, which is one of our faults we rather like. (Yes, oddly, we're rather fond of our faults, which is partly why they're so hard to resolve.) Then notice how we find the same fault highly irritating when we encounter it in someone else.

Here's another way to get at our faults. We can ask our partner—or someone who knows us well—to tell us what they see. *What are my faults?*

Such a question, of course, may feel loaded with a pile of dynamite. This is where things get interesting. Because the thing that typically motivates someone to give us feedback about our faults is that our fault is really annoying them. For in reality, people are constantly triggering each other with their faults.

So when we ask someone to share feedback with us, it may seem like an invitation for them to blow up on us. To bring out a sword and use it to be destructive, instead of constructive. In fact, most people—if they care about us and we ask nicely—will do their best to give us honest feedback.

Two suggestions for receiving feedback

If we have the courage to ask someone to help us see our faults—and if they have the courage to give us such a gift—there are two things to keep in mind. One is that we should always search for the grain of truth. Yes, the other person may bring their own distorted view. In fact, since they're human, they probably will. But if they are willing to try to help us, that's not nothing.

Second, we must be willing to give the other the benefit of the doubt. In other words, if they say something in a way that feels hurtful to us, it's possible they didn't mean to hurt us. For our old residual pain—which easily gets rubbed the wrong way—is not their fault. Or maybe they did mean to hurt us. Perhaps they didn't lay their sword of truth on its side. Then we might give them a chance to try again, but this time more gently.

Not a linear process

In my last job in the corporate world, I worked for a manufacturer of high-performance polymers for 15 years, moving through various positions in marketing communications, marketing, and sales. By far, my favorite role was working for six years as the manager of the marketing communications department, called marcom for short.

Marcom handles the many promotional activities for a company. This includes the company's website, brochures, technical manuals, press releases, trade advertising, trade shows, and the like. From a business-to-business ad agency's perspective, someone in marcom is often the client.

At times, our marcom department directed the process for naming products or product lines. To help us, we hired an outside agency who specialized in naming products. One of the most fascinating aspects of this process was that there was very little line of sight to the final name during any stage of the process.

Let's say we needed to meet with the product-naming agency four times for a particular project. In the first meeting, we would talk about various influences and factors to consider. Then the agency would come back with a list of name parts that were really more like syllables.

Without a lot of thought, each person on our team would select the ones we liked. In the next meeting, we would come down the funnel a little more. *Now which combinations of name parts do we like?*

Each time, the agency would do a trademark search and kick out anything we likely couldn't get a trademark for. But then even during the third meeting, I often couldn't see where we were going. And then, miraculously, it would all come together at the end. We would have a name we could get behind, and that we could trademark.

Open to the adventure

Similarly, sharing feedback with someone about their faults is not a linear process. So we shouldn't go into a fault-finding adventure with someone thinking we know exactly how this ends. This is not a time to say our peace and expect the other to simply agree. Because course-correcting is a co-creative process.

Once we become willing to open up and talk—to really try to both hear and be heard—the other person may offer a perspective we never considered. They may have a history behind their fault we never knew. In fact, there is always a story behind people's behaviors. The work is to sift through our stories and see where we strayed from the truth. *Where did we get lost?*

167

Fighting the good fight

Fighting is a fact of life, even though what we're ultimately fighting for is peace. Because on this plane of existence, people show up with all kinds of destructiveness in their Lower Self. So if we want the light to win, we're going to need to fight for it. We must fight the Lower Self, in whatever form it shows up.

The trick is figuring what is worth fighting for. What's truly in our best interest and what's just rebellion and resistance for the sake of spreading darkness? What are our motives? How are they mixed motives? And what's the best way to fight? What will carry God's goal of peace and harmony forward, and what will allow the forces of darkness to prevail?

The answers aren't going to be easy. The solutions aren't going to be simple. But if we are fighting for the cause of the light, and we are truly doing our own work to clear away our Lower Self obstacles, then we will be guided for going the distance. We will have insight about how to fight the good fight.

From Scott:

The story Jill tells here is true. I gave a lot of constructive feedback, but I was also harsh. I actually did use the word "terrible."

Overall, I didn't feel the piece could ever "get there." I felt it should be abandoned.

And yet when I read the final draft, everything worked. So although my feedback was helpful, I was also wrong. Very humbling.

(And yes, Jill edited this comment.)

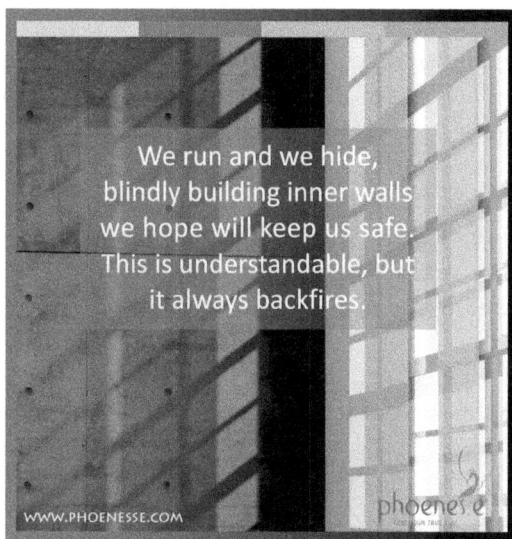

We run and we hide,
blindly building inner walls
we hope will keep us safe.
This is understandable, but
it always backfires.

WWW.PHOENESSE.COM

phoenesse

Essay 29

The truer way to freedom

In 1989, the world watched as something extraordinary blew up before our eyes. An author many of us had not heard of, Salman Rushdie, had written a book. And the blowback went viral. As in, it almost killed the host.

Those who were adults at the time may remember that Salman Rushdie, after publishing his novel *The Satanic Verses*, received a death sentence. The Ayatollah Khomeini, Supreme Leader of Iran at the time, had issued a *fatwa*—a legal ruling—calling for the death of the author.

In this essay, Jill shares some insights—not about *The Satanic Verses*, but about the author—gained from reading his memoir, *Joseph Anton*. This memoir tells Rushdie's version of what was happening behind the scenes, all those years ago.

Rushdie's defense of writing *The Satanic Verses* is, by now, somewhat legendary. After all, he basically spent a decade in hiding to avoid being killed and, at the same time, to defend this book. Yet if we focus only on things like freedom of speech, we may miss some equally important underlying pieces.

For it's a most intriguing question: What was behind Salman Rushdie's motivation for writing such an inflammatory story. *What made him do it?* Believe it or not, perhaps without realizing it, he tells us.

PART ONE: The lay of the land

Here in the United States, as in many parts of the world, we claim the right to free speech. Some might say this is the most important constitutional guarantee we have protecting our freedom. And freedom is certainly worth fighting for.

But what if someone claims to be fighting on the side of freedom but actually creates prison walls for themselves instead? Then the work must turn to understanding those walls. Where do the walls originate? For as the Pathwork Guide teaches, everything we create in the world—whether it's good or bad—has roots inside us.

When our creations are negative or destructive, they are always associated with untruth. This means our self-directed questions must be along the lines of, *Where is untruth hiding within?* For untruth is the scaffolding on which we build inner walls. And these walls then show up in the outer world as unpleasant developments.

"Anywhere that our conscious opinions, ideas and feelings are separated from what's in our unconscious, a wall is created in our soul. The walls we build in our outer material world are actually far easier to destroy than this inner wall.

"On this side of the wall lies everything we know about and are willing to face. On the other side of the wall is where we store all the stuff we don't want to face. This is a collection of unpleasant faults and weaknesses, along with whatever frightens us and confuses us. We seal all this shut using an unconscious wrong conclusion, like, if I see this about myself it will confirm that I'm bad. With that, we lock the gate and throw away the key.

"So what is this wall made of?...our wall will be made up, in part, from our goodwill that is ineffective due to our wrong conclusions and ignorance... In addition, we will find fragments of cowardice in our wall, along with impatience, pride and self-will. We can see evidence of our impatience in the mere fact that we've built this inner wall, hoping to reach perfection by piling our less-than-perfect parts behind it.

"Because heck, it sure is easier to put up a wall than take the time and effort needed to eliminate our misunderstandings and disharmonies. And let's face it, that kind of self-honesty doesn't happen without a lot of inner work. So let's go ahead and add laziness to our list of wall ingredients. Indeed, all these trends are the building materials we're using to make our inner wall."

– *Living Light*, Chapter 20: THE WALL WITHIN | Where, Really, is the Wall?

In *Joseph Anton*, Salman Rushdie gives us a view into what his inner walls may be made from. And they are worth exploring. After all, these limiting, self-made walls are part of the human condition. And learning to dismantle them is a key reason we are here.

Understanding the landscape

Here's what Rushdie said in his memoir regarding the Supreme Leader of Iran in 1989: "After he came to power the imam murdered many of those who brought him there and everyone else he disliked. Unionists, feminists, socialists, Communists, homosexuals, whores, and his own former lieutenants as well. There was a portrait of an imam like him in *The Satanic Verses*, an imam grown monstrous, his gigantic mouth eating his own revolution.

"The real imam had taken his country into a useless war with its neighbor, and a generation of young people had died, hundreds of thousands of his country's young, before the old man called a halt." (Prologue: The First Blackbird, page 11)

Rushdie knew this was the landscape in Iran in the 1980s as he was writing *The Satanic Verses*. He went on to say: "After that the dead cried out against the imam and his revolution became unpopular. He needed a way to rally the faithful and he found it in the form of a book and its author…This was the necessary devil of the dying imam." (Prologue: The First Blackbird, page 11)

The big question is: Why did Rushdie offer himself up to become their "devil"? *What compelled him to do it?* Recognizing that humans are so often a bag of mixed motives, what were some of the deeper pieces inciting him to write a book that would blow up his life?

Is it OK to say this?

Let's pause a moment to ask: Is it OK to be talking about Salman Rushdie like this? There are two reasons I am taking the liberty to use his story as a teaching opportunity. First, he told us his story himself. So I am not disclosing anything new or personal. And second, by virtue of becoming a successful author, he has become a public person.

That said, it's generally not good to not spell out someone's work for them. They must come to see it on their own. If we simply tell them what we see before they are ready to discover it for themselves, it will be a bitter pill to swallow.

What I am sharing here are my own perspectives. And I could be wrong. With this in mind—along with a lot of respect and sensitivity—let's push on.

PART TWO: Understanding negative pleasure

The Pathwork Guide teaches that everything makes sense once we see the whole puzzle. I can tell you the exact point in *Joseph Anton* when the pieces of Rushdie's life started falling together and making sense for me. It was when he shared this nugget about Marianne, his wife during the onset of this turmoil. They were well into the process of splitting up when he writes (and note, he writes about himself in the third person):

"He missed Marianne. He knew he must not try to go back to her after everything that had happened, after the CIA plot and the black journal, but, mind and body, he missed her. When they spoke on the phone, they fought. Conversations that began I wish you well ended with I hope you die. But love, whatever he meant by love, whatever she meant by it, the word "love" still hung in the air between them." (Chapter IV: The Trap of Wanting to Be Loved, page 251)

What was more likely hanging in the air between Salman Rushdie and Marianne was something the Pathwork Guide calls negative pleasure and the recreation of childhood wounds. It will help if we fill in more of the story before explaining how these work. For now, just consider you may have no idea what negative pleasure is. And chances are good, Salman Rushdie may not either.

The recipe for struggle

After marrying Marianne, Rushdie found out that many of his friends didn't like her. He had also caught her in a few lies. Rushdie said she often seemed angry, and he didn't know what she thought of him. He felt he had married a stranger.

He also reveals: "He had asked her to marry him in the highly emotional state that followed his father's death in November 1987 and things between them had not remained good for very long." (Prologue: The First Blackbird , page 10)

Now it's February of 1989, and the crowds in Tehran are carrying posters of Rushdie's face with the eyes poked out. "It was Valentine's Day, but he hadn't been getting on with his wife, the American novelist Marianne Wiggins. Six days earlier she had told him she was unhappy in the marriage, that she 'didn't feel good around him anymore,' even though they had been married for little more than a year, and he too, already knew it had been a mistake." (Prologue: The First Blackbird, page 3)

Let's add one more ingredient to this recipe for struggle. At another point in the book, Rushdie shared that "his mother had survived decades of marriage to his angry, disappointed alcoholic father by developing what she called a 'forgettery' instead of a memory. She woke up every day and forgot the day before. He, too, seemed to lack a memory for trouble, and woke up remembering only what he yearned for." (Chapter IV: The Trap of Wanting to Be Loved, page 251)

So, is that what made him miss Marianne and want to go back to her? Because he forgot what it was really like? That's a convenient explanation, but not very convincing. Here's something that makes more sense: He was attracted to Marianne because she was a great match for his troubled history. In short, she ignited his negative pleasure.

What is negative pleasure?

Woven through the fabric of life is a vibrant substance that has incredible power. This life force contains a stream of utter bliss, which the Pathwork Guide calls the pleasure principle. We will each experience this vibrant aliveness—this bliss—more and more as we do our inner healing work. Eventually, we will vibrate in harmony with the whole universe.

The greatest experiences we can have as humans are connected with this pleasure principle. And fortunately, we are all born pre-wired, if you will, for pleasure. But unfortunately, our parents were imperfect, just as all parents are imperfect. So although we sometimes experienced the pleasure that came from their love, we also experienced pain due to their limitations and faults.

Whenever a child experiences any kind of cruelty, the child's pleasure principle attaches itself to the cruelty. The wires become "welded" together to the same degree—and with the same flavor—as the cruelty that the child experienced and internalized. And note, there are different flavors of cruelty. Overt cruelty, such as hostility or aggression, is easier to spot. But covert cruelty, such as a parent withholding love through an inability to connect, is often just as damaging.

Did the child experience pleasure when they were rejected? No, of course not. Children simply do the best they can in a traumatic situation, meeting the rejection in a way that makes it bearable. This welding, or wedding, of the pleasure principle to cruelty, then, is not a conscious, deliberate process. We aren't even aware we are doing this.

Negative pleasure is the condition that develops in which we feel "pleasure"—perhaps very strongly—in the presence of cruelty. And it runs in both directions. So we may find our own cruelty leaking out when we are enjoying a pleasurable activity. And when we are cruel to others, we will experience a streak of pleasure. For our cruelty has "juice" and makes us feel alive.

This effect will show up in our adult relationships and in the way we engage with the world. Because, having not received sufficient mature love when we were children, we have a deep unfulfilled hunger for it now that we are adults. And we will spend our entire lifetime—this one and likely many before it—recreating our childhood wounds as we try to remedy the situation.

Although we're not consciously aware of why, we feel drawn to people and situations that are the ideal blend of our mixed-up childhood experiences. There will be aspects of the parent who most missed the mark, as well as aspects of the other parent who came closer to giving genuine love and affection. Now, as adults, any time we encounter the unique flavor of cruelty that resonates with our childhood, it activates our life force by exciting our negative pleasure.

A troubled relationship with storytelling

We see the origin of Rushdie's love for storytelling in the stories he tells about his relationship with his parents. They start off rather pleasantly, like this: "He was not raised in a very religious family. As a child, his father had taken him to Bombay, 'to pray on the day of Eid-al-Fitr.' There was the Idgah, and a good deal of up down forehead bumping, and standing up with your palms held in front of you like a book, and much mumbling of unknown words in a language he didn't speak. 'Just do what I do,' his father said. They were not a religious family and hardly ever went to such ceremonies. He never learned the prayers or their meanings." (Prologue: The First Blackbird, page 8)

Rushdie goes on to say that, as a small boy, his father shared the great wonder tales of the East with him at bedtime. His father told and re-told them, re-making and re-inventing them as he went along. "To grow up steeped in these tellings was to learn two unforgettable lessons: first, that stories were not true (there were no "real" genies in bottles or flying carpets or wonderful lamps), but by being untrue they could make him feel and know truths that the truth could not tell him, and second, that they all belonged to him, just as they belonged to his father, Anis, and to everyone else, they were all his, as they were his father's, bright stories and dark stories, sacred stories and profane, his to alter and renew and discard and pick up again as and when he pleased, his to laugh at and rejoice in and live with and by, to give the stories life by loving them and to be given life by them in return. (Chapter I: A Faustian Contract in Reverse, page 19)

Rushdie describes his mother, Negin, as also being a storyteller. But she was a world-class gossip. And she loved sharing her gossip with Rushdie. So her "delicious and sometimes salacious local news...hung with the juicy forbidden fruit of scandal." Gossip, he said, was her addiction. And she could no more give it up than his father could give up alcohol.

It's interesting to see how there's a mix of storytelling along with a twist into something dark. It's also interesting that Rushdie would marry Marrianne, who was also a novelist—a storyteller. But more than that, she was also unstable. Which as we'll see in a moment, is what made her a perfect match for him.

Finding the roots of negative pleasure

Here are two of the more tragic stories from Rushdie's youth, that expose the deep roots of his negative pleasure:

"Anis Ahmed Rushdie…inherited a fortune from the textile magnate father whose only son he was, spent it, lost it, and then died, which could be the story of a happy life, but was not…When he took them to the beach on the weekend he would be lively and funny on the way there but angry on the way home… when he was drunk he grimaced hideously at them, pulling his features into bizarre and terrifying positions, which frightened them horribly, and which no outsider ever saw, so that nobody understood what they meant when they said that their father 'made faces'…"(Chapter I: A Faustian Contract in Reverse, page 20)

And "Anis took his thirteen-year-old son to England in January 1961 and for a week or so, before he (Rushdie) began his education at Rugby School, they shared a room in the Cumberland Hotel near the Marble Arch in London. By day they went shopping for the school's prescribed items…At night Anis got drunk and in the small hours would shake his horrified son awake to shout at him in language so filthy that it didn't seem possible to the boy that his father could even know such words." (Chapter I: A Faustian Contract in Reverse, page 21)

Where we have positive experiences as children, our life force will be wired to meet a "yes" with a "yes". Then we respond to positive expressions of love, kindness or creativity in the same way. But where our wires have become crossed, we will be drawn to situations that energize our "no".

Returning to the description of his life with Marianne: "Conversations that began I wish you well ended with I hope you die." We can start to see the bright threads of negative pleasure connecting Rushdie's relationship with Marianne and his father, Anis.

PART THREE: Uncovering inner conflicts

There were several other sad stories that Rushdie shared about his father: "Anis took a photograph of his son outside his boarding house…and if you looked at the sadness in the boy's eyes you would think he was sad to be going to school so far from home. But in fact the son couldn't wait for the father to leave so that he could start trying to forget the nights of foul language and unprovoked, red-eyed rage." (Chapter I: A Faustian Contract in Reverse, page 21)

Also, "…perhaps it was inevitable that he would make his life as far away from his father as he could, that he would put oceans between them and keep them there. When he graduated from Cambridge University and told his father he wanted to be a writer a pained yelp burst uncontrollably out of Anis's mouth. 'What,' he cried, 'am I going to tell my friends'?" (Chapter I: A Faustian Contract in Reverse, page 21)

Life is a mixed bag

Rushdie's father was no longer alive when *The Satanic Verses* came into the world. But Rushdie felt his father would have supported him: "Without his father's ideas and example to inspire him, in fact, that novel would never have been written." (Chapter I: A Faustian Contract in Reverse, page 22)

Such a flip of perspective about his father cascaded from the closure Rushdie experienced with his father in the months before Anis's death at 77. Anis shared with him how carefully he had read each of Rushdie's books. Anis even said he looked forward to reading more. His father told him he felt a profound fatherly love that he had spent half his life not expressing.

What Rushdie received from both his father and mother, then, was a mixed bag. There was both the love for the craft of storytelling, and the twisting of the story into something dark. There were unsupportive comments, as well as unexpressed support.

These kinds of conflicting experiences are common among humans, as we all have both lightness and darkness inside. And through our experiences in childhood, we set the stage for seeing our pre-existing buried conflicts. Why does this happen? So we can heal them. For healing is the whole reason we are here.

In Rushdie's case, regarding his parents, he went on to say: "*They fuck you up, your mum and dad?* No, that wasn't it at all. Well, they did do that, perhaps, but they also allowed you to become the person, and the writer, that you had it in you to be." (Chapter I: A Faustian Contract in Reverse, page 22)

Perhaps, indeed. For the stage had been set to write a critically-acclaimed novel that would become, in many ways, a disaster.

PART FOUR: Discovering images

I have written about what the Pathwork Guide calls "images" in other essays. In brief, images are wrong conclusions we draw about life at an early age. To us, they are iron clad understandings about how the world works. But they are based on our very limited perspective at the time. As such, they are never in truth. And as a result, they color the way we behave in the world.

When we are living in truth, the rolling pictures of our life story are free-flowing and alive. When there is untruth, they become frozen, like a snapshot. This is why the Guide calls them images. And they act like a boulder in our psyche. Due to their rigid and distorted nature, they cause us to think and act in ways that will make them seem to be true.

But because images are untrue, they don't align with the truth of our being at our core. As such, they keep us locked out of our own divine self and forced to live from our ego. For our ego cannot let go and live from our Higher Self with these big boulders in the way.

Plus, by acting from these untruthful hidden beliefs, we repeatedly create ever more painful life experiences for ourselves. For our inner conflicts always get out-pictured into the world. This lets us see them, so we can face them and transform them. But our external conflicts are never the true cause of our problems. *We are.*

How images create more and more pain

One doesn't need to read *Joseph Anton* to know that Salman Rushdie has images. He's human, and all humans have them. But by reading his story, one image in particular jumps out. It might go something like this: "I am rejected by unstable people." Or "I am abused by unstable people."

We can see the origin, in this lifetime, of such a belief in Rushdie's relationship with his father. We can see it in his marriage to Marianne. And we can see it in spades in the reaction he got to his book, *The Satanic Verses.*

In the end, both the author and his most famous book experienced rejection and abuse from an arguably unstable world leader, as well as from many people who lined up behind that leader. Why did this happen? Because we are all amazing creators. And we create from what we believe to be true.

PART FIVE: The life-altering impact of splits

Rushdie's writing career got off to a very slow start. In a nutshell, his first attempts at writing books weren't good.

"He was already beginning to understand that what was wrong with his writing was that there was something wrong, something misconceived, about him." (Chapter I: A Faustian Contract in Reverse, page 53)

This is the nature of having an inner split: We can sense that something's off inside. After all, a split is a simultaneous belief in two opposing beliefs that can never be reconciled. It's not that reconciling a split is hard to do; it's impossible. Because unlike the truthful opposites that our Higher Self can hold, both halves of our split are based on untruth.

Here's how Rushdie describes what he was feeling inside:

"It was unsettling not to understand why the shape of life had changed. He often felt meaningless, even absurd. He was a Bombay boy who had made his life in London among the English, but often felt cursed by a double unbelonging...The migrated self became, inevitably, heterogeneous instead of homogeneous...more than averagely mixed up." (Chapter I: A Faustian Contract in Reverse, page 53)

Unrest points to an inner split

About going off to boarding school in England, far from his home in India, Rushdie said: "When he turned away from his father...and plunged into English life, the sin of *foreignness* was the first thing that was made plain to him. Until that point he had not thought of himself as anyone's Other. After Rugby School he never forgot the lesson he learned there: that there would always be people who just didn't like you, to whom you seemed as alien as little green men or the Slime from Outer Space, and there was no point trying to change their minds." (Chapter I: A Faustian Contract in Reverse, page 26)

He went on to say, "At an English boarding school in the early 1960s, he quickly discovered, there were three bad mistakes you could make, but if you make only two of the three you could be forgiven. The mistakes were: to be foreign; to be clever; and to be bad at games...He made all three mistakes. He was foreign, clever, non-*sportif.* And as a result, his years were, for the most part, unhappy..." (Chapter I: A Faustian Contract in Reverse, page 27)

Rushdie waxes on about the many possible reasons he went to boarding school in England, saying no one had forced him to do it. Later in life he wondered at this choice his 13-year-old self had made. I'll offer another possibility he didn't mention. It happened due to his inner split, which was then out-pictured in his life.

Can outer changes fix inner turmoil?

During his time at Rugby School, Rushdie—a young boy from India going to boarding school in England—did his best to fit in. He learned the rules, both written and understood, and he followed them. For example, putting both hands in your pockets was against the rules.

But more than once, he came back to his little study to find an essay he'd written torn to shreds. Someone once wrote "Wogs go home" on the wall of his room. Another time, a bucketful of gravy and onions were dumped on his wall. The school demanded he pay for the damage, or he wouldn't graduate.

He told no one, including his parents, about this. He tried to be like the others and to join in. It turns out, he was learning lessons about life that the school didn't know it was teaching. To add insult to injury, when he graduated from Rugby School, his parents didn't even attend the graduation. "His father said they couldn't afford the airfare. This was untrue." (Chapter I: A Faustian Contract in Reverse, page 47)

He would go on to college at Cambridge, his father's alma mater: "Cambridge largely healed the wounds that Rugby had inflicted, and showed him that there were other, more attractive Englands to inhabit, in which he could easily feel at home." (Chapter I: A Faustian Contract in Reverse, page 36)

But did it? Can moving to a different school resolve the inner tangles? "In later life he often spoke of the happiness of his Cambridge years, and agreed with himself to forget the hours of howling loneliness when he sat alone in a room and wept…" (Chapter I: A Faustian Contract in Reverse, page 37)

Does intentional forgetting—like his mother tried to do—really work? Or does it just make us forget ourselves? Ultimately, doesn't it just make us forget to search within for the truth of who we really are?

Speaking and healing our split

Just as it's important to find the right words to express our images, we must work to give voice to our inner split. What are the opposite beliefs we believe to both be true? Usually, one side comes from our mother and the other from our father. In Rushdie's case, it seems the influence from his father was far greater than from his mother. This might indicate an imbalance within that largely cuts off the allowing side of life.

If I were to take a stab at Rushdie's split, it might be something like this: "I can't find peace here. And I can't go home and find peace." Or it might be, "It's painful to be here, where I feel rejected, and it's painful to be somewhere else where I feel rejected." In either case, such a split might lead to creating life conditions in which there is no place to go and feel at home.

Healing a split involves learning to hold opposites. And this will necessarily require transitioning from an ego-centered life to living a life that's centered in our Higher Self. To do this, we will need to unravel the untruth held in both sides of our split. Then we must unearth the truth and imprint it on our soul.

The critical question we must explore is this: *What is the truth of the matter?* In this case, it might be something like: "When I find my true home within, I will be able to live in peace." But finding our true home requires we clear away the obstacles—the boulders—of untruth and residual pain that block the way. For they are what's keeping us from discovering the truth of who we are.

Getting to the real root

It's tempting to view our life story through the lens of our struggles, believing our painful experiences created our wounds. And for sure, they did leave a mark. But really, life works the other way around. Meaning, our wounds—our inner images and splits—cause our painful experiences. For they compel us to behave in ways that will surface them. If we want to have more pleasant life experiences, our work must be to heal ourselves.

All deeply rooted beliefs, such as images or splits, are carried forward from previous lifetimes during which we failed to sort them out. If that weren't the case, we would see the error of our ways more readily and correct ourselves. Instead, we dig in and end up repeating the same painful patterns over and over, life after life. If we are ready to unearth them, we only need to look at the patterns on display in this lifetime. *What are we creating?*

In the case of *The Satanic Verses*, Rushdie received considerable literary acclaim for his writing. Critics lauded his ability to interweave story lines with subplots. But the flow of his rich storytelling was also woven with powerful threads of cruelty directed toward Islam and its leaders. Only by examining the patterns of what we're creating in life can we surface the hidden wrong beliefs, which is why we must each do our inner work. No one else can, or should, do this for us.

Once we identify such hidden wrong beliefs, the next step—and perhaps one of the harder steps to take—is to turn the question around and ask: How does this hurtful untruth live in me? In the example given of a possible image of Rushdie's, one might ask: Where and how do I reject and abuse people? Where and how am I unstable? How do I use my own cruelty to hurt others?

Perhaps it will help to look at what was happening in his creation of *The Satanic Verses*. What was Rushdie rejecting? Who was he abusing? And how did doing so cause him to imprison *himself*, living for a decade as he did without a place to call home and feel at peace. For the threat against him was considered to be very serious.

In reality, it is only by diving to such inner depths that we find the way to escape our self-made prisons.

Finding middle ground

Although self-healing is an inside job, it also makes sense for us to take action to correct seeming injustices in our outside world. For in the greater reality, life is not *one thing or the other*—as it seems in duality—but *both/and*. And we can only experience this both/and way of living by dipping into another level of reality: the level of unity. This is where our Higher Self resides.

The ego, by design, exists only on the level of duality. So, from our ego's perspective, we each have to choose which horse we want to ride. And we can only choose one horse. For the ego does not have the ability to entertain opposing views. On the level of the ego, the choice seems to be we either stand up for personal freedom of expression or we will have no freedom.

The problem is that this is a false choice. For the opposite of "I must have freedom" is not "I do not have freedom". Rather, it is "everyone must have freedom." And that changes the whole conversation.

These teachings from the Pathwork Guide advise us to always search for the middle ground. So, yes, we must stand up for the right to express ourselves, even if others don't like it. But since we live in big groups—we live in communities that are part of a bigger world—we must also consider other people and their rights.

Half-truths build prison walls

In the case of freedom of speech, at least in the United States, personal freedom of expression stops at the doorway of a crowded theater when someone wants to yell "Fire!" for no reason. This kind of ruling arises from a legal system that's basically designed to protect its citizens from the Lower Self of other citizens.

If people had no Lower Selves—no darkness within—we wouldn't need such outer laws. Because we'd already be living in the harmony of our Higher Selves—of our inner light. And once we get *there*—by clearing away our inner obstacles, letting go of our ego, and aligning with our inner light—we'll discover we're already divinely connected. That if I hurt you, I hurt myself; and if I hurt myself, I hurt you.

In other words, when we take steps to live in the truer reality of unity—living from our Higher Selves—what's in the highest interest of one person will not conflict with that of others. But when our motivation for freedom is based on a half-truth—believing that our individual freedom is the only freedom that matters—we will not come any closer to real freedom. Rather, the opposite will happen. Our choices will create something that looks more like a prison.

In Rushdie's situation, his powerful push to secure his own freedom of expression negatively impacted other people's right to also have freedom. For the publishing of *The Satanic Verses* threatened many people's lives, not just his own. These included the lives of his former wife and son, his Special Branch protectors, and people involved in publishing and selling his book.

People attacked, and sometimes killed, those involved with translating the book. There were bomb scares to his publisher and evacuations of buildings. Several bombs actually exploded at various bookstores and department stores that were selling *The Satanic Verses*. And there were many, many death threats. "We know where you live. We know where your children go to school."

(Chapter III: Year Zero, page 148)

Other people were also fueling this fire by adding their own lies. Like saying Rushdie compared Britain to Hitler's Germany. "The author of the unloved book found himself shouting at the television. 'Where? On what page? Show me where I did that.' (Chapter III: Year Zero, page 152)

What's more, the longer he stayed alive, the more people wondered if anyone was really trying to kill him. People were asking, *Why does he get to be treated like a king?* "It was hard to convince people that from where he was standing the protection didn't feel like movie-stardom. It felt like jail." (Chapter III: Year Zero, page 178)

Rushdie came up with the pseudonym Joseph Anton at the request of his security detail, who then called him Joe for eleven years. For his own safety, Rushdie's goal was to become invisible: "Only Joseph Anton existed; and he could not be seen." (Chapter III: Year Zero, page 176)

In a certain way, this is what we all do. We run and we hide, blindly building inner walls we hope will keep us safe. This is understandable, even though it always backfires. Then we send our own unique flavor of cruelty—based on what we internalized from childhood—back out into the world, often without being aware we're doing this.

These cycles repeat across generations, sending hopelessness down the line and making authentic, loving experiences impossible. It's hard to admit all this, so we cover it up by blaming something outside ourselves for our lot in life.

The work of healing involves getting past shame and recriminations, and starting to unwind our problems at their root. This is the truer way to freedom.

Salman Rushdie, I honor the magnitude of the task you took on in this lifetime. And I thank you for letting me use your experiences to teach about doing the work of self-healing.

Humor is a fabulous God-given quality. But is laughter always filled with only light?

WWW.PHOENESSE.COM

phoenesse

Essay 30

Humor can heal,
but sometimes it just hurts

In this world of duality, generally speaking, to feel good is to be happy, calm and connected. To feel bad is to feel sad, mad and/or separate. Living in illusion means we try to live on only the happy side of life. In such a case, smiling becomes our main goal. Laughing out loud, then, becomes our Mount Olympus. But seldom—if ever—in this world, is anything all one thing or another. And humor is no different.

No doubt, a good laugh does feel good. After all, humor is a fabulous God-given quality. But is laughter always filled with only light? Does being funny—or attempting to amuse—always make things better? When we make fun of someone or something, is that fun *for everyone?*

Why does humor sometimes cross a line and go from being funny to being hurtful?

Humor wears many faces

It's often the case that laughing in the face of our struggles can lighten our load. For laughter can be very healing. But humor is also a funny thing (pun

183

intended). It can wear many faces. Depending on what's going on inside us, our sense of humor may carry a mix of both lightness and darkness.

As such, we can look at the way we use humor—at the kind of humor that tickles us—to learn some things about ourselves.

Sarcasm

Take sarcasm, for instance. When we make a sarcastic remark, we use words that mean the opposite of what they say. Sometimes we do this just to be funny. But often we use sarcasm when we want to show our irritation—without sounding mean—or deliver an insult. Like we might say someone is really on top of things when we want to point out how disorganized they are. If our words backfire, we fall back on, "I was only joking!"

When we use sarcasm this way we are using irony to mock. This is one way to "make fun of" something or someone. What we are often really doing is conveying our judgment or contempt. We are pointing a sarcastic comment at a person with an intention to criticize.

Sarcasm vs Irony

Similarly, but somewhat differently, we are being ironic when we communicate the opposite of what we notice, but do so in a general way. So while people make sarcasm happen, irony is just there.

With irony, there may also be wit or a clever play of words. Like this line in the movie *Dr. Strangelove:* "Gentlemen! You can't fight in here! This is the war room!" The term "war room" was originally the location where military strategies were discussed. Funny side note: When I worked in advertising, the war room was where the creative team met to brainstorm headlines for advertising campaigns.

Cynicism

Being cynical is not the same as being sarcastic. Cynical people don't trust that others are sincere or in integrity. So a cynical person is generally pessimistic about others, believing that everyone is motivated by their own self-interest.

A cynical person will always look for—and so, of course, also find—the negativity and selfishness in the way people behave. Such a person will tend to use sarcasm to sneer at others. Politicians are an especially easy target.

Cynics often think they are "just keeping things real." But in reality, this is a world of duality, so there is both good and bad in nearly everything in life. Hence, although there is certainly some truth to being cynical, it lacks the perspective of seeing the whole truth.

"Your sarcasm, your cynicism, in certain ways, your irony is not only a defense against the world, but it is perhaps even more so a defense against yourself. It's the only way the rebel nature in you—the violence in you, the rage in you—can seek a modified outlet.

It is as though a tremendous power is only allowed to trickle out in a very ineffective way. And by this very ineffective way puts you in a greater problem with the world and therefore with yourself."

– Pathwork Guide Q&A #166 on Sarcasm

Humor translates

During my years working in the corporate world, I had the good fortune of traveling to many other countries. My travels took me to Europe, including England, Belgium, France, Germany, Spain and Portugal. I also got to visit several countries in Asia, including Japan, China, Singapore, Malaysia and Taiwan. My many international colleagues were always bilingual, if not multilingual, which was also my very good fortune.

Over the course of many visits to various customers in Japan, I became friends with one of my Japanese colleagues. I was in marketing and Saito-san was in sales. He was smart, kind and very funny. And since he was also bilingual—my gratitude for all my bilingual colleagues ran very deep—when I gave presentations to a roomful of engineers in Japan, Saito-san would translate for me.

From time to time, during in-depth conversations with a customer, the whole room would laugh about something he said. Then my friend would translate back to me what had made them all laugh. And every time, I also thought the comment was very funny. What I learned is that, by and large, humor translates. Everyone, all around the world, laughs at the same things.

Good humor can carry a lot of light

The most wonderful thing about my colleague's humor was the way he could be funny, without leaning on criticism. He had a genuine talent for making people laugh without cutting anyone down. His words would delight, so people would gravitate to him. He was very well-suited for being in sales.

Another Japanese colleague once told me this joke. It landed well for me because it revealed a simple truth. He said: What do you a call a person who speaks two languages? I said: Bilingual. He said: What do you call a person who speaks three languages? I said: Trilingual. He said: What do you call a person who speaks one language? I said: I don't know. He replied: American.

This joke poked fun at me a bit—along with most of my fellow Americans—but it didn't hurt my feelings. For I had a good relationship with this person. So he could tell me this joke, knowing I would understand there wasn't any malice behind it. I laughed, *because it's so true!* This is good reminder that it's important to know our audience when we use humor.

"The more you mature emotionally, the more awareness do you gain, the more this will emanate from you and, in some way, it will find expression spontaneously, creatively, in your activities, whatever they are. Whether you are a doctor, a teacher or a shoemaker, makes no difference. You will influence your surroundings, not so much by what you say or preach, but by your mere being, by your emanations."
– Pathwork Guide Lecture #105 Q&A on Self-Development

The way we use humor matters

Done well, humor can illuminate without hurting. Maybe even inspire change. (I've been working for several years now to become bilingual*.) Which is why people often use humor to soften the blow, if you will, in pointing out something in need of fixing. It can be an effective tool when used right.

But depending on how it's oriented, it can elicit emotions that may not feel good. For there are always two aspects to consider in life. There is 1) what we do, and there is 2) how we go about it.

Where I worked, employees were assessed on these two considerations separately. So you could receive high marks for getting a project done. But if you "leave dead bodies along the way," as one of my managers put it, you would wipe out most of the credit you got for completing the job.

It's like this with humor. It can land differently, depending on how it's done. Because there's what you say—the real message you are wanting to communicate—and there's how you say it. Sometimes humor lands well because it simply reveals a truth. Like that joke in Japan. Other times, humor is a thinly veiled criticism. Then it's funny, but it also stings.

And sometimes humor crosses the line. Especially when it is intentionally used as a blowtorch. In such a situation, one side laughs while the other side burns. Duality at it's finest, folks. (Yes, that was sarcasm.)

Words can be pointed, like a knife

To be human means we have various conflicting parts. Some parts carry light, while others are still stuck in darkness. To whatever extent we still have inner darkness, we may hone the edge of our humor so that it cuts like a knife. Or we will gravitate to those who do so.

So someone may have an uncanny ability to spot the distortions in situations. But instead of using their insight to help straighten things out and restore connections, they will use their cleverness to shred people. Consider political cartoons that make a point about a political personalities or current event. They are in every daily paper, but they are not in the comics section. Rather, they are next to the editorial columns where people write essays to express their opinion.

This type of cartoon will typically use exaggeration and labels, along with symbols, analogies and irony. They can be a powerful way to interpret and reflect on the news of the day. They capture the human nature of their subjects, and may either humanize it or make fun of it.

Political cartoons—also called editorial cartoons—may reveal a truthful perspective. But at the same time, they often deliver an insult. This is what happens when people use humor to turn the sword of truth into a weapon, intending to wound others. But honestly, do insults work to motivate others to change?

We see this a lot where cruelty cloaks itself as amusement. Under the guise of humor, people routinely tell jokes aimed at other political groups, other religions, other nationalities. These are basically insults masquerading as being funny. Sure, there's a genuine aspect of humor in the mix. But when it's so tainted with negativity, it's not possible to *not* be an insult.

Satire

Satire is a literary device that artfully ridicules the vice or folly of a person or situation. Think: the 2021 movie *Don't Look Up*. Satire combines tones of amusement with indignation, scorn and contempt to highlight a flawed subject. The intention is to expose and create more awareness with the hope of inspiring change.

But again, when the mix becomes overly dark, the intention can shift from increasing awareness to just insulting a person, group or situation. The art lies in how you go about it.

Sometimes it's just not funny

I once spent some time around a family that had developed a difficult dynamic of laughing at another's misfortune. Like, hit your head on an open cabinet door…ha ha ha. In a nutshell, this is humor that's just a hair away from cruelty. Classrooms can be a hotbed for this kind of thing.

Practical jokes fall into this same category. They involve intentionally planning a scenario that will scare, embarrass or anger someone. Probably all three. I know of a parent who set their son's clock forward an hour. Because it's hilarious to watch a teenager wait an extra hour, in the dark, for the bus.

People can also develop a habit of laughing after saying something that has no humor in it. This could actually be a defense. The unconscious intention may be to make the other person also laugh or smile. Because the hidden belief may be "if you are happy, I am safe." This might stem from growing up in a household where people were not happy, and it was not safe.

Transforming our humor

The trouble is, we are often particularly attracted to the kinds of humor that are loaded with negativity. Why? Because along the way our own wiring has gotten twisted. So now we need a certain flavor of negativity to turn on our lights. In fact, we actually like our distortions due to the way they light us up.

To make things worse, we believe that if we give up our distortions—such as our enjoyment of dark humor—we will have no fun at all. But this is not correct. This confusion is a key reason we stay mired in conflict and struggle. Because negativity is highly charged. *We get such a kick out of biting sarcastic remarks or making fun of others!* This makes our negativity incredibly hard to let go of.

In truth, since all our negativity towards life is always something positive that's gotten twisted, it can always be unwound. We can transform ourselves. In other words, it is possible to have the same amount of excitement, pleasure and fun, without the jagged edge.

This is what self-development is all about: Restoring ourselves to our original light-infused form. One way to do this is by paying attention to the kind of humor that attracts us. With awareness, we can then make new choices.

But if we allow ourselves to steep in the kinds of humor that debase others, build on pessimism, or spiral around in cruel and bitter criticism, we'll miss out on the true humor of life. We'll miss the genuine blessing of bright and joyful laughter.

*Prior to a trip to Brazil in Spring of 2019, Scott and I were taking weekly Portuguese lessons for nearly four months. In one exercise, our teacher asked us to spell out Portuguese words to each other, using the proper Portuguese pronunciation for the letters.

The day before, I had stopped by Scott's office to pick him up to go skiing. But the front parking lot had been completely full. I saw a sign that said Additional Parking in Rear of Building, so I texted Scott where to find me.

Since we had just learned the Portuguese words for "car" and "parking lot" in class, I was excited to try texting him in Portuguese. With a little help from Google Translate, I was able to tell him "Meu carro está no estacionamento traseiro," which means "My car is in the rear parking lot."

When it was Scott's turn to spell a word for me, he picked one from this text. Our teacher's eyes began to widen around the fourth letter…t…r…a…s… and by the time we got to the end, she was clearly surprised.

"Where did you learn this word?" she asked. So we told her what had happened. Then we all laughed when she explained that Scott was spelling the Portuguese word for "ass."

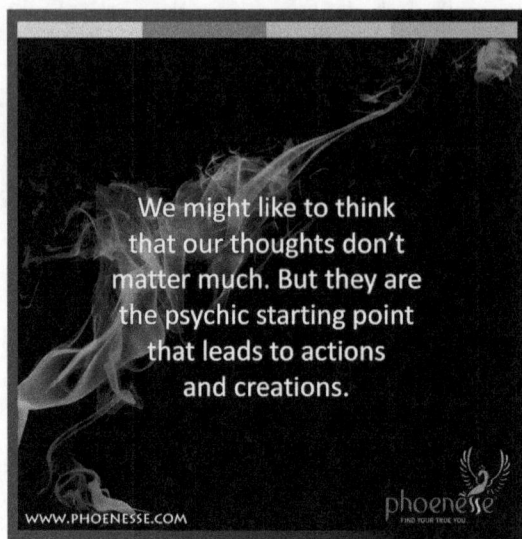

We might like to think that our thoughts don't matter much. But they are the psychic starting point that leads to actions and creations.

WWW.PHOENESSE.COM

phoenesse
FIND YOUR TRUE YOU

Essay 31

Making life better by changing what we create

The whole point of walking a path of spiritual development is self-transformation. For it's only by changing ourselves that we can change the life we're creating—for ourselves and for others. So then by changing what we create, we can make life better.

Why does it work this way? Because each of us have some parts of our psyche that have become twisted, or distorted. As a result, we each have areas in ourselves—and therefore in our lives—that function in a discolored, negative way. Now we need to unwind them and restore them to their original bright and shiny condition.

And this, friends, is exactly what the teachings from the Pathwork Guide can help us do. They can help us change what we're creating in life by helping us regain our inner light.

Yes, if we want to start making things better, we've all got some work to do.

Working with the creative process

We'll start out talking about some general creation concepts in Part One. In Part Two, we'll explore the illusion of time and some of the ways we attempt to take shortcuts. Then in Part Three we'll move into specific ways we can use these truths in our own personal lives. We'll especially explore the three most common ways people attempt to escape living in the present.

Part One
Crations springs from swirling starting points
  • Two simple examples of psychic starting points
Part Two
Understanding time and the "now point"
  • Our many shortcuts to bliss
Part Three
The way out of misery
  • Three common ways we escape the "now point"

Every metaphysical truth offered by the Pathwork Guide can be applied immediately to our lives, regardless of where we are in our spiritual development. But also keep in mind that what the Pathwork Guide is sharing in this teaching is a highly simplified version of things. Try to listen with your inner ears so you can hear the wisdom that echoes the truth of a greater reality than the one we know.

Essay 31 | Part One

Creation springs from swirling starting points

For creation to happen, two essential principles must meet. In human terms, we can think of these as the receptive and active principles. These are two aspects of one complete whole, and they permeate through everything in all of creation. It's not possible to create anything without having both of them come together.

In order to make a positive creation, these two principles must meet in a way that is harmonious, flexible and mutually beneficial. Alternatively, when we make a negative creation, these two principles clash with each other and are mutually exclusive. Either way, the same receptive and active principles are involved.

Regardless of whether the interaction is constructive or destructive, when these two principles meet, the force created is tremendous. For they unite in a strongly concentrated form and converge into a single point. The Pathwork Guide calls these "psychic nuclear points."

We can think of them as "nuclear" because each meeting forms a nucleus, or center starting point. And this nucleus is so highly charged with creative material that it can't help but set off a powerful chain-reaction that is self-perpetuating. These points are the fundamental principle underneath every form that gets created.

We can also think of these points as being "psychic" in that they are not made of physical material. Rather, they are something that comes from consciousness, or the psyche. They come from our thinking, planning minds. So, we can't see them in our 3D reality. We can, however, perceive them though inference, intuition and even by using our powers of deductive reasoning.

But don't get confused. We're not talking about "psychic phenomena" here. We're just pointing out that we can't create anything without having a conscious intention somehow embedded in the force that is bringing it forth. After all, the universe is made up entirely of energy and consciousness. These two things cannot be separated, although the limited human way of perceiving things may see these two things as two separate factors.

The power of intention

In principle, energy and consciousness are one. Said another way, consciousness can't exist without also being energy at the same time. Consider then that every thought is also highly charged energy. What's more, energy can't be anything but an expression of consciousness. You simply can't have one without the other.

It's through our intention, then, that consciousness sends out energy by way of our thought processes. And our intentions are affected by our attitudes towards everything that is, as well as towards whatever it is that we're creating. In short, we can't create anything without having an intention, a purpose, a thought going on somewhere in the background.

Psychic nuclear points—which going forward we are going to call "psychic starting points"—are actually a series of psychic events. For there can't be just one psychic point, or just one psychic event. Because one thought leads into another in a logical sequence.

By stringing together a series of thoughts, this leads us to actions and reactions. And these cause new facts to be born. These, in turn, lead to even newer facts. And all these facts create a series of chain reactions that interact and are also interdependent.

Visualize it this way: We have a thought and it brings about a certain result. Then that result elicits a feeling and an attitude. These then lead to an action. And that action will bring forward a reaction. Which brings forward yet another reaction. And the process continues, on and on.

Swirling in circles

These chain reactions don't follow a straight line. Instead, they go in a circle. And don't forget, they are highly charged. Instead of dying out, the chain reactions build momentum, growing stronger and stronger. And not only are they self-perpetuating, they are self-feeding. Meaning they grow with ever-increasing speed. Plus they are self-revolving. So they form an ever-increasing swirl of energy that is highly charged.

Eventually, the momentum reaches its maximum charge, and then an explosion happens. This is the peak point for a specific creation. Now the creation takes form. And then a new set of chain reactions is kicked off.

Think of the momentum traveling around a spiral where the movement keeps going faster and faster until it finally converges into a single point. This point is so tiny that no smaller measurement seems to be possible. And yet, at the same time, this one point still consists of all those forces that went into the series of events that led up to this one creation.

Size can be misleading

Note, terms like "size" or "time" or "measure" are part of the state of consciousness that we humans are in. But these no longer apply to the concepts we are discussing here. As a result, these teachings may be misleading if we don't try to listen with our intuition and perhaps even consider all this symbolically, and not literally.

For example, big and small are not necessarily about size. Rather, these words can be used to describe the significance of a particular creation. So say, for example, that a thought which brings forth something new is very strong, very unified, and full of purpose for supporting the creative plan of evolution. There are no countercurrents going in opposite directions because the thought aligns with all universal spiritual laws.

In this case, the psychic point will be extremely large. That is, it will be powerful and will have a lasting impact. The charging and recharging of the cyclic movements will go on in a seemingly endless process.

On the other hand, if the thought that sets off a chain of events is insignificant and full of wrong beliefs, the result will be less intense. It might seem powerful, but it won't have much impact.

Psychic starting points are everywhere

The entire universe is made up of these psychic starting points. They exist in the most simple creations as well as the most complex systems we can imagine. They're in every particle of air and in every cell that is created. Each leaf comes from a complex reaction of many psychic starting points. Even a gust of wind has psychic starting points behind it.

The air we breathe as well as our muscles, skin, bones and organs are all created from this same origin: a highly complicated system of intricate connections between psychic starting points. Which doesn't mean that all psychic starting points exist on the material level. Many we cannot measure but can only understand through logical reasoning.

Such nonmaterial psychic starting points are crucial for things that exist on the nonmaterial level. And they are just as important as what exists in our material world. For they also affect us. After all, our own beings are made up of the material parts—our bodies which we can see and touch—and our nonmaterial parts, such as our beliefs and attitudes. So we are just as affected by the psychic starting points we can't see as the ones we can, regardless of whether we're aware of our nonmaterial parts or not.

This means that whatever situations we find ourselves in right now, and whatever life we are creating for ourselves, come from very complicated systems made up of psychic starting points. Some of these points converge. Some of them contradict or fight with each other. Others reinforce each other. It's all built on our long history of thoughts, intentions, actions, feelings and attitudes.

Changing the patterns

What we are experiencing right now, in this moment, is basically a psychic explosion that has been running through thousands of years to arrive at the last half hour we just lived. And it all culminates in the exact thoughts we are thinking this very minute. Once the pieces of this psychic explosion fall into place, they may re-form and create the same pattern. Alternatively, they may create a new form, depending on whether we take a turn in our consciousness—in our thoughts, attitudes and beliefs.

For our minds can always be changed. There are, in fact, infinite possibilities for making infinite changes going on all the time. Which means we don't have to live with negative creations. They can be altered.

It's vitally important to realize that when we start working deeply with these teachings from the Pathwork Guide, we will start to uncover how we are the ones creating the chain of events that we are now experiencing as "my life."

What we will discover—become aware of—is that these highly charged psychic starting points seem to have created a life of their own. For they are self-perpetuating. But they always begin with us. And we can learn how to change the course that our life is taking. So, if we're miserable, we don't have to stay that way.

We keep making more of the same

When we find ourselves lost in the illusion that we are helpless, what we've really lost is our connection to our intention that created this situation. We don't realize that we have the ability to change a psychic starting point that has now materialized. Because whether we create something positive or negative, it's still the result of our thoughts and intentions.

We mentioned that psychic starting points are self-perpetuating. Consequently, the more we love, the more love there will be in us and coming to us. We'll keep recreating a stronger and stronger capacity for loving, and it will just keep growing. The more love we give, the more we will have. This is why it is said in the Bible that "to those who have, more will be given."

But weak, negative and counterproductive psychic starting points work the same way. They still build momentum until they explode. But the impact won't be so great as a positive, focused psychic starting point. Because the explosion will occur before a greater force could gather.

Whatever it is we are creating, we will keep creating more and more of it. For the momentum of a psychic starting point creates more and more of the same thing. That is, as long as our consciousness doesn't change and just keeps going along with it.

This applies to everything. To knowledge, to negative intentions, to talents, to our attitude towards life. And it all depends on whether we are in truth or in error. What we are thinking will breed more of the same. Until we decide to stop going down the track we are on.

We are all amazing creators

Most of the time, we are oblivious to these psychic starting points. What we notice is the end creation. The explosion. And then what we see appears to be a fixed thing. But when we start doing our personal healing work, we start to see our hidden inner attitudes.

We do this by dissolving our inner blocks and our resistance to seeing ourselves in truth. In this way, we tune into what amazing creators we are. And we start to see how we are living in a world of our own making.

It's through these ongoing explosions of psychic starting points that we renew ourselves. This is the case when we go through significant changes in our lives, including any crisis that seems, in the moment, to be traumatic. As such, an unpleasant event is an explosion that creates an opportunity to re-form our life, hopefully in a better way. Even if our minds stubbornly refuse to understand this, a crisis is a chance for renewal.

But let's say we keep going down a negative road, creating and re-creating negativity. Ultimately, things will reach the point of absurdity, and then can no longer keep functioning. To be in a crisis, then, means we refused to heed the warning signs and we deliberately failed to find a way to steer ourselves in a better direction.

A major crisis then can be a wake-up call. It's a chance to struggle for more awareness of what's really going on. It's a time to see how we are using our creative energies.

Working with the creative charge

Creation is endless. It is ongoing explosions, which are always a climax that releases new energies that form new spirals. These energies keep filling the void with the glory of divinity and consciousness. There is no end to this charge.

But the charge can be dimmed when we fear it. When we doubt it. When we counteract it with our preposterous ideas. Even then, though, the charge is not lost, but just held back and prevented from manifesting. Nonetheless, it keeps gathering steam behind the scenes, so to speak, and it will remain there until we are ready to use it.

Our task is to figure out where we are blocking that creative charge. How are we diminishing the light in our own life? We can start right now to use the part of our mind that is able to observe our own thinking. We must start to see that what we are thinking—behind our negative creations—is absurd.

Facing our numbness

We might like to think that our thoughts don't matter much. But they are the psychic starting point that leads to actions and creations. And therefore our thoughts actually have huge consequences.

Our work is to use our own mind to pinpoint the crazy or foolish starting points. And then search to find the corresponding truth. We can set our intention toward straightening ourselves out, using that same energetic power to shift our thinking into truthful channels. And then we can start to build positive self-perpetuating starting points.

Let's say we find a part of ourselves that is deadened. Numb. And we are afraid of waking it up and bringing it back to life. What's happening is that psychic starting points in our system are going in a negative direction, and these are frightening to us.

At some point in our past, we had the intelligence and a strong enough mind to realize that this was happening. And it seemed we had two choices. We could either express this flow of energy and act out, which would often mean extreme destructiveness. Or we could deaden these energies, and thus protect ourselves from them.

This is a common predicament for people to discover at some point in our development. What happens is that we feel this great rush of energy when we become enraged or destructive. This is something we simply never get to experience in a positive way.

When we start to do our personal healing work, we must learn how to express this energy in a way that doesn't harm others. We can take responsibility for these expressions and vent them in an environment—with a trained healer, therapist or counselor—where no one is hurt by us. But then we're stumped. Because we fear releasing them any further. We'd frankly rather be numb than destructive.

When we arrive at this juncture, we don't yet realize that there is a choice.

The momentum of charge that our negative attitudes creates was frightening to us. So we slowed things down. Now it's time to revive things. But it's not enough to bring these energies back to life without also understanding the consciousness that lies behind the numbness. For all deadness comes from a negative intention.

What we must also come to see—to completely understand—is how our negative intent is based on a false idea. It's only when we have this specific understanding that we can dare to revive all that energy that is living constantly in every particle of our being. Then we will be able to allow that charge to flow freely once again. But now it can start to feel good.

A recap of the phases of self-development

Let's recap the phases we go through in the course of following these teachings from the Pathwork Guide. First, we search to find our conscious negativities. This is the stuff we already know about. Our hate, our spite, our angst, and our desire to make somebody else pay for our pain. Then we must seek out our hidden unconscious negativities. Second, we need to own all of this in a spirit of wanting to be in truth. We don't deny our negativities, but we also don't annihilate ourselves for them, believing that that part of us is all of who we are.

Third, having discovered the false ideas that are buried inside our negative attitudes, we articulate them clearly. It can be a bit of a battle to become clear about what we currently think and believe. Then, in the last phase, we change our intention. This requires a clear formulation of our commitment to move from the negative to the positive.

These phases often overlap and don't always go in this exact sequence. But you get the idea.

Beware of stubbornness

In a moment, we'll get to some practical steps for working through these phases. For now, just notice that we may find—illogical as it seems—that we resist this process. Despite our intellectual understanding that this is the way we must go, we are reluctant to energize the matter in us that is now numb.

The reason for this reluctance is that we aren't quite clear yet about our specific false idea. What do we believe that is not true? In what way is it false? What's the right idea? It's only by answering these questions that we can embrace our positive intent. As long as this isn't clear, we will fear the energy that sets off a negative chain reaction. We'd rather remain numb and half-dead than risk blowing up our life.

But don't be too hard on yourself. For until we're ready to become aware of ourselves and to raise our level of consciousness, this temporary numbing serves a neutralizing function. So we really can't jump to any conclusions about whether being numb is good or not good.

It's equally true that at certain stages in our development our negative intention will cause a crisis in our life. And this crisis will serve the purpose of helping us grow. When that's the case, we waste time by stubbornly holding onto these stuck energies and needlessly procrastinating.

Be on the lookout for stubbornness. It's an inner wall that sides with our fear and scattered thoughts to shut out the divine guidance that wants to flow from within.

Two simple examples of psychic starting points

When we start to examine more and more deeply what we are creating with our mind and our intentions, we can explore both our positive creations and our negative creations. What we'll find is that the same principles exist either way. So it will help us greatly to understand how this process works. Otherwise, we will see the world out of context, because we will fail to see how everything interconnects.

But by seeing how individual psychic starting points roll up to create a larger process, we start to see how we fit into the world. And we begin to see how our thoughts contribute to our environment. For every pattern is a creation within itself, and at the same time, is part of a larger pattern of creation.

Here are two fairly simple examples of how this works.

Example 1: Walking to the corner

Let's say we decide to stand up, move through the room we're in, walk down the stairs and go outside to a street corner, for whatever reason. We can look at this as one plan, one configuration, one spiral. When we get to our destination, the plan fully manifests, which is the explosive, climactic point. So this particular creation showed up on this level of reality.

But before it could fully come into being, we had to take many smaller steps. And each of those steps could be considered a plan in itself. For there had to be an intent to move our muscles, even though we do so automatically by now. Still, there was an intention to walk to the corner. And our movement was because of our intention to follow a particular plan.

Altogether, it was the purpose, the plan, and the execution of each step—of each smaller starting point—that led us to complete this small creation. But our walk to the corner is not an isolated creation. It too is part of a larger plan. This simple example is important to understand because it shows us how the scheme of creation works.

Example 2: Building a house

Here's a second example. Let's say we want to build a house. All the same principles will apply with a number of smaller psychic starting points converging into a whole. And then these keep rolling into larger spirals. Starting out, it may take many years to buy a property and hire an architect to design our house. The architect, in turn, will execute their own plan, and also hire contractors to organize the construction process. Various subcontractors will also be involved who will need to cooperate with each other. Then landscapers and interior decorators may be involved until the house is finally finished.

Each step along the way is a creation in itself. What's more, the house itself is a single step in a series of creative events. It's one small step that is part of a larger scheme in perhaps a neighborhood, a city and a state. Yes, it's a house. But it's also part of something bigger.

The value of seeing the bigger picture

These examples are simple. Yet they can help us get an intuitive feel for how many psychic starting points must weave together to form a whole network. They keep moving, creating, exploding, falling apart and reforming new patterns. And it's all related to the larger plan. Yet it's hard for us to imagine the purpose and meaning behind all of this. Nonetheless, doing so can give us a glimpse of the Divine Mind that is always at work, bringing forth its loving wisdom through the power of creation.

Walking to the corner may not seem like much. But it is indeed a creation that requires setting brilliant creative genius into motion. It requires the coordination and control of muscles in addition to innumerable other components. Yet this walk to the corner is not an isolated creation. We must have a reason to walk there. And that reason is also part of a bigger plan.

In life, we are forever weaving and enlarging these creative patterns that are self-perpetuating. Each fragment is a little piece of perfection that helps form a larger fragment. Imagine the complexity involved in creating a human being. A mathematical system. How about a galaxy? There are systems within systems within systems. And yet it's always this same creative process at work.

Now let's go back to looking at our inner thoughts and reactions, and our tendency to see the world out of context. The less we are able to see that each smaller part of creation is a fragment of a whole, the more we'll believe that the smaller particle is all there is. That it has no connection to anything else.

Many of us feel separate simply because we can't perceive more. This is a reflection of how fragmented we are inside ourselves, in our current state of awareness or consciousness.

But the more we are able to perceive that everything we experience is just a smaller part of a bigger, ongoing plan—just like the steps we take in our walk to the corner, and how that walk was part of a larger plan in our mind—the more aware we will be of how we're connected with the Whole. That we're part of the all-is-one consciousness. And that, friends, brings us closer to bliss.

The Fall keeps on occurring any time we cause our consciousness to fragment.

WWW.PHOENESSE.COM

phoenesse
FIND YOUR TRUE YOU

Essay 31 | Part Two

Understanding time and the "now point"

Time is another thing that results from fragmentation. For time is really just the illusion that gets created by having a disconnected view of reality. To continue using one of the examples for this topic, time is the perception of only the partial steps, those smaller creative units. Too often we can't see the whole structure that this particle of time is part of. And this causes us to suffer from the feeling that things are senseless.

Part of the issue is that we only see things in a linear way. For that is what the human mind is capable of, living in this limited state of consciousness. In this state, we are fragmented, so we can't perceive any more fully than we do. We are oblivious to the larger process.

This means we can't take in endless dimensions of width, depth or scope. So when we experience time, we are experiencing what is happening as a sequence, rather than seeing it as part of a whole. Yet each moment of time—each fragment of a second—is one of those psychic starting points that contains meaning and consciousness, along with purpose.

If we were able to string together seconds, not just in a line but also in depth and in width, we would be able to perceive that there is no time. We could see that each point in time—each "now point"—is a point of creation that is endless and always there.

Occasionally, we may get a sense of this "now point." But to live there all the time requires we reach higher states of consciousness. And *that* we must work for.

But as we keep growing and maturing—transforming more and more of our conscious and unconscious negativity—we will perceive that life is made up of not only the immediately obvious fragments. We will begin to sense how each fragment is part of a larger fragment. And eventually, we will become ready and able to experience the "now point."

Perhaps we've already had inklings of this kind of perception. If so, that will be enough to imprint in our minds that there's so much more to life than what is in front of our eyes.

Being in the now

What does it look like to live in the "now point" and be completely in the now? It is to have a sense of the eternal. And *that* is true bliss. For then we are fearless, truly secure, and totally certain of the meaning of life. We know—not as wishful thinking but rather with absolute certainty—that life does not stop simply because a certain momentary manifestation stops.

When there is no longer any fear, there can be complete relaxation. This is an entirely fearless state in which there's no tension and no contraction. But this doesn't mean we're in a totally passive state. We're not flaccid or motionless. Rather, we're in an ever-moving flexible state that is open and receptive.

We tend to associate flexing with tightening and defending. But in the pure state, tightening is what gives spring to the creative movement. It's a kind of charge. By alternating between charging and letting go we have a creative whole. But both movements are relaxed, without fear or defensiveness.

In such a state, we are able to experience bliss. And we are in a deep state of knowing that all is well. Deep down, we all long for this. But then along the way, we fragmented our consciousness. And so we are now creating this false reality we call our three-dimensional world.

Way deep down inside ourselves, though, we never lose our connection with the greater reality of our eternal being. That's the part of us that's still capable of experiencing the "now point." And our human consciousness continually strives to regain this eternal state, whether we realize this or not.

Our motivation to make things better

It's our striving for this other, better state that motivates us to keep growing, keep searching and keep moving. Along the way, we must accept that we are facing temporary hardships which we ourselves have created. And we must walk through them as we would go through any tunnel, as a way to free ourselves from our inner obstructions.

No doubt, this will require a bit of motivation.

A big part of walking a spiritual path has to do with the battle we face between wanting to move ahead—following our longing for freedom and peace—and our resistance. And yet when we give up our striving for what our heart knows could be possible, we give up on our own freedom. We all have to go through such an inner war.

Until at some point, we win this struggle by committing to movement, even if that brings momentary hardship or discomfort. Of course, it's an illusion that we can avoid hardship or discomfort. These things are going to happen, whether we decide to move in the direction of our own inner divinity or not—even though this is always our final destiny anyway.

Actually, though, it's only by following the way of movement that we can understand what the hardship is about. And this needs to happen for us to really dissolve it. So while denying any hardship may seem to temporarily eliminate it, later, when we decide to turn inward and face ourselves, it will seem like doing so is what creates the hardship. But this is also an illusion.

Our many shortcuts to bliss

Our striving to make life better motivates us. And eventually this inner motivation is what tips the scales in this battle between moving and stagnating. Between reality and illusion. And between feeling fulfillment or despair. Keep in mind, when we choose movement and reality, we find fulfillment. And in the end, this is what we're all really searching for.

At one stage or another, we'll get there.

But we're still also human. And so we look for shortcuts. We think we can get the goodies—fulfill our deepest longing—and not have to pay any price for it.

What is the price we must pay? It's the hard work of searching and finding, of learning and growing, of changing and purifying ourselves. We must travel through all the pain we have created for ourselves. We must see where darkness—and all darkness is some form of evil—lives in us.

What are some of the shortcuts we try to take? Here are a few:

Sexual activity as a shortcut

We'll start with sexual activity. In the sexual experience, we can experience the blissful experience of now, but rarely can we sustain it. As such, we may try to use sexuality as a way to escape our problems. When we use sex—by itself—as a way to avoid the unpleasant parts of reality, this is basically a cheap way to get some semblance of bliss. Of course, any kind of cheating can never work. As a result, this bliss will be short-lived and likely problematic.

Alternatively, when two people experience honest growth together, their sexual union will be an expression of bliss. For it will result from two people relating deeply and fusing spiritually, emotionally, mentally and physically. So, through mature, healthy sexual union, the true "now point" can be temporarily experienced.

Drugs as a shortcut

The most blatant way that people search for an experience of the "now point" is through drugs. For drugs have a way of removing our three-dimensional physical boundaries and revealing what lies behind the great veil. But when we have such a revelation without earning it—which can only be done by making our state of consciousness compatible with such an experience—then the price we pay will be very high. The same thing goes for using alcohol as a shortcut to bliss.

People choose such shortcuts because their soul remembers that such a blissful state exists. But at the same time, the person is resistant to doing the work to get there. So escaping into drugs and alcohol are an attempt at a compromise that doesn't work. Worse, the inevitable fall from the state of bliss feels all the more painful. And the person's ordinary state of consciousness is all that much more dark.

Holy Moly: The Story of Duality, Darkness and a Daring Rescue tells the story about the Fall of the Angels. As in Scripture, the Fall tends to be seen as symbolizing a one-time event. In truth, the Fall takes place outside of time. It occurs—and keeps on occurring—anytime we violate spiritual law, causing our consciousness to keep fragmenting.

Whenever we search for the "now point" in a false way, we are trying to gain the result without paying the price. We insist on wanting to be in heaven, but we don't work to make ourselves ready for it. And so we end up plunging ourselves into hell.

Meditation exercises as a shortcut

A third shortcut that some people use is through meditation exercises. At first glance, this appears to be an honest search. After all, it typically involves a long practice of concentration exercises. Sometimes there will also be an ascetic lifestyle designed to prepare a person for this kind of experience. But sometimes, this is also all an illusion.

For it is possible to produce "results" through extended fasting, chanting, reciting self-hypnotic meditational phrases and doing concentration exercises.

By way of such techniques, one can have a short-term experience that, once again, reveals what lies beyond the veils. But if we're doing these things as a substitute for true self-development and deep self-transformation—for the kind of self-searching that leads to real change in our deeply hidden distortions—the result will be similar, in essence, to the more obviously destructive shortcuts just mentioned.

Reaching the blissful "now point" can only truly happen as a result of unification. And this we must earn slowly through our personal development work for it to truly be ours. Otherwise, we'll put a lot of effort into something—like meditation exercises that are mechanical—that we can't maintain with a feeling of ease.

Eventually, this part splits off from our parts that remain undeveloped, which we push out of our conscious awareness. Now a big contradiction happens. For due to our shortcuts, instead of becoming more unified, we have become even more split. Actually, the personality of someone following such a shortcut was less split when it began than it will be after sampling and savoring the blissful "now points" achieved by artificial means, such as through mechanical practices and exercises.

The harm of daydreaming

Many people have a tendency to daydream. And most of us don't think there is anything wrong with this. It seems to be a harmless pastime that doesn't hurt anyone. And yet when we daydream, we are deeply harming ourselves.

When children daydream, it is fine. But as we mature, we will naturally stop doing this. If, however, we continue to daydream as adults, this indicates we really haven't matured. We harbor fragments that are still stuck in childhood. For if we have really matured, we will live in reality and not in fantasy.

When we are daydreaming, we are escaping reality. If life seems very difficult, we may try to escape from it by conjuring up ideas of how we would like it to be. Unfortunately, we can't solve our real-life problems when we are not willing to look at them and find their roots.

All thoughts have form or substance in spiritual spheres. Daydreams, too, create forms, but these thought forms stand in the way of any real fulfillment we might want to bring about. While it seems tempting to escape in such a harmless way, we must not let ourselves be tempted like this. Because doing so is a waste of our time.

Instead, all the time we invest in such a pastime could be better used to see what is blocking us from truly fulfilling ourselves and our mission in life.

As such, we can liken daydreaming to taking drugs. If we take a drug one time, it will probably not harm our body or our spirit. But once we start, there is a danger we won't be able to stop. In truth, there are many people addicted to daydreaming, and they are using up their available energy to build worthless structures. They essentially withdraw from the reality of life and give up the future reality they *could* create—one that's satisfying and rewarding—if they didn't indulge in daydreaming.

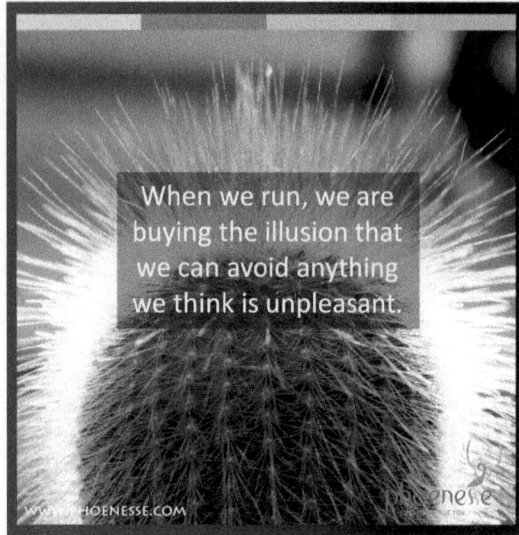

When we run, we are buying the illusion that we can avoid anything we think is unpleasant.

WWW.PHOENESSE.COM

Essay 31 | Part Three

The way out of misery

If we truly want the unlimited dimensions of reality to be revealed to us—if we want to attain the blissful "now point"—there is only one safe and secure way to do it. Simply put, we must fulfill the task we have come here for. And it is by walking an authentic spiritual path—such as the one laid out for us by the Pathwork Guide—that we can do so.

We have to learn to travel through our pain. This includes the pain of our guilt, of our illusions, and of our side that is still undeveloped. Ultimately, that's what it really all comes down to.

Living outside the "now point"

If we're not currently living in bliss, this means we have lost our connection with the "now point." In other words, we feel cut off from spiritual reality. So we think that the temporary reality we've created for ourselves—which is an illusory reality, if we may use such a seemingly paradoxical phrase—is the only reality.

Now here's the most important part of this teaching to understand: Being in the "now point" means we are intensely aware of what this "now point" means.

Anytime we try to run away from the "now point," we lose our awareness of what it means. Then we create a false reality that we superimpose over our life.

We do this in several ways. First, we live in either the past or in the future, not in the present. Sure, we might be present to some degree, but we're not truly aware of the "now point." In each minute, our mind is already running ahead—perhaps into the next minute, the next hour, the next day. We might even be in some faraway future, in a wishful daydream of how it could be one day, or should be, or might be if we only had some magic.

As a result, we bypass the "now point" that could give us the key to actually reaching that future point we cherish so much. Either that, or we hang onto something from the past that has a hold on us, possibly without our even realizing it.

When we begin to work deeply with the teachings from the Pathwork Guide, we start to come into contact with both of these. Most notably, after much hard work, we begin to see how our past is still influencing us. This influence makes us react to something happening now as if we were still living in the past.

Because we are caught with distorted vision, we actually believe that what's happening now is the same as what happened in the past. Not that we are aware of this belief. If we were aware of it, we would be a lot closer to that "now point." The fact that we think the way we're reacting now is appropriate is a good ruler for measuring how alienated we are from the "now point."

How to stop "time projection"

In short, we lose touch with the "now point" by being lost into the past as well as the future. And we are doing this kind of "time projection" all the time. We often believe we are acting freely, based on what's currently going on. But our behaviors are not actually freely chosen at all.

They are reactions determined by events in the past. And our reactions may or may not have been appropriate back then. Regardless, they are not appropriate now. And they lead us to distort reality, meaning we blot out our connection with the real reality happening now.

To put it frankly, it's our lack of awareness about what's really taking place in the moment that creates the illusion we call time. To put it another way, our lack of awareness and the false reality that accompanies it causes fragmentation. And this fragmentation is the reason we're disconnected from living in the present moment.

The way forward, however, is not something we can determine by using our mind through an act of will. The use of our will comes into play by using our mind to develop more self-awareness regarding those parts of ourselves we don't want to face and deal with. For that's the only way to bring ourselves back into alignment with the truth. We can only make life better by establishing a better sense of reality.

Once we do this, a new sense of timelessness will come about on its own. It will happen almost effortlessly, when we least expect it. Because it comes as a byproduct of our searching to be in truth.

Over time, after we go through some of our self-exploration, the past will stop bleeding into the present. When that happens, we will be able to trust that the future will be fine, since it can only be an extension of the now. Once we no longer feel the need to escape the present, we will stop toying with the future with our wish-making mind. Then the now turns into our new reality, forever.

Three common ways we escape the "now point"

There are three fairly well-known ways that we lose the "now point." They are 1) displacement, 2) projection, and 3) denial.

Displacement

First let's look at displacement. Say we love someone dearly, but they do something to hurt us or make us mad. We don't want to offend this person, and we know that if we let them see how we feel, they might push us away. And we need them and depend on them! So we want to avoid such a pain.

Still, they did something that causes us pain and anger. We fear that if we acknowledge our pain, we might destroy our little bubble of illusion, which we don't want to give up. Our illusion might be that our beloved person really should be perfect. They should never do anything that would hurt us. The reason we have this illusion is so we can avoid anything unpleasant ever happening. In this case, confrontation would be very unpleasant. And we sure don't want to risk losing their love.

Our goal is to avoid all discomforts, risks and pains. To do this, we must build an illusion. And then we must invest quite a lot of energy into maintaining this fictional version of reality. Nonetheless, the energy of the pain and anger we're feeling is real, so we need to get rid of it.

For it's also an illusion to think that just by ignoring our pain and anger, it will go away. How do we "solve" such a problem? Often, our solution is so automatic, we don't even realize we're doing it. We dump our feelings onto someone else, possibly for an entirely different issue.

After all, this other person may not mean nearly as much to us. If we make this other person mad, their retaliation or rejection might not matter so much. The outcome is less "dangerous." Or maybe we're so secure in this other person's love and tolerance for us that we can safely unload on them and get away with it. In this way, we solve our problem by finding an outlet for this tight ball of energy, and we don't put our relationship with the all-important person at risk. That's displacement.

Not only does this shrewd device cause us to feel guilty for our dishonesty, it creates a false version of reality. So now we are living in a world that's really not based on reality. And there's no way for us to be aware of the "now point" with this going on. Whatever meaning or message might come to us about ourselves in this situation, we won't be able to hear it until we set everything straight.

Here's something else that's helpful to realize. After we get underway in doing our personal development work, we will discover that by fully facing into even the most undesirable, dishonest pieces of untruth in ourselves, we arrive into a feeling of bliss. We reach it even before we've had a chance to change that part of ourselves. Bliss arises from simply dealing honestly with an issue.

Why does this happen? Because we're now in the specific "now point" of our untruthfulness. We're in the "now point" of our negativity and our deceitfulness. Displacement, on the other hand, turns everything into chaos and disorder. It takes what is really happening and turns it into total confusion. It completely disconnects us from our inner divine self, and that always creates fear and fragmentation.

We do this displacement thing much more than we think. We shift something off one person and put it on someone else. We take things from one situation and move it to another. Sometimes we're just too lazy to deal with the real situation. Or maybe we have a habit of being resistant. But if we don't stop doing this, we can never shift into the ongoing "now point."

To get started, we must make up our mind that we want to see what we are doing. And we want to see the full extent to which we are doing this. For our lack of awareness makes every problem bigger. The minute we realize that we have a problem with automatic displacement, our problems already come down a notch.

Projection

We are likely a little more familiar with projection, which is about seeing in others what we aren't willing to see in ourselves. Nonetheless, we are still often blind to how we're reacting to others when there's something in ourselves we don't wish to see. At times, the other person might actually have the undesirable trait we don't want to see. Other times, they may not. But whether or not they do or don't really doesn't matter.

What matters is that when we're projecting, we're abusing the energy that should go toward facing ourselves. We need to be turning our attention toward confronting and dealing with something unpleasant in us. Instead, we become angry and annoyed by the other person. In this case, we want to maintain an illusion about ourselves—namely, that we don't have the trait in question.

Denial

Last is denial, which doesn't need much explanation. We don't displace and we don't project. We simply attempt to deny a problem exists at all.

In all these cases—whether we're running from the past, pretending about the future, or displacing, projecting or denying—we are trying to get away from the "now point." We're buying the illusion that we can avoid anything we think is unpleasant.

But the new reality we are creating—using the force of our will—is not based on truth. And that, friends, is an abuse of the creative process. All we actually accomplish is to create more fragmentation, and we become further and further alienated from the center of our own being. We lose our connection with our "now point," with all its amazing meaning and relationship to the whole. To the greater One.

Approaching more joy

The Pathwork Guide points out that these two lectures on Psychic Nuclear Points and the process of being in the now were especially joyful to give. In fact, he said, the Spirit World had been preparing them for a "very long time"—with time, of course, being a very human way of understanding their considerable effort.

For one thing, those who would hear these lectures needed to be ready to receive them. Also, it took some work to massage the terminology so that humans could even understand them. This was not easy to do. Because human language does not make much room for talking about such ideas.

Yet if we can understand this material, simplified as it may be, it can help us to raise our level of consciousness. It can help us to intuitively understand how the creative process works, and *that* can make it easier to deal with ourselves.

Accelerating our spiritual progress is tremendously joyful for everyone. Not only is this the way to create more joy, it leads to more peace, more excitement and more fulfillment in our lives. Until one day we realize that it's totally safe to live in a highly charged state of being, as long as the charge is a positive one.

We can all start today by actively working with the creative process to make life better. For all of us.

Blessing from the Pathwork Guide

"Be blessed in the world of love that surrounds and permeates you. This is the only unalterable reality that ever exists. Be blessed."

– Pathwork® Guide Lecture #215: Psychic Nuclear Points Continued—Process in the Now

Adapted from Pathwork Guide Lecture #214: Psychic Nuclear Points and #215 Psychic Nuclear Points Continued—Process in the Now

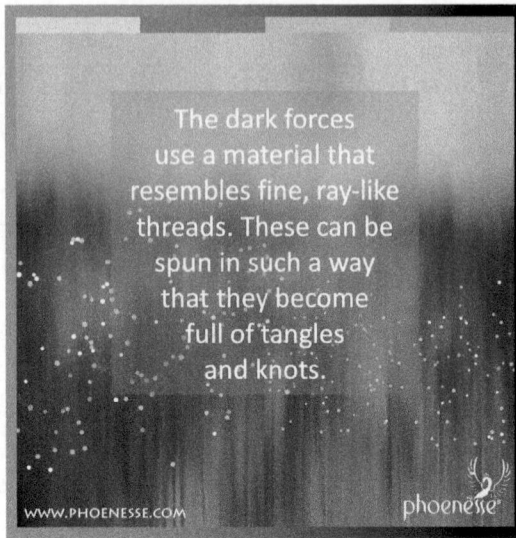

The dark forces use a material that resembles fine, ray-like threads. These can be spun in such a way that they become full of tangles and knots.

WWW.PHOENESSE.COM

phoenesse

Essay 32

Untangling the twisted threads of friction

I recently spent some lovely summer days with family at my parent's cabin in Northern Wisconsin. During our visit, we got to enjoy a much-loved Packers-Vikings football game together. Fortunately, with family living on both sides of the Wisconsin-Minnesota border, such a spirited game brings out the good sport in everyone.

Our pre-game activity involved reconfiguring the cabin furniture, returning it to its original layout. Because a different layout had been tried and nearly everyone disliked it. As my brother, Jeff, quipped while moving and remounting the TV screen: "Wisdom comes from experience, and experience comes from bad decisions."

How can we tell a bad decision from a good one? Bad decisions tend to create friction.

Why friction is good

Over time, we are all becoming more and more spiritually developed (sometimes quickly, sometimes slowly). As a result, humanity will gradually become more and more unified. Eventually, according to the Pathwork Guide, different races won't even exist. The Guide postulates that in about 1500 years, we will notice the effect of our development in the way our nations, religions and races will have so few remaining differences.

This will be a sign showing how far we have grown through improving our self-knowing. It will be a sign of how unified we have become *within ourselves*. But for now, people have their differences.

"Differences will exist as long as disunity exists on Earth and humanity has not learned to overcome it. As any difficulty or apparent disadvantage can be a cure, which it must be if the person is on the right path, advantage can be a cure, too.

"Through differences of race, religion, nationality, or various other categories, humanity can become stronger and advance faster in spiritual development precisely because frictions exist. Without friction, development can never proceed.

"It is only a question of how the difficulty is met, always; how is it met individually and collectively."

– Pathwork® Guide Q&A #25 on Races

Let's talk about tests

When there are storms in our life, we are being tested. With this understanding, it's possible to face into storms and approach them with more awareness. Often, tests come in the form of a person. For nearly every group of people—whether a family, a community, or a team of co-workers—will include at least one person who is there to test everyone else.

This person will still be so low in their development they easily become a plaything for dark forces. That doesn't mean the person is evil. No, it's enough that such a person—despite having some very good qualities—does not have much self-honesty.

They don't strive to align with the truth of their own inner self. And therefore the dark forces have easy access to influencing them. In other words, with our lack of self-discipline and lack of self-awareness, the dark forces have everything they need to create chaos.

Chaos, tangles and knots

The dark forces use a material that resembles fine, ray-like threads. But because truth and awareness are lacking, these rays are dull in color and texture. These threads can be spun in such a way that they become full of tangles and knots. Eventually, such a tight ball of confusion forms that it becomes incredibly hard to unravel it.

But the materials for confusion don't only come from the person low in development. Everyone involved also contributes their share. They furnish their own mistakes and weaknesses, in the areas where they too violate spiritual laws. This is how life goes, as we keep spinning more and more of the same somber yarn.

Until no one can figure out what's the truth anymore.

Untangling the threads

The truth can be hard to sort out. This is also true for those who are further along on their path, and whose sight is therefore clearer. Often, it takes tremendous effort to discover the truth that's gotten buried under mounds of confusion. It's hard to know how to even behave in the middle of such tests.

After all, the dark forces are clever. They know, all too well, how to make an untruth look like a truth, and how to make a truth to look like an untruth. They know how make us think that something evil is good, and that something good is evil.

And so we get confused. This even happens to those who want to be in truth, who are striving to develop higher levels of spiritual awareness. For we're all still human, with our own issues to work out. When we lack the clarity to perceive what's really happening, we don't know how to unravel chaotic situations. So we may inadvertently darken a difficult situation some more.

Parting the clouds

The only way to help part the clouds—to help see the truth—is for us to become schooled in developing our own self-awareness. For if that is not our conscious intention, we too will become playthings of dark forces. Our boat will be tossed around by the waves, and we will no longer be able to steer our life. Or at least not as well as we could.

But let's say we are really willing to make an effort to see the truth. We want to get to the core of any problem. Even with the best of intentions, none of us can part the heavy clouds by ourselves. We need the guidance of those who have gone this way before us.

We need to learn what to do, and also what not to do. And we can do this best by embarking on a spiritual path such as the one given to humanity by the Pathwork Guide. Then we will develop the discipline to go into our inner stillness—even when wild storms are raging all around us—and connect with God within. This is also the way to contact the forces of light, which are God's divine spirits.

Main steps on a spiritual path

Walking a spiritual path is the way to open ourselves to truthful inspiration from within. Then, from this new vantage point, we will be able to observe our faults and overcome our resistance. Our development will follow certain steps.

Starting out, we will do well to control our actions. This is the level humanity was at when we received the Ten Commandments. At that time, "thou shalt not lie" and "thou shalt not steal" were a big ask. Even today, many people are still at this beginning level of development.

As we develop control over our behavior, we must also learn to cultivate our thoughts and feelings. At the time Christ came to Earth, we were ready to understand that our inner thoughts and feelings contribute to events in our outer lives. That we could "sin" in our thoughts and attitudes, as well as in our deeds.

Then we move onto understanding and unwinding our emotions, which is the most difficult level. Only when we are at a higher level of development will we be able to penetrate into these deeper levels of reality.

Why working with emotions is hard

Correcting our actions may be fairly straightforward. But the deeper reasons for our sideways behaviors are harder to untangle. For many of our feelings have become buried in our unconscious. So we feel them, but don't understand their origin. This means we must work diligently—using both our willpower and our patience—to make them conscious.

Even then, we can't control our feelings as directly or as immediately as we can our thoughts and actions. Yet if we continue to deceive ourselves about our real feelings, there will continue to be conflict within ourselves and with others, and we will become lost. For we will never be able to steer our little boat effectively if we refuse to discover the true origin of our conflicts.

First, we must make the effort to sort out and clean up our thoughts. Then we must make the unpleasant and often painful discovery that our unconscious feelings and beliefs don't match our conscious thinking.

This, friends, is exactly what it means to do spiritual work. We must untangle our hidden twisted threads. And this is neither simple nor quick to do. If we keep at it, though, we will eventually master the ability to know the truth, even when the seas are surging. Even when—and maybe especially when—we are in the middle of a test.

Through our persistent efforts to head in the right direction, we will eventually scatter the clouds. We will untangle the ball of threads and unravel the knots of our life one by one. The extra effort this requires is exactly the effort that God wants us all to be making.

Bringing clarity helps everyone

These tangles and knots create an actual spiritual form that surrounds groups of people. As mentioned, everyone contributes their share to these tangles, which the dark forces so masterfully tempt us to create. And yes, there is usually one person who adds more to the confusion than most.

But what if someone decides to take the spiritual high road? If they begin to gradually loosen one knot, and then another. Eventually, when there are no more knots, everything becomes clear. The beauty of making such an effort toward true clarity is that it helps even the weaker people to stop deceiving themselves.

Of course, at first there will be resistance by such people, as they cling to their Lower Self ways. But if we keep doing our own work, we will keep bringing forward more and more truth. And truth has a way of illuminating things with its clarity.

This is something we all can be doing. Instead of taking the path of least resistance—which is always the path of the Lower Self—we can seek to enlighten situations that are cloaked in shadow. We can do this by making the effort to gain clarity inside ourselves, working at whatever level we're at.

Being of service

If we're more advanced in our spiritual development, we will more readily disentangle the knots surrounding us. And this will naturally help clear up situations where there's confusion. Being of service in this way will keep cycles of happiness open and flowing.

So then more light—more guidance and grace—will keep flowing into us. Because a person with this kind of intention—being of service in restoring divine laws—is worthy of receiving special help from the divine.

"Yes, my dear ones, few people think this way. They go to God and make wishes and demands, but they are not willing to give anything to God's world, to the great struggle which is so crucial. Think about this, all of you.

"All who approach God in this way can be given more light and help to disentangle the knots and to have the strength to steer their little boat well, even through a storm, so that they come through it strengthened and enlightened, as is the will of God."

– Pathwork Guide Lecture #1: The Sea of Life

If we are able to courageously face ourselves, time and time again—overcoming our own mountain of pride in the process—then we will gain a true perspective about others and outer situations. And we can use our understanding to help untangle the knots we've made with others.

But if we stay blind to our own truth, we'll also remain blind to the truth of others. And then we'll remain lost, drifting aimlessly in the sea.

Adapted from Pathwork Guide Lecture #1: The Sea of Life.

When we see clouds
gathering on the horizon, we
once again have the chance
to pick up the oars.
To direct our life.

WWW.PHOENESSE.COM

phoenesse

Essay 33

So, how's your little boat doing?

If we were standing in the Spirit World looking at Earth, we would see this ocean of humanity. For all of us are living in a sea of life. And each life is a little boat. In this picture of things, the sea of life may be stormy and the sky might be grey. But then out comes the sun again, calming the choppy waters. Until another storm comes along.

Isn't that just the way of life, always alternating between storms and sunny skies? Until one day, we reach our destination.

And what is our destination? Firm land. It sounds backwards, but that's what God's Spirit World actually is. The firm ground of the divine is our true home. And getting there all depends on how we direct our little boat. How good are we at navigating life?

How well do we handle storms?

Let's say we're someone who feels well-prepared for life. We've been well-trained and we've got some experience. So we're a skillful captain who is not afraid of danger. As such, we will steer our little boat well through howling winds and high seas.

Then, when the gentle periods of calm return, we relax and gather our strength for the next storm. For we know there will be rough weather again. And we'll be ready for it.

Another person gets nervous every time another storm starts brewing. If that's us, we keep losing control of our life. Yet another person gets so scared they don't even try to steer their boat. They just drift through the storms of life, hoping for the best and not learning anything.

We need to realize that these difficult conditions in life—these sudden storms—are tests. When we see clouds gathering on the horizon, ushering in another disturbance, we once again have the chance to pick up the oars. To direct our life. Perhaps if we look around—look at our life—we can sense where our boat is now.

The symbol of the sea

The sea is a symbol telling us loudly and clearly that nothing is ever lost. We can see this in the way the tide ebbs and flows. It flows forward in great waves, only to recede. Where does it go when it seems to disappear and no longer exist?

From where we're standing on the shore, there was water a moment ago and now it's gone. But we know the water does not disintegrate into nothing. It continues to exist in the bigger pool of water, without ever losing its unique quality. And it will return.

Maybe it's the same with us.

Why go through all this effort to cleanse and develop ourselves—to grow and expand—if there isn't any purpose? Well, in fact, the more connections we discover between our inner attitudes and our experiences in life, the more we will understand that nothing is arbitrary. Every experience has meaning. There are no coincidences.

Our life is a direct reflection of who we are now, on the inside. How we express ourselves determines what we create. And this is true whether we are creating deliberately or unconsciously. Once we start unraveling the tangled threads—gaining awareness of these connections—life will make sense in a whole new way.

We'll then see that nothing is for naught. There's a magnificent design at work, trying to bring everything into harmony. Once we discover how the storms in our life connect to the storms in our soul, we will understand the construction of the fabric and see the wisdom woven into it. Seeing how we've had a hand in making this fabric will bring us peace.

Rhythms of the sea

The sea ebbs and flows, following a very particular rhythm. Its rhythm may be temporarily disrupted—by earthquakes or tidal waves or human interference—but it is never broken. Following a crisis, the sea will work to reestablish its unique rhythm so that once again, it is in harmony with the rest of creation.

The sea is wise in the way it follows this pattern. Humans, on the other hand, with our busy and distracted minds, often tune out our unique rhythm patterns.

If we look at the time span between the ebb and flow of the sea—between high tide and low tide—it's never exactly the same. One will last longer than the other. It's the same with our human rhythms. Sometimes, things come to fruition more quickly. In other areas, the waiting may last longer.

When we are out of rhythm with ourselves, it can help to pray to see connections between events and our inner selves. But maybe the answers don't come right away. Then we could use this waiting time to learn more about ourselves. To learn things that only show up in times of ebb, not in times of flow.

Sensing our rhythm in all things

Our job is to learn to sense our own rhythm in all things. If we learn to rest and to play—to work and move in harmony with our own unique rhythm—we will live a more fruitful life. We will be more creative, more joyful, and more peaceful. Restlessness will fall away and we won't feel so burdened by life.

To reach this way of living, we must raise the level of our consciousness. Just sitting with the reality that this possibility exists can help us get there. We can stir our imagination and feel into what it would be like to live a day in rhythm. *Imagine smooth sailing.* Then compare that with the way life usually feels. The way it feels to unconsciously follow a rhythmless existence.

By visualizing the difference daily, we can start to tune into our little boat and see how we are doing. We can ask for personal guidance that flows from within, to help us stay focused on this. And to stay, more and more, in our own rhythm pattern.

Losing our rhythm

We all have days when we feel out of sorts. This happens when there is something tangled up in our consciousness that we aren't yet aware of. And it makes us feel disconnected from whatever we are experiencing. If we can accept this rhythm pattern, respecting it and using it in a constructive way, then our rhythm will take its natural course and return to flowing once again without disturbance. Just like the sea.

But instead, we tend to respond destructively, delaying the return of our rhythm pattern to its natural flow. We do this by doubting and rebelling, by deciding this is a meaningless universe after all. Or maybe we get angry because we are suffering. Equally disruptive is having a self-rejecting attitude that says, "I am such a bad person. I deserve to be punished like this."

According to the Pathwork Guide, nothing is more painful and more frightening than not seeing the connection between a painful event in our lives and its inner cause. To have storms arise for seemingly no reason, and to feel we have no say. Once we start establishing the inner causes, however, what we will feel is relief.

Get a better boat

A better response to difficulties in life would be: What can I learn from this? What can I learn while the tide stays out that I couldn't learn after it flows in? What inside me do I not yet see? Have I lost sight of the fact that I am a unique expression of God? Am I aware that God always loves me?

These are positive ways to respond that will help our rhythm return to a more harmonious course. Then, taking their own time—and probably when we least expect it to happen—connections will start to open up. Suddenly, truthful understandings may pour forth in an abundant river of awareness. Our woe will disappear, and our suffering will transform into the rich blessing it always had the potential to be.

And the one who is always standing ready to help us make these connections? None other than Christ. We can actively help ourselves find harmony in our lives by making personal contact with Christ. But rhythm patterns are at work here as well.

In our minds, we might be completely comfortable with the reality of Jesus Christ. In our will, we may be willing to surrender to Christ, and we might really mean it. But we may not yet have felt, in our emotions, the sweet and loving presence of Christ in our life.

Perhaps we're still waiting for this happen. So then we may become impatient that it ever will. We'll start to doubt. And that's how we disrupt the seeds we have sown.

When we wait, but the emotional experience fails to arrive, it's not that Christ is keeping us waiting. It's that we still have inner barriers that need to give way. And this will happen once we restore our unique personal rhythm.

"Please, my friends, remember these words well, because here your personal contact with Jesus Christ is again your best solution. Only through allowing yourself to know—and later to feel—His love and total acceptance of who

223

you are now, no matter how flawed, imperfect and destructive your lower self may be, will you be able to do the same. Only then will you trust your ultimate divine nature.

"Then you will be able to afford the luxury, if I may put it this way, of accepting your distortions—your sins, if you will—without losing the ground under your feet. And that is the healthy position which allows you to reach truth and harmony with yourself, with others and with life."

– Pathwork® Guide Lecture #258: Personal Contact With Jesus Christ—Positive Aggression—The Real Meaning of Salvation

When we are ready to do deeper spiritual work, then we are ready to get a better boat. And in this new boat, we can feel held and guided by Christ, and able to rest. This will give us the sustenance we need to fulfill our task in life.

Even if our senses can't yet perceive it, Christ cares about each of us. It will help for us to remember this, and not turn to despair. Christ is here, helping us learn to navigate life well, and to guide our little boat to our true destination.

Adapted from Pathwork Guide Lecture #258: Personal Contact With Jesus Christ—Positive Aggression—The Real Meaning of Salvation.

Appendix A

Five ways to learn about
the Fall and the Plan of Salvation

1. Read *Understand the Teachings*, Parts 2 & 3

This online overview of the teachings from the Pathwork Guide is available in three parts at www.phoenesse.com

    1. **The Work of Healing** | What We're Here to Learn (Part One)

    2. **The Prequel** | How We Arrived Here (Part Two)

    3. **The Rescue** | The Mission That Built Us a Bridge (Part Three)

2. Read or listen to *Holy Moly: The Story of Duality, Darkness and a Daring Rescue*

This is an easy-to-read version of 10 lectures from the Pathwork Guide about the life and mission of Jesus Christ, and the origin of duality and darkness.

    1. Read chapters online with membership

www.phoenesse.com

    2. Get the eBook, paperback or audiobook from online book retailers

      1. Google Play (eBook)

      2. Amazon (eBook, paperback or audiobook)

      3. Apple Books (Included in 3-book collection)

      4. Barnes and Noble (Included in 3-book collection)

    3. Listen to free podcasts of each chapter in *Holy Moly*

      1. Apple Podcasts

      2. Google Podcasts

      3. Spotify

      4. Stitcher

      5. Phoenesse website

    4. Get the story of *Holy Moly* in nutshell on Phoenesse

3. Read the 10 original Pathwork lectures included in *Holy Moly*:

    • Original Pathwork® Lecture: #18 Free Will

    • Original Pathwork® Lecture: #19 Jesus Christ

    • Original Pathwork® Lecture: #20 God: The Creation

    • Original Pathwork® Lecture: #21 The Fall

    • Original Pathwork® Lecture: #22 Salvation

- Original Pathwork® Lecture: #81 Conflicts in the World of Duality
- Original Pathwork® Lecture: #82 The Conquest of Duality Symbolized in the Life and Death of Jesus
- Original Pathwork® Lecture: #143 Unity and Duality
- Original Pathwork® Lecture: #247 The Mass Images of Judaism and Christianity
- Original Pathwork® Lecture: #258 Personal Contact with Jesus Christ—Positive Aggression—The Real Meaning of Salvation

4. Read *Jesus: New Insights Into His Life and Mission* by Walther Hinz

Based on channelings by Beatrice Brunner in Germany, this book tells a similar story to *Holy Moly*, offering greater detail in certain areas. Ebook available on Amazon.

5. Read *Keywords*: Answers to Key Questions asked of the Pathwork Guide

Read *Keywords:* Answers to Key Questions asked of the Pathwork Guide, This is a collection of Jill Loree's favorite Q&As with the Pathwork Guide:

www.theguidespeaks.com

Appendix B
Deep Prayer for healing
Cultivating an in-depth intention to heal

It is important we bring the full weight of our soul to this work. For it takes a fierce commitment and *full emotional investment* to reach our destination: returning home to God. Consistently saying this deep prayer can provide a personal compass for navigating the high seas of life.

Scott Wisler, Jill Loree's husband, developed this prayer in 2001, after studying these teachings for several years. Its powerful spiritual momentum has helped carry him through many difficult times. Consider reading it a few times to see the deep beauty it holds.

Prayer

I give my heart and soul to God.
I commit myself to listening for the will of God.
I serve the best cause in Life.

I want to expand my life.
I want health and fulfillment and abundance in every area of life.
I want rich, intimate, vibrant relationships.
I want to experience total love and pleasure supreme, without holding back.
I intend to give myself completely to life. I am willing to give to life as much as I wish to obtain.
It *is* possible to have such a rich, good life.

To do so, I ask for Divine Guidance and Divine Help:
I want to see and find *all* places in me where there is selfishness, self-centeredness, negativity, and destructiveness—I want to see all falseness, no matter how hard this may seem.
I want to see and find all places in me where there is pride, self-will, untruthfulness, and fear.
I want to find every place inside me where I wish to cheat life by secretly wanting more than I am willing to give.
I intend to shed all illusions I have about myself. To see the raw, naked truth about my current inner state. This is the price I will pay to have the life I want.

I want to overcome every pride, vanity, willfulness, and shame that make me hide behind pretenses. And to find every subtle inner dishonesty where I am too self-indulgent to face myself and change.

I am willing to shed my ego defenses and face directly into all negativity.

I am willing to accept all difficulties that arise in my life, because whatever life brings, I know that, somehow, I have created it. I accept utter self-responsibility for my life.

I am willing to grow from my difficulties, rather than childishly complaining about them, as if someone else had given them to me.

I trust that in truly accepting life's difficulties, I can find and heal the roots of them inside me. In facing life's difficulties, I will be capable of receiving the good of life.

I invest the best I have into my life. I will not withhold anything of myself.

I want to contribute to the cosmic unfoldment and Christ's Great Plan with all the faculties I have—those already manifest, but perhaps not used in this way, and those that are still dormant in me.

I want to contribute and be of service. And only as a thoroughly fulfilled and happy person can I do so—not ever as a suffering one.

The route through my inner negativities requires becoming emotionally healthy and mature. So I wish to truly know what I feel and how I block my feelings.

I wish to see the superimposed, intellectualized concepts that block my feelings without judgment or moralizing.

And I wish face and feel my fear of experiencing defeat, pain, loss and the unknown.

I am willing to look at myself naked, as I truly am, without emotional defense.

I am willing to patiently look without haste or hurry, or try to get it over with immediately.

I beg of you God, help educate me, to fully know and experience what I really feel.

Help me see the distinction between superimposed will and real feelings.

I ask my Higher Self—God in me—to show my mind, inspire me to be receptive, and gently, gently let my feelings come up, whatever they may be.

I have the strength to endure a little real pain. Real pain is the gateway to pleasure and fulfillment. I welcome my real pain, my real emotions. I gather all my faculties, all my resources, and use all the ground I have gained to fully experience all fear of deep painful, hurtful, frightening feelings in me. With all my heart, all my strength, and all my gentleness I intend and wish to recognize the cause of all life's difficulties within myself.

I intend and wish to go in and through my deepest fears and wounds.
I intend and wish to experience all accumulated feelings in me and rid myself of all toxic emotional waste. I summon my faith that "going in" will not annihilate me.

I intend and wish to face the discrepancy between what I claim to believe and actually do believe about going into my feelings. And I wish to be aware of my special methods of avoidance and no longer want to deceive myself like this.

I accept the life I have created for myself and in this way, I can change the parts I don't like.
I dedicate myself to being of service to life.

Amen

Appendix C
Understand these spiritual teachings

Understand These
Spiritual Teachings

Learn About **Self-Transformation**

The *Real.Clear.* series is a 7-book collection of Pathwork Guide teachings. Each lecture has been recreated and repackaged to make this marvelous body of work easier to access. Diving deeply into them is the best way to surface our inner obstacles and find freedom. But it's also helpful to see the lay of the land, to understand these spiritual teachings about self-transformation from a bigger viewpoint.

Gain an eye-opening perspective on life and the work of self-transformation with this overview of the spiritual teachings you'll find throughout Phoenesse.

THE WORK OF HEALING
What we're here to learn

We can boil down our entire journey of spiritual growth and personal healing into two key ideas. **Self-responsibility** is one of them, and **waking up** is the other.

While reading through this overview of these spiritual teachings, consider how we can learn to take responsibility for all of our life experiences by seeing where and how they originate inside of us. If we do this, we will gradually become aware of aspects of ourselves we simply hadn't been aware of before. Then we can wake up from duality and start to live, more and more, from our true inner center rather than our ego.

Learn about the work of incarnating as a human into this land of duality, and the steps we can take to unwind our difficulties and free ourselves from struggle. This world needs more light, and the work of self-transformation turns on the switch.

Important aspects to consider

- Soul splits
- Unmet needs
- Faults
- Body blocks
- Defenses
- Idealized Self-Image
- Inner critic
- Negativity
- Hidden wrong conclusions
- Recreating childhood hurts
- The ego
- Transformation

THE PREQUEL
How we arrived here

Duality didn't just happen. We each made choices that led us to experience everything in its distorted, or negative, form. How did this come about? Here is a story of events—an incredibly shortened version of an immensely huge understanding—that may help us see the truth of cause and effect.

Learn about the series of events that unfolded in the Spirit World, landing us here in this difficult dimension.

Important aspects to consider

- Creation
- Divine qualities
- Lucifer
- The Fall
- The Plan of Salvation
- Positive to negative
- Influence of dark and light

THE RESCUE
The rescue mission that built us
a bridge to get back home

These teachings from the Pathwork Guide and this work of Phoenesse have a particular mission. It is to explain the reason for our existence, who came to our rescue, and what we must do to come to terms with duality so we can return home.

Unfortunately, many people have had experiences involving church that cause us to reject anything remotely sounding like religion. As a result, we turn away from hearing a perspective that offers a markedly different take on things. Consider the possibility that there's another way to see Christ, in a new light. The invitation is to listen with fresh ears.

Learn what happened when we lost our free will, how we got it back, and who we should thank.

Important aspects to consider
- Deal with the devil
- Ascending
- Rescue the Bible

www.phoenesse.com/about/about-spirituality

Appendix D
Ways to learn more

1 Jewels in the heart
- Read or listen to original Pathwork lectures on the International Pathwork Foundation website: www.pathwork.org
- *Living Light*, Chapter 6: TRANSFERENCE VS. PROJECTION | The World is Our Mirror

2 A simple test for life
- What it means to be spiritual
  www.phoenesse.com/spiritual-teachings/what-it-means-to-be-spiritual/
- *Bones*, Chapter 13: The Ubiquitous Faults of Self-Will, Pride and Fear

3 The Real Self vs the True Self
- *Bones*, Chapter 7: Love, Power and Serenity in Divinity or in Distortion
- *Spilling the Script*, Part II: Masks & Defenses

4 Finding the light switch: My husband, the ego and imposters
- *Gems*, Chapter 4: Claiming Our Total Capacity for Greatness
- *Spilling the Script*: LETTING IT GO | The Ego

5 From believing to knowing: The trip of a lifetime
- *Why We All Need Philosophy* by Mark Manson
  www.markmanson.net/why-we-all-need-philosophy

6 Taking the more mystical way home
- *Bible Me This*, Chapter 7: Reincarnation in the Bible
- Appendix A: Five ways to learn about the Fall and the Plan of Salvation
- *The Guide Speaks*, Topic: So Many Religions • Self-Development

7 Two Martin Luthers, two kinds of faith
- *Pearls*, Chapter 13: Uncloaking the Three Faces of Evil: Separation, Materialism and Confusion

9 After isolation: Approaching the Great Transition
- *After the Ego*: Insights from the Pathwork Guide on How to Wake Up
- *Blinded by Fear*, Chapter 6: The Painful Predicament of Both Desiring and Fearing Closeness

- *Bones*, Chapter 12: Finding Out the Truth about Ourselves, Including Our Faults

10 Paying attention: The life-changing process of waking up
- *Spilling the Script*, Part II: Meeting the Selves
- *Blinded by Fear*, Chapter 6: The Painful Predicament of Both Desiring and Fearing Closeness
- *After the Ego*, Chapter 6: Self-Identification Through the Stages of Awakening Consciousness

11 Living on the good side of life
- *After the Ego*, Chapter 5: Living with Polar Opposites and Finding the Good in Being Selfish
- *After the Ego*, Chapter 15: Cause and Effect on Various Levels of Consciousness

12 How inner obstacles let in dark forces
- *Bones*, Chapter 8: How and Why we Recreate Childhood Hurts
- *Bones*, Chapter 10: Unpacking the Pain of our Old Destructive Patterns
- *Bones*, Chapter 17: Overcoming our Negative Intention by Identifying with our Spiritual Self

13 Closing the gaps in our awareness
- *Bones*, Chapter 12: Finding Out the Truth about Ourselves, Including Our Faults
- *Bones*, Chapter 13: The Ubiquitous Faults of Self-Will, Pride and Fear
- *After the Ego*, Chapter 10: The Three States of Consciousness

14 What's hiding beneath our stories?
- *Healing the Hurt*: How to Help Using Spiritual Guidance

15 Suffering? It's time to search for images
- *Bones*, Chapter 9: Images and the Deep, Deep Damage They Do
- *Bones*, Chapter 19: Giant Misunderstanding About Freedom & Self-Responsibility

16 Four hard lessons about immaturity and images

- *Find your images:* www.phoenesse.com/spiritual-teachings/
  10-steps-on-spiritual-path/find-your-images/
- *Spilling the Script:* UNDERSTANDING THE INNER CHILD | The
  Little-L Lower Self

17 Why did God make war?

- Appendix A : Five ways to learn about the Fall and the Plan of Salvation

19 What's behind all the resistance?

- *Pearls*, Chapter 10: Two Rebellious Reactions to Authority
- *Blinded by Fear*, Chapter 7: How Fear of Releasing the Little Ego Spoils
  Happiness

20 Feeling lost? Here's how to find yourself

- *Spilling the Script:* Finding the Treasure
- *After the Ego*, Chapter 12: Creating from Emptiness
- *Gems*, Chapter 9: Why Lazy is the Worst Way to Be

21 Healing from every angle, in body, mind and spirit

- *Pearls*, Chapter 5: Preparing for Reincarnation: Every Life Counts
- *Pearls*, Chapter 11: Bringing ourselves to Order Inside and Out
- *Bones*, Chapter 2: The Importance of Feeling All Our Feelings, Including
  Fear
- *Bones*, Chapter 18: How to Use Meditation to Create a Better Life
- *The Guide Speaks*, Topic: Body & Health/Vision

22 The tricky thing about self-responsibility

- *Pearls*, Chapter 17: Discovering the Key to Letting Go & Letting God

23 How to swim with life, by evolving and resolving our splits

- Appendix B: Deep Prayer for healing
- *Finding Gold*, Chapter 5: Self-Alienation and the Way Back to the Real Self
- *Bones*, Chapter: 11 Our Habit of Transferring our Split onto Everyone
- *Blinded by Fear:* Insights from the Pathwork Guide on How to Face Our
  Fears
- *The Guide Speaks*, Topic: Evolution

24 Playing the long game
- *Walker*: A memoir
- *Keywords*: Answers to Key Questions Asked of the Pathwork Guide
- What I realized while writing *After the Ego*
  www.phoenesse.com/spiritual-books/after-the-ego-wake-up/
  what-i-realized-while-writing-after-the-ego/

25 The key to a happy marriage? Honesty
- *The Pull,* Chapter 6: The Forces of Love, Eros and Sex

26 The story of our lives: Why look within?
- Appendix A: Five ways to learn about the Fall and the Plan of Salvation
- *Bones*, Chapter 14: Exposing the Mistaken Image we have About God
- *The Guide Speaks,* Topic: How to Find God
- *The Spiritual World,* Issue 3, May/June 2022 (in English)
  www.glz.org/en/spiritual-world-online/issues/spiritual-world-3-2022

27 How to heal a country
- *Pearls*, Chapter 3: Exploring the Spiritual Nature of Political System
- *Gems*, Chapter 6: Finding Balance Within Instead of Banking on Outer Rules
- *The Guide Speaks*, Topic: Wasted Lifetimes • Compassion vs Pity
- Appendix C: Understand these spiritual teachings
- All Phoenesse spiritual podcasts

28 Learn to fight the right way, for the right thing
- *Finding Gold*, Chapter 8: Winner vs Loser: Interplay Between the Self and Creative Forces

29 The truer way to freedom
- *Living Light*, Chapter 20: THE WALL WITHIN | Where, Really, is the Wall?
- *Bones*, Chapter 16: How Pleasure Gets Twisted into Self-Perpetuating Cycles of Pain

30 Humor can heal, but sometimes it just hurts
- *The Guide Speaks*, Topic: Sarcasm • Self-Development
- *Salty*: The Colorful Adventures of a Well-Seasoned Seadog by Lon Calloway

31: Part Three The way out of misery

- *Blinded by Fear*. Chapter 9: Our Fundamental Fear of Bliss
- *Gems*, Chapter 2: The Evolutionary Process & Why We Can't Stop It

32 Untangling the twisted threads of friction

- *The Guide Speaks*, Topic: Races

What is Pathwork®?

This remarkable collection of spiritual teachings has been selected by Jill Loree from the body of material collectively known as the Pathwork spiritual materials. The teachings of the Pathwork are contained in about 250 lectures that were given in the 1950s, '60s and '70s by a Vienna-born New Yorker named Eva Pierrakos. The teachings are unparalleled in their wisdom, scope and practicality, and therefore also in their effectiveness.

By following these Pathwork teachings, we embark on a lifelong spiritual journey of self-discovery that allows us to heal our emotional wounds, understand the true workings of life, and foster harmony and balance within our own being, as well as with others and God.

Perhaps the least interesting thing to know about these lectures is that they were channeled. This relevant-yet-insignificant fact is often one of the first things that tumbles out when one tries to explain the Pathwork. It is a relevant point of interest because this material is often of great interest to people who have curious minds and would like to understand the origin of these teachings. At the same time, it is insignificant because it doesn't really matter where they came from. As the Guide often said, you shouldn't believe anything—no matter who said it—unless it makes sense to you.

Who is the Pathwork Guide?

The Guide is the entity who is actually speaking, using Eva as the medium, or channel, through which he spoke. Through Eva's dedication to her task—including her willingness to do her own work—the material continually evolved and deepened over the course of the 22 years she gave monthly lectures.

Pathwork is a trademarked word owned by the Pathwork Foundation, a non-profit organization. It was coined along the way by Eva and other followers of the Guide based on the fact that he so often spoke of "being on a path," and the reality that it is hard work to follow such a path.

In truth, every human being is on a spiritual path, whether they know it or not. Today, however, many more people are becoming conscious about their spiritual journey. For hard as it may be to look directly at our own faults and negativity, at some point we realize we can't keep looking away from ourselves and hope to find solutions. And that, in a way, is the heart of what the Guide teaches: The only way to get to the other side of our struggles in life is by stepping through the gateway of self-responsibility and finding our true selves.

The lectures are available online in the form of printed transcripts, free audio recordings and, for a fee, the original recordings by Eva:

www.pathwork.org

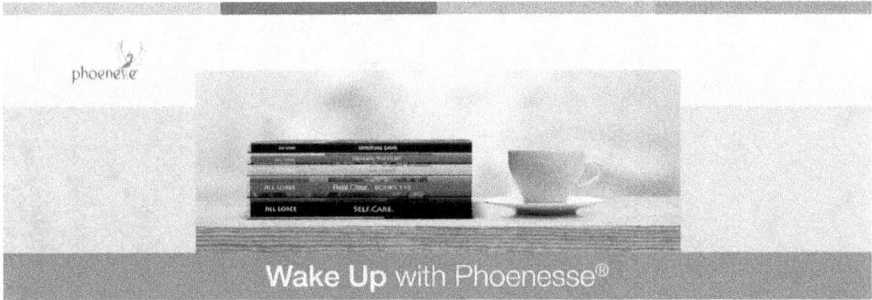

Wake Up with Phoenesse®

What is Phoenesse®?
Founder of Phoenesse

The Guide offers profound teachings that are only valuable if they are put into service in understanding and unwinding our everyday disharmonies, both large and small. One has to actively apply the Guide's teachings to be served by them. That's really the key.

But the lectures are long—roughly 10-12 pages each—and dense, so it takes some mental stamina to get through them. This is where Phoenesse can help.

Doing the Work

Inspired directly by the Guide, Phoenesse offers a fresh approach to these timeless spiritual teachings. Phoenesse—pronounced "fin-ESS"—is a registered service mark of Phoenesse LLC, founded by Jill Loree.

In the *Real. Clear.* seven-book series, Jill Loree has rewritten nearly 100 of the teachings using easier-to-read language, and organized them by topic. Podcasts of each teaching are also available online.

In the *Self. Care.* How-to-Heal teaching series, Jill Loree offers a high-level overview of the work, identifying the various parts of the self and showing how to actually go about doing the work of healing.

In the *We Can Heal* series, Jill Loree provides guidance for facing our fears and waking up. Podcasts of each teaching are available.

You can also read an overview of the Guide's teachings on the Phoenesse website:

www.phoenesse.com

phoenesse
FIND YOUR TRUE YOU.

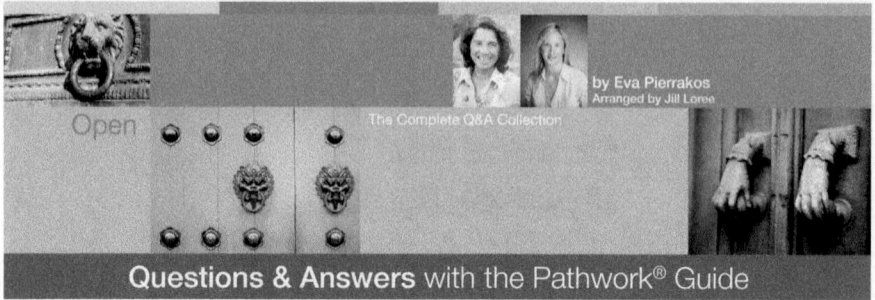

Questions & Answers with the Pathwork® Guide

What is *The Guide Speaks*?
The Complete Q&A Collection

By Eva Pierrakos
with Jill Loree

After each lecture, attendees were encouraged to ask questions. In addition, once a month Eva and the Guide would hold dedicated Question & Answer sessions. Unlike the original lectures, which were prepared by a council of spiritual beings, the Pathwork Guide answered these questions himself. For this reason, the Q&As embody a somewhat different energy from the lectures, which—in addition to their shorter length—makes them easier to digest.

The Q&As were either related to the lecture just given, to a person's personal issues, or to life in general. They offer a wisdom and perspective that has the potential to change a person's worldview.

On *The Guide Speaks*, Jill Loree opens up this fascinating collection of thousands of Q&As answered by the Pathwork Guide, all arranged alphabetically by topic. This website includes hard-hitting questions asked about fears, hate, anger, health, relationships and so much more.

www.theguidespeaks.com

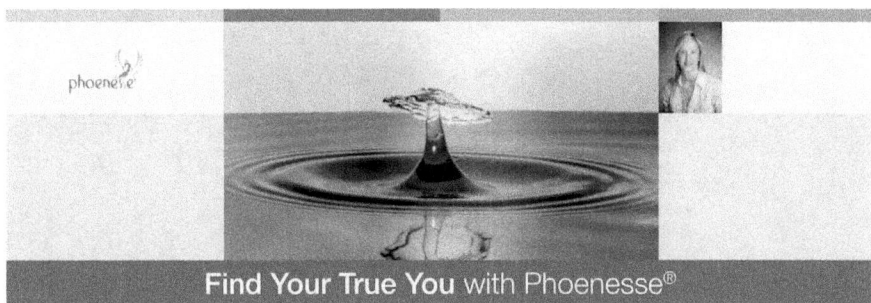

Find Your True You with Phoenesse®

Acknowledgments

Special thanks to Charlie Sanders, my awesome editor for this book. Your suggestions were insightful and spot on. *This book wouldn't be the same without your help.*

Jill Loree | Founder of Phoenesse

About Jill Loree
Founder of Phoenesse

Jill Loree grew up in northern Wisconsin with parents who embraced their Norwegian, Swedish and German heritage. Foods like lutefisk, lefse and krumkaka were prepared every Christmas. And of course there was plenty of beer, bratwurst and cheese all year round.

She would go on to throw pizzas and bartend while attending college at the University of Wisconsin, and then moved into a career in technical sales and marketing. She would settle in Atlanta in 1989 and discover the sweet spot of her career would be in marketing communications. A true Gemini, she has a degree in chemistry and a flair for writing.

One of Jill's greatest passions in life has been her spiritual path. Raised in the Lutheran faith, she became a more deeply spiritual person in the rooms of Alcoholics Anonymous (AA) starting in 1989. In 1997, she was introduced to the wisdom of the Pathwork Guide, which she describes as "having walked through the doorway of a fourth step and found the whole library."

In 2007, she completed four years of training to become a Pathwork Helper, and stepped fully into her Helpership in 2011. In addition to offering individual and group sessions, she has been a teacher in the Transformation Program offered by Mid-Atlantic Pathwork. She also led marketing activities for Sevenoaks Retreat Center in Madison, Virginia and served on their Board of Trustees.

In 2012, Jill completed four years of kabbalah training and became certified for hands-on healing using the energies embodied in the tree of life. She began dedicating her life to writing and teaching about personal self-development in 2014.

Today, Jill is the proud mom of two adult children, Charlie and Jackson, and is delighted to be married to Scott Wisler. She's had more than one last name along the way and now happily uses her middle name as her last. It's pronounced *loh-REE*. In 2022, Scott joined her full time in their mission to spread the teachings of the Pathwork Guide far and wide.

Catch up with Jill at www.phoenesse.com.

After the Ego
Insights from the Pathwork® Guide
on How to Wake Up

Whether or not we lead meaningful and fulfilling lives depends entirely on the relationship between our ego and our Real Self. All these teachings from the Pathwork Guide are pointing to this, prying at it from a multitude of directions to help us open to this truth as our personal experience. For if this relationship is in balance, everything falls nicely into place.

But now, as a new world unfolds from the new consciousness sweeping Earth, many are struggling to find their footing. What every soul on Earth is actually noticing is where they currently stand on their personal journey to find their Real Self and live from this truthful inner space.

After the Ego reveals key facets of the complex and fascinating phenomenon behind the inner "earthquakes" now shaking so many people, and walks us through the vital process of awakening from duality.

Now is the moment for all of us to pay attention—not just to the unprecedented outer events in our world, but to what is happening within.

Now is the time to wake up.

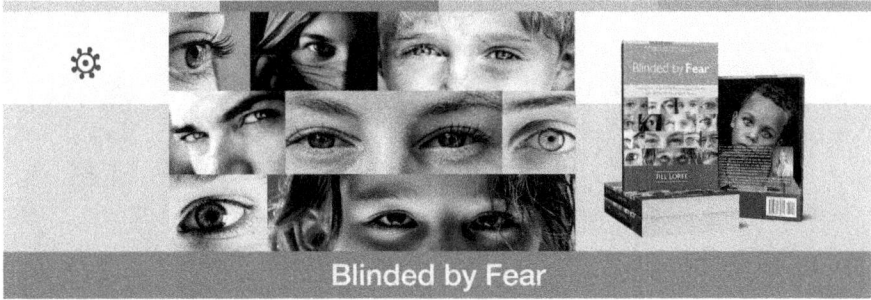

Blinded by Fear

Blinded by Fear
Insights from the Pathwork® Guide
on How to Face Our Fears

It's an error to think that becoming aware of our fears—of turning towards them and facing them in the light—will give them more power. Yet too often we turn a blind eye, hoping to avoid something unpleasant.

In truth, it's not awareness of our fears that causes us problems, but our fearful attitude about even looking at them. By not facing our fears, we keep fighting the parts of ourselves that happen to be in fear, right now. We cramp up our whole being—including our bodies—bracing ourselves against feelings of fear.

In this collection of insights, fear is illuminated from many perspectives. Because it's only by bringing our fears into the fresh air of our conscious awareness that they lose their terrible roar.

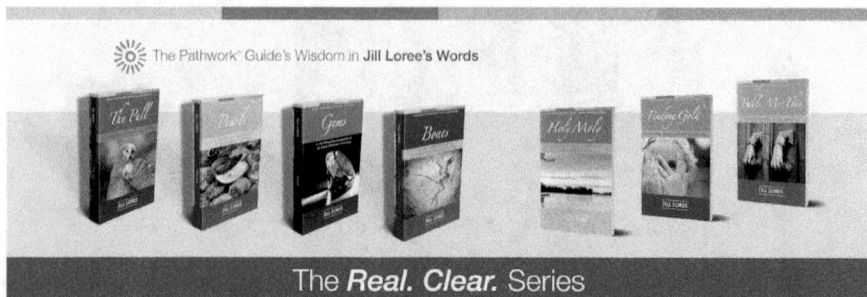

The *Real. Clear.* Series

The Real. Clear. Series
A Seven-Book Series for Spiritual Clarity

The *Real. Clear.* series offers a fresh approach to timeless spiritual teachings by way of easier-to-read language; it's the Pathwork Guide's wisdom in Jill Loree's words. Each book is written with a bit of levity because, as Mary Poppins put it, "A spoonful of sugar helps the medicine go down."

HOLY MOLY: The Story of Duality, Darkness and a Daring Rescue

There's one story, as ancient and ageless as anything one can imagine, that lays a foundation on which all other truths stand. It exposes the origin of opposites. It illuminates the reality of darkness in our midst. It speaks of herculean efforts made on our behalf. This is that story.

FINDING GOLD: The Search for Our Own Precious Self

The journey to finding the whole amazing nugget of the Real Self is a lot like prospecting for gold. Both combine the lure of potential and the excitement of seeing a sparkling possibility, with needing to have the patience of a saint.

It helps to have a map of our inner landscape and a headlamp for seeing into dark corners. That's what Jill Loree has created in this collection of spiritual teachings called *Finding Gold*.

BIBLE ME THIS: Releasing the Riddles of Holy Scripture

The Bible is a stumper for many of us, not unlike the Riddler teasing Batman with his "Riddle me this" taunts. But what if we could know what some of those obscure passages mean? What's the truth hidden in the myth of Adam & Eve? And what was up with that Tower of Babel?

Bible Me This is a collection of in-depth answers to a variety of questions asked of the Guide about the Bible.

THE PULL: Relationships & Their Spiritual Significance

The Pull is about discovering the truth about relationships: they are the doorway through which we ultimately can come to know ourselves, God and another person; through them, we can learn to fully live. Because while life may be many things, more than anything else, it is all about relationships.

The Pull walks us through the delicate dance of intimate relationships, helping us navigate one of the most challenging aspects of life.

PEARLS: A Mind-Opening Collection of 17 Fresh Spiritual Teachings

In this classic, practical collection, Jill Loree strings together timeless spiritual teachings, each carefully polished with a light touch. Topics include: Privacy & Secrecy • The Lord's Prayer • Political Systems • The Superstition of Pessimism • Preparing to Reincarnate • Our Relationship to Time • Grace & Deficit • The Power of Words • Perfectionism • Authority • Order • Positive Thinking • Three Faces of Evil • Meditation for Three Voices • The Spiritual Meaning of Crisis • Leadership • Letting Go & Letting God

GEMS: A Multifaceted Collection of 16 Clear Spiritual Teachings

Clear and radiant, colorful and deep, each sparkling gem in this collection of spiritual teachings taken mostly from the final 50 lectures out of nearly 250, offers a ray of light to help illuminate our steps to reaching oneness.

BONES: A Building-Block Collection of 19 Fundamental Spiritual Teachings

This collection is like the bones of a body—a framework around which the remaining body of work can arrange itself. Sure, there's a lot that needs to be filled in to make it all come to life, but with *Bones*, now we've got the basic building blocks in place.

NUTSHELLS: Short & Sweet Spiritual Insights

Nutshells are short-and-sweet daily spiritual insights carved from three books: *Pearls*, *Gems* and *Bones*. Meaningful inspirations and memorable phrases are woven together to create a new creation that largely resembles the original form. Like the acorn that contains the potential for the oak tree, these nuggets of wisdom hold the power to change our whole perspective on life.

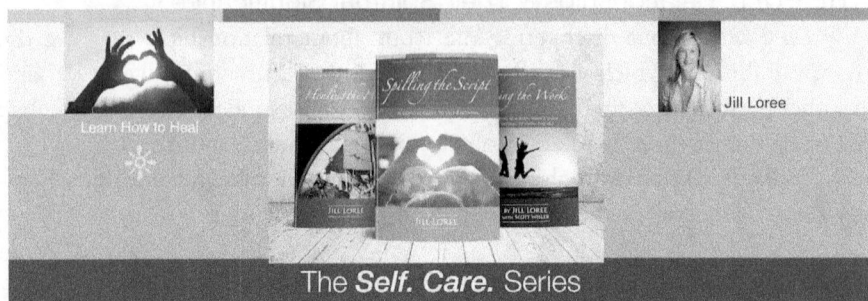

The *Self. Care.* Series

The Self. Care. Series
A Three-Book Teaching Series

The *Self. Care.* How-to-Heal series offers a bird's-eye view of the Pathwork Guide's teachings and shows us how to apply them in working with ourselves and others.

SPILLING THE SCRIPT: A Concise Guide to Self-Knowing

Now, for the first time, powerful spiritual teachings from the Guide are available in one concise book. Jill Loree has written *Spilling the Script* to deliver a clear, high-level perspective about self-discovery and healing, giving us the map we need for following this life-changing path to oneness.

The goal of this spiritual journey is to make contact with our divine core so we can transition from living in duality to discovering the joy of being in unity. For even as we believe ourselves to be victims of an unfair universe, the truth is that we are continually guarding ourselves against pain, and through our defended approach to life we unknowingly bring about our current life circumstances. But we can make new choices.

Bit by bit, as we come out of the trance we have been in, we begin to see cause and effect, and to take responsibility for the state of our lives. Gradually, our lives transform. We once again can sense our essential nature and eternal connectedness with all that is.

"You will find how you cause all your difficulties. You have already stopped regarding these words as mere theory, but the better you progress, the more will you truly understand just how and why you cause your hardships. By so doing, you gain the key to changing your life."
–Pathwork Guide, Lecture #78

HEALING THE HURT: How to Heal Using Spiritual Guidance

The work of healing our fractured inner selves takes a little finesse, a lot of stick-to-it-iveness, and the skilled help of someone who has gone down this road before. Being a Helper then is about applying all we have learned on our own healing journey to help guide others through the process of reunifying their fragmented hidden places.

That may sound simple, but it's surely not easy. It's also not easy to be the Worker, the one who does this work of spiritual healing. Now, with *Healing the Hurt*, everyone can understand the important skills needed by a Helper to assure Workers find what they're looking for.

DOING THE WORK: Healing Our Body, Mind & Spirit by Getting to Know the Self | By Jill Loree with Scott Wisler

Many of us have an inkling there can be more to life: that more meaningful moments are possible, and more satisfying experiences are attainable. Well, we're right. And fortunately, the tools for bringing this about are not really a secret. They're just not obvious. Herein lies the crux of the problem. We must come to realize what we have not been willing or able to see before.

Truth be told, no one gets out of planet Earth alive. But we can come out ahead by learning to make the best use of our time here. And that starts the day we begin doing the work. So let's get at it.

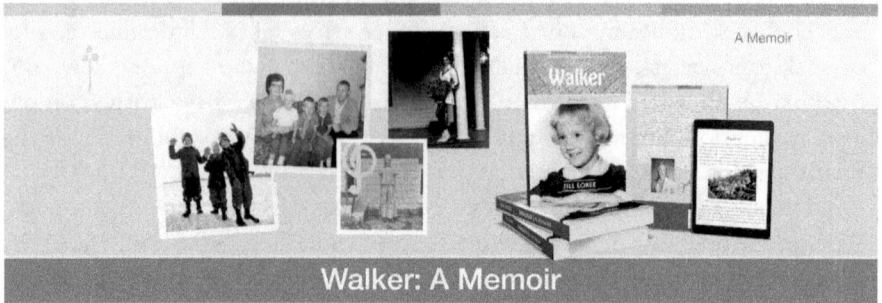

Walker: A Memoir

Walker
A Memoir

Walker is a memoir about one woman's spiritual journey to open her heart and develop compassion. Through it all, her own gumption would be her steady companion.

It starts out with a young girl raised in a singing Lutheran family where things looked good on the outside. But inside, Jill Loree was struggling. Later, she would "trudge the dreary road of happy destiny," as the AA Big Book puts it, getting sober at 26 and picking up only one white chip. That's not nothing, considering that most of Jill Loree's childhood memories are infused with her father's drinking. Her mother, on the other hand, had a controlling, co-dependent streak that wouldn't end. Sounds dreary indeed, right?

In this spiritual memoir however, Jill Loree artfully lifts the story out of the ditch and finds the grace weaving between the lines. *Walker* also merges in a touch of poetry—her own, her sons' and even her Dad's—adding heart, depth and levity to the telling. Her gentle wit and brisk writing pace keeps things moving along. True to the title, there's no need to sit and stew in misery.

Today, Jill Loree's spiritual path is filled with the light of Christ, which is what she has discovered emerges from the core of one's being after clearing away the detritus accumulated in youth—just as the Pathwork Guide said it would. That's the deeper message she is now passionate about sharing, and which shines through in this warm telling of the story of her life.

By Jill Loree & Scott Wisler

Word for Word

Word for Word
An Intimate Exchange Between
a Couple of Kindred Souls

By Jill Loree and Scott Wisler

What does it really look like, not just to talk the talk, but also to walk the walk of a spiritual path?

Surprisingly insightful and at times pretty funny, *Word for Word* is a unique collection of text and email messages written back and forth between a couple of died-in-the-wool spiritual seekers, Jill and Scott, as they walked head-long into a new relationship that would prove lasting.

Typos and punctuation have been cleaned up to aid readability, but believe it or not, nothing has been added or subtracted nor has any-thing been tweaked so the two don't look too strange. You'll see.

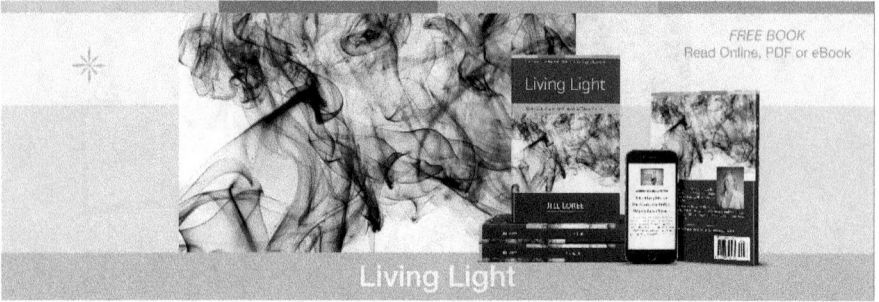

Living Light
On Seeking and Finding True Faith

What greater gift could we give ourselves than to wake up and bring forward the Christ consciousness that dwells within. To become a living light. Indeed, every time we listen for the truth, we will find the light of Christ within. And there is nothing greater for us to uncover than this, and to find true faith. For that's the moment we'll know there is truly nothing to fear.

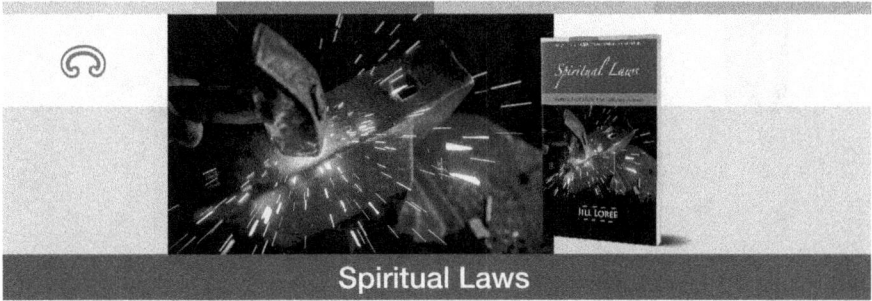
Spiritual Laws

Spiritual Laws
Hard & Fast Logic for Forging Ahead

Just what are the laws that rule this precious land? Turns out, there are an infinite number of laws that govern everything that happens. And while *Spiritual Laws* does not claim to be comprehensive in covering them all, this sampling of teachings from the Pathwork Guide does a nice job of explaining how this sphere works.

Understanding this will help us grasp the truth that behind our trials, there is a method. That someone or something is behind life, working out a plan. So gather round and listen up, because there are important guidelines we could all stand to know more about, and the hammer is about to drop.

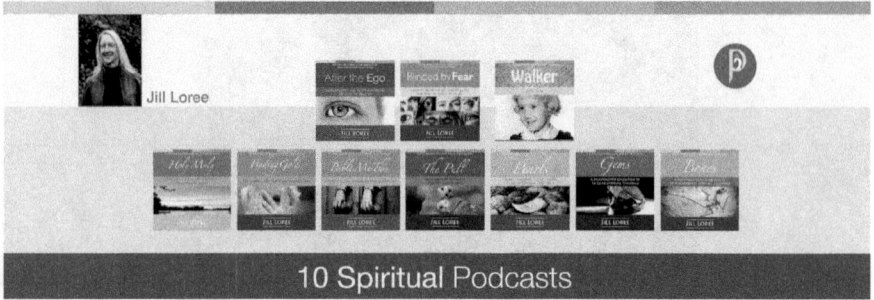

10 Spiritual Podcasts

Spiritual Podcasts
Available on Phoenesse

These spiritual podcasts are available for free, from Phoenesse. You can also access them from Audible, and using the apps for Apple Podcasts, Spotify, Google Play and Stitcher. Listen to *Walker: A Memoir* on Phoenesse with a Full Access Membership.

www.phoenesse.com/spiritual-podcasts

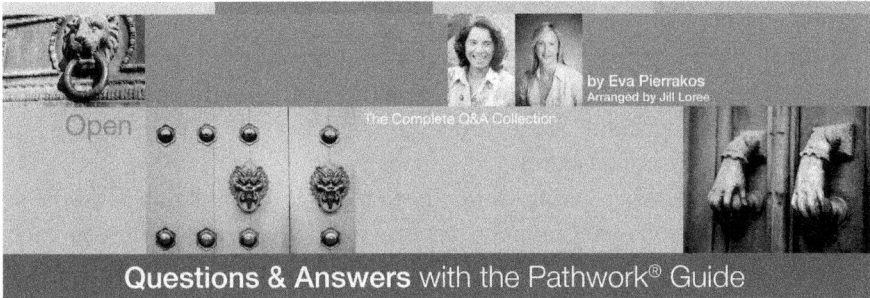

Questions & Answers with the Pathwork® Guide

The Guide Speaks
The Complete Q&A Collection

by Eva Pierrakos with Jill Loree

On *The Guide Speaks*, Jill Loree opens up this fascinating collection of thousands of Q&As answered by the Pathwork Guide, all arranged alphabetically by topic. This website includes hard-hitting questions asked about fears, hate, anger, health, relationships and so much more.

www.theguidespeaks.com

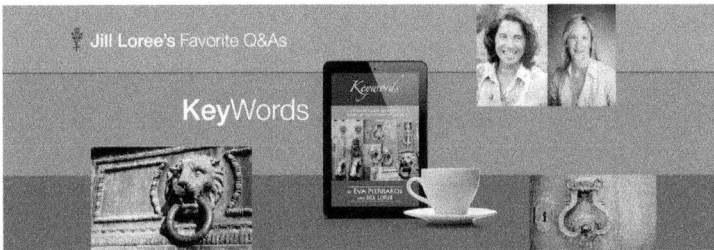

Keywords
A Collection of Jill's Favorite Q&As

Jill Loree has combined her favorite questions about religion, Jesus Christ, the Bible, reincarnation, the Spirit World, death, prayer and meditation, and God into a single "Best Of" collection. You can read this collection online or download *Keywords:* Answers to Key Questions Asked of the Pathwork Guide.

255

"There are so many questions you need to ask, personal and general ones. In the end they become one and the same. The lectures I am called upon to deliver are also answers to unspoken questions, questions that arise out of your inner yearning, searching, and desires to know and to be in truth. They arise out of your willingness to find divine reality, whether this attitude exists on the conscious or unconscious level.

But there are other questions that need to be asked deliberately on the active, outer, conscious level in order to fulfill the law. For only when you knock can the door be opened; only when you ask can you be given. This is a law."
– The Pathwork Guide in Q&A #250

www.theguidespeaks.com/keywords-from-Pathwork-Guide

Brought to you by Phoenesse®

phoenesse®
FIND YOUR TRUE YOU.